Dissent into Treason

rgus **Whelan** has worked for thirty years in the trade
ion movement and has been an officer of the Irish
ngress of Trade Unions since 1995.

McBride is Senior Lecturer in Early Modern and Irish
y at King's College London. He has written on
ects of modern Irish history and recently
ral history of Ireland between 1688 and
enth-Century Ireland.

FERGUS WHELAN

DISSENT INTO TREASON

Unitarians, King-killers and the Society of United Irishmen

To my old comrade
Brendan
Best wish

Fergus Whelan

BRANDON

A Brandon Original Paperback

First published in 2010 by Brandon
an imprint of Mount Eagle Publications
Dingle, Co. Kerry, Ireland, and
Unit 3, Olympia Trading Estate, Coburg Road, London N22 6TZ, England

www.brandonbooks.com

ISBN 9780863224102

2 4 6 8 10 9 7 5 3 1

Cover design: Anú Design, with Barry Kidd
Typesetting by Red Barn Publishing, Skeagh, Skibbereen

Contents

For my children Paddy Nickel, Karl and Rosa

Illustrations

The cover illustration, *Dr Priestley's House and Laboratory, Fair Hill, destroyed in the Birmingham Riots, 14th July 1791*, is reproduced by permission of Dickinson College, Carlisle, PA.

The images of Rev. Stephen Charnock, Rev. John Owen, Rev. John Abernethy, Great Strand Street Baptismal register, Rev. William Bruce, and the Robert Emmet signature are all reproduced, with the assistance of Steve DePaor, courtesy of the Dublin Unitarian Church. The Great Strand Street image is reproduced courtesy of the National Library of Ireland.

Thanks to

Rosheen Berry, Professor Paul Bew, Frank Cuneen, Rev. Bill Darlison, Rory Delany, Dr Diarmuid Ferriter, Marius Harkin, Senator Eoghan Harris, Diarmuid Harte, Professor Gerry Hughes, Ken McCue, Kieran McGovern, Hugo McGinnis, Nuala Monaghan, Liz Morris, Theresa Moriarty, Tom Mulligan, Albert Murphy, Rev. Dr J. W. Nelson, Naoise Ó hAnnain, Phillip Orr, Bill O'Brien, Peter Rigney, Dr Margaret Robson, Dr Elaine Sissons, Rob Taylor, Tom Wall, John Ward, Padraig Yeates and Sheila Hanley.

FOREWORD

Irish republicanism, the central ideological force in the history of modern Ireland, had its origins in Belfast and Dublin in the 1790s, when admirers of the French Revolution established the Society of United Irishmen. Dr William Drennan, the pamphleteer and poet, first proposed the new initiative during the preparations for the Bastille Day celebrations of 1791. Lamenting the fact that "distinctions of rank, of property and of religious persuasion" had erected "brazen walls of separation" among the inhabitants of Ireland, Drennan called for the formation of a new society, an "Irish Brotherhood", which would communicate with radicals in Britain and the Jacobin Club in Paris. Inspired by events in France, Drennan hoped to abolish those artificial distinctions of rank and religious affiliation, and to unite the inhabitants of Ireland in a single "political faith". The body that eventually emerged from the celebrations of 14 July 1791, the Society of United Irishmen, went on to adopt Drennan's oath or "test", committing its members to the extension of a "brotherhood of affection" among Irishmen.

Few events have received more attention from Irish historians than the campaign of the United Irishmen, the loyalist backlash that resulted and the explosion of rebellion in 1798. The entire eighteenth century is often treated as merely an extended prelude to the bloody denouement at its close. To some extent, too, the political history of Ireland since 1798 can be understood as an attempt to

7

work out the radical democratic ideas first crystallised in that revolutionary decade. In recent years a flood of books and articles have analysed the United Irishmen and their extraordinary achievement in constructing the largest insurrectionary movement in Irish history. As long as those "distinctions of rank, of property and of religious persuasion" endure, new generations on both sides of the border and beyond will return to the original United Irish vision for inspiration. And yet many aspects of the 1790s remain underexplored.

Everyone knows that Wolfe Tone laboured to bring together "Protestant, Catholic and Dissenter". We all know – or at least we think we know – what "Protestant" and "Catholic" mean. But how many of us really understand the third force in eighteenth-century Ireland, the "Dissenter"? It is Fergus Whelan's great achievement in *Dissent into Treason* to reconstruct the mental and social world of the most advanced Dissenters of the revolutionary period, and to remind us of their distinctive contribution to Irish republicanism.

Dr Drennan was the son of a Dissenting clergyman who first ran an academy in Dublin with the enlightenment philosopher Francis Hutcheson, and then ministered to the Rosemary Street meeting house in Belfast. In Dublin, where Drennan settled as a practising physician, he affiliated to the Great Strand Street congregation, where he rubbed shoulders with Archibald Hamilton Rowan, the Emmets and other supporters of the revolutions in America and France. Unlike traditional Presbyterians, these congregations defended the right of private judgement against the interference of church and state alike. They had come to believe that personal persuasion was the very essence of religious belief, and that the imposition of creeds and confessions was part of the tyranny and superstition that the French Revolution confronted.

These two congregations form the central pillars of Fergus Whelan's story, a vivid story in which the elegance and refinement of Georgian Ireland intersect with the radical aspirations of the common people. Along the way, he introduces a wide range of Dissenting voices in Ireland and explains their connections with Oliver Cromwell, the Commonwealthman and scholar John Toland, the English philosopher and radical Joseph Priestley, the pioneering feminist Mary Wollstonecraft, the Scottish Unitarian and reformer Thomas Muir, exiled to Botany Bay in 1793, and the young reformer Robert Stewart, who would later put down the 1798 rebellion as Viscount Castlereagh. Particular attention is paid to the intellectual and personal links with Britain and the United States, and also to the role of female radicals such as Oliver Bond's wife Eleanor, who administered the United Irish oath "to several ladies".

In 1791, the United Irishmen rejoiced that they were living in an age of revolution, "when unjust governments are falling in every quarter of Europe" and, equally importantly, "religious persecution is compelled to abjure her tyranny over conscience". Drawing on the archive of the Dublin Unitarian Church, never before exploited by historians, Fergus Whelan provides a compelling portrait of Ireland's enlightened vanguard and helps us to understand the ideals that mobilised thousands of people in 1798.

Ian MacBride

INTRODUCTION

Oliver Cromwell and his government in Ireland sponsored two congregations of Protestant Dissenters in Dublin between 1649 and 1660, one of which met at Wood Street and the other at "Saint Nicholas within the Walls". Both of these communities flourished from the mid seventeenth century well into the nineteenth century. For more than 140 years, the ministers at these meeting houses preached a passionate commitment to notions of civil and religious liberty. The radical religious and political principles which they developed contributed to the foundation of the Dublin Society of United Irishmen and inspired the rebellion of 1798 and its aftershock, Robert Emmet's rebellion of 1803.

The Wood Street "meeting", which later located to Great Strand Street, was founded by Puritans who settled in Dublin to escape persecution in England during the reign of Elizabeth I.[1] Their ranks were swollen in 1649 by the arrival in Dublin of soldiers of the New Model Army. A notable new arrival in Dublin at this time was Rev. John Owen, who was born in Wales in 1616. He was one of the most eminent Puritan theologians of his era. He came to Ireland with Oliver Cromwell and was his personal chaplain during the Irish campaign. During his stay in Dublin, Rev. Owen was an "occasional preacher" at Wood Street. Rev. Stephen Charnock was another eminent Puritan preacher who preached at Wood Street from 1653. Charnock was personal chaplain to Oliver Cromwell's son

Rev. Stephen Charnock

Henry, who was appointed by his father to the post of military commander in Ireland in 1655.

The "meeting" which initially gathered at St Nicholas was founded in 1650 by Rev. Samuel Winter. Winter was born in Warwickshire and was sent to Dublin by Cromwell to become the eleventh provost of Trinity College. John Owen had probably suggested Samuel Winter for the Trinity post.[2] Rev. Winter's congregation initially had great political influence, and four of his adherents served as mayor of Dublin during the Commonwealth.[3] However, at the Restoration of Charles II in 1660, Rev. Winter was ejected from St Nicholas's and imprisoned. Forced out of Ireland for a short time after his release, he soon returned and based himself at New Row, off Thomas Street, where his congregation was to remain for more than sixty years.

Introduction

These Protestant Dissenters were constantly reinterpreting scripture and reviewing their beliefs in their search for truth. At some point, both the Wood Street and New Row ministers altered their theology and ceased to subscribe to the doctrine of the Trinity. They no longer accepted that the godhead consists of the Father, Son and Holy Spirit; for them there was only one god, "the Father". They denied that Jesus Christ was God or the son of God.

Rev. Owen, who had mustered the considerable power of his pen and intellect to publish a refutation of Unitarianism at the request of Oliver Cromwell in 1654, could never have imagined that the descendants of his associates in Dublin would eventually embrace the "abominable heresy" of Unitarianism.

The Cromwellians who gathered at Wood Street and at New Row had come to Ireland to establish a Protestant colony and to extirpate the native Irish population and the Roman Catholic faith. Yet nearly a century and half later, their descendants emerged as the advocates of a union of Catholics, Protestants and Dissenters in support of political and economic reform.

Although the evolution from sectarianism to liberalism within the congregations was a process of profound change, there is also a pattern of continuity and consistency through the generations. The change involved the gradual shedding of notions such as predestination: that is, that God has decided who is elect and who is damned. Indeed, their optimism regarding the essential benevolence of the Deity led them to reject the very idea of eternal damnation. While they jettisoned beliefs they judged irrational, they retained core values. Their most cherished principle was the right of the individual to freedom of conscience. Every person should be guided by his conscience, and no civil or church authority should presume to tell a person what to believe or to punish unorthodox belief or opinion.

These Dublin-based Dissenters were also unwavering in their opposition to the Established Church: the Anglican

Church had been "established" by law as the national church of England and Ireland, and such a church was regarded as a tyranny which sought to impose beliefs from on high. They believed that a religious congregation should govern itself and be free from the control of bishop or priest. Their abhorrence of the arbitrary power of civil or religious "tyrants" such as kings and bishops marked them off from the mainstream of loyal Irish Protestants. Those elements of their Cromwellian legacy not only survived into the late eighteenth century but sat easily with the enlightened liberalism of the Society of United Irishmen.

When Protestant Dissenters established the Dublin Society of United Irishmen in 1791, it was a step on a very long journey towards liberty which started when their ancestors executed their "tyrant" king, Charles I. In the 1790s, the descendants of the king-killers of 1649 emerged as advocates of religious toleration, freedom of conscience and democracy. The democratic republicanism of the United Irishmen was not an aberration; rather it was a product of the interaction of the politics of the Age of Reason and the Cromwellian tradition of Protestant dissent.

Notes to Introduction
1. Smyrl 2009, p. 49
2. Gribben 2007, p. 147
3. *Ibid.*

Chapter One

THE RISE AND FALL OF THE REPUBLICANS

August 1649, the Puritans Arrive in Dublin

A vengeful Puritan, regicide army has landed at Ringsend. They come as the "Israelites about to extirpate the idolatrous inhabitants of Canaan".[1] The great guns of Protestant Dublin boom out to welcome the army and its commander, Oliver Cromwell. A vast concourse of people has come to see the man they have heard so much about. "Old Ironsides" steps forward flanked by his chaplains, Rev. Hugh Peter and Rev. John Owen. Rev. Peter had gained notoriety a few months earlier when he addressed King Charles I the night before his execution. As Isaiah once told the king of Babylon, Peter told Charles "thou hast destroyed thy land and slain thy people". Rev. Owen told the regicides that their deeds "are the Lord's doing and most marvellous in our eyes".[2]

Cromwell believes that victory in Ireland will confirm the Lord's favour at the execution of Charles. He tells the admiring crowd that he hopes that "their hearts affections are real for the great work against the barbarous and blood thirsty Irish… and for the propagating of the Gospel of Christ".[3] The battle-hardened veterans of the New Model Army have come to crush the Irish. The pious and godly preachers at Cromwell's side have come to do battle against Popery and the Antichrist.

The English Civil War

The English Civil War ended with the execution of Charles I on 30 January 1649. Charles's reign began in 1625, and for much of the next twenty-four years, he was in conflict

15

with many of his subjects on the question of his powers to raise taxes and his duties and obligations to the parliament of England. Infuriated by insults to his authority, he had dissolved his parliament in 1629. In fact, throughout the 1630s he flatly refused to call another parliament for more than a decade, dispensing entirely with the services of those "turbulent and ill-affected spirits" of the House of Commons.[4] During the period of Charles's "Personal Rule", matters of taxation, foreign policy and religious observance and practice were decided by the king alone without reference to the so-called "people's representatives" in parliament. In the view of his opponents, Charles was drifting towards tyranny, and discontent was rife in England.

By the late 1630s, discontent was also growing in Ireland. The king's representative, the abrasive Thomas Wentworth, known to the Irish as "Black Tom Tyrant", squeezed the Protestant Irish to raise revenue for his sovereign. Wentworth treated all Irish Catholics, both Old English (the landed families who had come from England and who remained loyal to their old faith after Henry VIII had broken with Rome) and native Irish alike, as disloyal.[5]

In England, the religious controversy, which was the locus of much conflict, was essentially about the different forms of Protestantism which were contending for dominion in the hearts of the people. Protestant Dissenters, or Puritans as they were then known, sought a "true" Protestant reformation. The term Puritan is problematical in that it can have many and even contradictory meanings. The term has even been described as "an admirable refuge from clarity of thought".[6] One bishop suggested that a Puritan "is one who loves God with all his soul but hates his neighbour with all his heart". A less hostile view of what it meant to be a Puritan was that of Arthur Haslerig when he said, "I was bred a Puritan and am for public liberty."[7] The term Dissenter is almost as ill-defined as Puritan. It encompasses those on the extreme of religious radicalism as well as more conservative Presbyterians. Yet it denotes those who could not accept the king's or the bishops' authority over their religious consciences.

Preaching the word was what mattered to most Dissenters. They believed that a man can find his way to God through scripture and required no priest, no ceremony, no bishop or state church to act as mediator. Dissenters denied the authority of the hierarchy of the Anglican Church of England, which they came to regard as a mirror-image of the Roman Church. They disapproved of its high church ceremonies, its pomp and its rigid orthodoxy. The Established Church, that is the Church of England of which Charles was head, enforced its spiritual authority through the civil magistrates: a secular judge could send a man to prison for interpreting scripture according to his conscience, and a magistrate could condemn a man simply for failing to attend the services of the Established Church.

Archbishop of Canterbury William Laud (1573–1645), Charles's most trusted churchman, attempted to streamline Protestant worship and practice in the 1630s. He sought "to keep an uniformity in the external service of God according to the doctrine and discipline of the Church".[8] He intended that all clergymen should be ordained by a bishop of the Church of England and that they should run their services according to the strictures of the Book of Common Prayer. Laud, enthusiastically supported by the king, also insisted on a form of ceremony of worship which shocked many Dissenters who regarded such practices as Popish priestcraft. However, Laud's efforts provoked a split in the Church of England. Ministers who would not accept his innovations were ousted from their livings, many were imprisoned, and he thus created a new generation of "true" Protestant martyrs.

As Laud sought to enhance the authority of his bishops, the Puritans feared that his real objective was a gradual return to Popery. The wearing of a surplice by ministers, the location of the communion table and pulpit, the presence of altar rails all became matters of conflict and division. Many thousands of Dissenters escaped what they regarded as the Laudian persecution by leaving England. A few communities came to Ireland, to places such as Baltimore and Bandon in County Cork as well as Dublin. A far larger number made the hazardous journey across the Atlantic to settle in New England, where they were able to gather religious congregations free from interference by bishops or king. However, many who were preparing to follow their brethren to America changed their plans when they detected that Charles's regime was not as invulnerable as it had once seemed.

Laud's efforts to impose his version of Protestantism on Presbyterian Scotland provoked the first "Bishops' War" of 1639, the crisis which finally led to the English Civil War. The defeat of Charles by the Scots forced a very reluctant king to recall parliament; he needed money to rebuild his army, and he could raise taxes only with parliamentary consent. After years of pent-up frustration, "the turbulent and ill-affected spirits" of the House of Commons were back with a vengeance. The new parliament refused to vote new taxes, and it lasted only three weeks before Charles lost patience, dismissed them and sent them home. Unable to raise new taxes by other means, Charles was soon forced to call what became known as the Long Parliament. This parliament proved strong enough to deny the king his traditional power to dissolve parliament.

The Earl of Strafford, "Black Tom" Wentworth, was recalled from Ireland to help rescue the king's fortunes. He left behind him in Ireland a strong Roman Catholic army, which many in the English parliament believed would be used to intimidate them or dissolve parliament by force. The king's enemies in parliament, who sought the destruction of the king's "evil councillor", accused him of treason. In spite of Charles's efforts and promises of protection, the king could not save his friend, and Wentworth was executed in May 1641. Wentworth had left a power vacuum in his wake after his departure from Ireland. With the king and parliament at loggerheads, the English government in Ireland was paralysed. In October 1641, the Irish Roman Catholics rebelled in furious anger.

The rebellion started in Ulster under the leadership of Sir Phelim O'Neill, Conor Maguire and Hugh Óg Mac Mahon. Although the rebels' plan to capture Dublin was betrayed and consequently failed, the rebellion soon spread throughout the country. This was a war between neighbours of different religious persuasions, each thinking of themselves as civilised and their enemies as barbarians. There were also custom and language issues involved. All of this would have been enough to ensure the conflict would be bloody and merciless, but there was another dimension to the conflict which determined that atrocities involving men, women and children were more common than set-piece battles in the field. The Protestant settlers held land that had once belonged to the Catholics, and competition for land can bring out the savage in otherwise civilised men, whether they are dispossessed natives in rebellion or colonising settlers. This rebellion was a most terrible affair. Toby Barnard writes:

> Opportunists robbed neighbours, carried off clothing and furnishings, felled timber, maimed livestock, snatched horses and pillaged barns and mills. On occasions the robbers desecrated objects, notably bibles sacred to Protestants, and even dug up their corpses from graveyards. Whether this was a symbolic act aimed at removing the pollution arising from heretics or a device to make saltpeter needed for gunpowder can be debated. Protestants were killed. Reports soon put the total at 154,000. Panic resulted and did not make for a cool appraisal of what was afoot. Modern research has reduced the deaths to a more plausible but still alarming 3,000–4,000.[9]

Pamphlets published in London contained illustrations

of women and children being tortured, mutilated and burnt to death. Many of these depicted the murderers in the vestments of Romanist priests.[10] Many refugees from Ireland arrived in England telling stories of cruelties and Roman Catholic barbarism that lost nothing in the telling. At any rate, this rebellion proved to be the longest and bitterest of the many rebellions which characterised the relationship between England and Ireland.

The failure of Charles to intervene to protect his beleaguered Irish Protestant subjects became another grievance for his enemies to exploit. The Irish Catholic rebels claimed they were fighting on behalf of Charles and had forged a warrant to that effect. The House of Commons was only too willing to believe this and blame the king for the terrible events in Ireland. Atrocity stories from Ireland fuelled Dissenter propaganda. The propagandists could have it both ways: Charles was in league with the Popish rebels and was a knave; otherwise he was incompetent and incapable of protecting his Irish Protestant subjects.

Events in England dictated that Ireland could not be given the required attention. It would be eight years before matters had settled in England to such an extent that the new regime could send an army of sufficient strength to put down the rebellion and reconquer Ireland. Charles had raised his war standard against his parliament at Nottingham on 22 August 1642. He forced all of his subjects into deciding whether they owed their loyalty to their king or their parliament. When word that the Civil War had begun reached New England, many of the exiles returned to fight for parliament and against the king. There followed years of civil war involving massive set-piece battles, sieges of major cities and towns and spectacular cavalry raids. The battles of Edgehill, Marston Moor and Naseby involved huge armies on both sides. At Marston Moor and Naseby, the parliamentary forces were the victors, but both sides suffered massive casualties on the field. In the nature of seventeenth-century warfare, there were also huge casualties afterwards when men died from untreated wounds and disease. By December 1648, Charles had been defeated and was a prisoner in the hands of an army who blamed him for all the strife and bloodshed of the previous six years.

Charles had lost the war, his power and his kingdom, and Oliver Cromwell was about to emerge as the most powerful man in England. The soldiers who idolised him now called him "Old Ironsides" or "Nol". MP for Huntington and an otherwise almost unknown country gentlemen when the war began, by the war's end he had established himself as England's finest general.

Throughout the Civil War, the Established Church stood with the king, and the Dissenters were solidly for parliament. Laud, imprisoned by parliament during the early stages of the Civil War, was executed in 1645. When these differing theologies collided on the battlefield, the king and his Established Church were defeated.

The Dissenters were now determined to organise their religious affairs as they pleased without the interference of prelates. However, the Dissenters were not a homogeneous group, and when the war was over, they began to fall out amongst themselves. Tension arose between the New Model Army that had fought the war and the parliament that benefited from their victory. Cromwell, who founded the New Model Army in 1645 because he felt that only a modern professional army could deliver a decisive victory which could end the war, insisted that "no good soldier should be excluded from the new army merely because his own way to God differed from the orthodox way of the Presbyterians".[11] Many of his soldiers had been recruited in the eastern counties from a body known as the Eastern Association. The men were drawn from Essex, Hertfordshire, Norfolk, Suffolk, Cambridgeshire, Huntingdonshire and Lincolnshire. In these areas, religious "Independency" was strong, rather than Presbyterianism.[12] For Presbyterians, religious authority resided in the synod and presbytery. Independents were sometimes called Congregationalists, because they held that such authority resided in the individual congregation.

The Presbyterian majority in parliament were moderate Puritans or Dissenters who sought to replace the Anglican Established Church with a Presbyterian church establishment. The army was a power base of religious Independency. Independents rejected any form of church establishment and saw it as a threat to the authority of Independent congregations.

The Presbyterians knew that if their plans were to succeed, they would have to break the power of the New Model Army. The Presbyterian majority in parliament tried to clip the army's wings by disbanding several regiments and getting the more radical regiments out of the way by sending them to the war in Ireland.[13]

The army was enraged by the lack of gratitude of parliament to the fighting men who had suffered much in its cause. After the battle of Naseby, Richard Baxter, one of the best known Puritan ministers of his era, came down to the army. He found that controversy was rife in the ranks and that "their most frequent and vehement disputes were for liberty of conscience as they called it... that every man might not only hold but preach and do in matters of religion what he pleased".[14]

William Bray, an army captain, linked liberty of conscience with political freedom when he declared, where civil liberty is entire it includes liberty of conscience and where liberty of conscience is entire it includes civil liberty, they are the inseperable right of the people.[15]

The soldiers maintained that a parliament that would impose Presbyterianism on unwilling people was a tyranny little different from that which they had overthrown. "Independency in religion led to independency in politics and the soldiers discussed civil democracy as well as church democracy."[16] Cromwell was a strong Independent and was therefore distrusted by many of the Presbyterian majority in the House of Commons. He wrote to the speaker of the house after the battle of Naseby and pointed out that "those who had ventured their lives for the liberty of their country trust God for the liberty of their conscience and the parliament for their civil liberty".[17] In other words, parliament should not interfere with a soldier's religion.

Religious authority from above had been overthrown. In the vacuum left by the fall of the Established Church, a bewildering array of radical religious and political sects filled the void. The Independents who had broken with the Church of England were now demanding to worship according to their personal consciences, with their services conducted according to the preferences of their congregations. Some Dissenters, influenced by Dutch Protestantism, formed separate congregations which accepted only believers into their membership, and they baptised converts upon their profession of faith. Their opponents nicknamed them "Baptists", and the name stuck. Quakerism also began to attract a following from "those who trembled in the fear of the Lord", and they spread their message fearless of oppression.

These groups came to be collectively described as "the Sects". The new "heresies" all espoused that the individual Christian may directly relate to God, free from the intervention of priests and, more particularly, bishops. Most of the new heresies also contained elements of egalitarian politics and republicanism in that they were anti-hierarchical and gave precedence to individual opinion over the dictates of social superiors. The world had been turned upside down.[18]

The Levellers and the Good Old Cause

In October and November 1647, representatives of the New Model Army debated the future constitution of England at a small church in Putney. It was during this debate that the demand for universal male suffrage emerged alongside the demand for complete religious toleration. This was when the "Leveller" Colonel Thomas Rainsborough made the oft quoted demand for democracy when he said:

> I think that the poorest he that is in England hath a
> life to live, as the greatest he; and therefore truly, sir,
> I think it's clear, that every man that is to live under
> a government ought first by his own consent put him-
> self under that government.

The Leveller movement was an informal alliance of civilians and soldiers. The Levellers did not choose their title but were branded with that name by their opponents. Their enemies argued that if the franchise was extended to the "poorest he in England", it would pose a threat to private property, since the poor would dispossess the wealthy and "take away all the property and interests that a man hath".[19]

Rainsborough championed their cause at Putney when Henry Ireton, Cromwell's son-in-law (and second in command of the army) expressed the views of the so-called army grandees that only men of property could have a say in the affairs of England. In a bitter cry for justice for the common soldier, Edward Sexby said, "We ventured our lives and it was all for this: to recover our birthright and privileges as Englishmen... I wonder we were so much deceived."[20]

In their many petitions and pamphlets, the Levellers called for the extension of the franchise to all men, equality under the law and religious tolerance for all, including Roman Catholics.

The range of principles they espoused came to be called "the Good Old Cause". The Good Old Cause had at its core freedom of conscience in religious matters. It also comprehended political principles such as "no rule by one man", "a constitutional republic", "annual election of a parliament responsible to the people alone", "the right to trial by jury", "no capital punishment or imprisonment for debt; freedom of the press and no license on printing".

Richard Overton, another Leveller, in his pamphlet *A Remonstrance of Many Thousand Citizens...*, addressed to the members of the House of Commons, demanded:

> We are men of the present age and ought to be absolutely free from all kinds of exorbitances, molestations or arbitrary power; and you we chose to free us from all, without exception or limitation either in respect of persons, officers, or things; and we were also full of confidence that ye would have dealt impartially on our behalf and made us the most absolute free people in the world.[21]

There were two tendencies or political factions within the Levellers. There were those who dreamed of a social republic in which there would be no private property or land, no buying or selling and neither rich nor poor.[22] However, the majority merely sought civil democracy, and the chief points in their programme were universal manhood suffrage, annual parliaments and complete religious liberty. As universal male suffrage was not achieved in Britain until the mid-nineteenth century, it could be said that even the moderate wing of the Levellers were two and a half centuries before their time.

"Freeborn John" Lilburne was the Levellers' most famous leader. He single-handedly reformed the British legal system by winning the right to fair procedures in his many courtroom battles as a defendant during the Interregnum (the period between the fall of Charles I and the restoration of Charles II, i.e. 1649 to 1660). Lilburne insisted on the right to be tried by his peers and got his way. He established the right of an accused person to reasonable comfort when he urinated on the courtroom floor when refused the use of a toilet.

The Levellers had taken advantage of the fall of the king and the Established Church to open new political possibilities. The floodgates to heresy were also thrown open. Without the constraints of a conservative hierarchy, Protestants were prone to drift towards schism and heresy. Roman Catholics could read scripture only in Latin or Greek. This ensured that the reading and the interpretation of scripture remained the preserve of the clergy and an elite group of scholars. Restricted access to scripture acted as a bulwark against "error".

Protestants had access to the scriptures in English and could read the Bible. Soldiers listened to lay preachers preaching as they pleased. Some of the new preachers were working men with no formal training in the ministry and were dismissed by their critics as "mechanic preachers". The soldiers were told by the new preachers that God had given them the victory over the king and his church. They were told that they were the "saints" or the "godly" and that their enemies were the tools of Satan or the Antichrist.

Parliament attempted to halt what they perceived to be a slide into religious anarchy. A gathering of Presbyterian divines was summoned to Westminster Abbey in 1643 and produced the "Westminster Confession of Faith". This document, running to thirty-three chapters, amounted to a Calvinist and Presbyterian orthodoxy which all Protestants would be required to accept. The Presbyterians' efforts to make Presbyterianism the established state religion failed. The major obstacle was Oliver Cromwell's rigid Independency and the strength of the Sects within the ranks of the New Model Army.

The Sects believed that no group – of priests, bishops of the Anglican Church, much less a high priest such as the Pope or even the Calvinist majority in the House of Commons – had a monopoly of truth in theological matters. The state had no business interfering in individual religious opinion. The Westminster Confession was a man-made test, and scripture held precedence over man-made tests, which might contain human error. The Sects held that religious congregations should have a say in choosing their minister: ministers appointed by a hierarchy become unresponsive to the needs of their congregation, and congregations would judge if a new minister was what they wanted and feel free to look elsewhere if they found the applicant unsuitable.

Men were reading scripture, interpreting it in different ways and reaching different conclusions; some were improving their knowledge of scripture and changing their opinions. There was no longer simply one truth, with all other views error and heresy. The Sects held that differences should be tolerated. When the demand for complete religious tolerance was argued through to its logical conclusion, it had revolutionary implications for political thought. When different religious views are tolerated, then different views on politics were also deserving of toleration. Toleration of diverse views on politics is the central principle of modern secular democracy.

Religious controversies were therefore a catalyst for further radical political thought. For instance, the Quakers, rejecting a convention which had existed for centuries, would not doff their hats to a "social superior" because they saw it as social submission and anathema to their egalitarianism. They used "thee" and "thou" rather than the formal "you" because they saw no man as their better regardless of his title or position. It is hardly surprising then that this attitude made princes, bishops and the social hierarchy uneasy. The Quakers' enemies wanted them suppressed, claiming that "those such as now introduce thou and thee will (if they can) expel mine and thine... dissolving all property into confusion".[23]

Anglicans and Presbyterians fought on opposite sides in the Civil War, but they had more in common with each other than the Presbyterians had with their former allies in the Dissenting Sects. Anglicans and Presbyterians believed that there should be a national church to which all citizens should belong. They differed, of course, in that both believed that it was their own church that

27

should be established and the competition suppressed. Independents, Congregationalists, Baptists and Quakers saw religious affiliation as a matter of individual choice or conviction.

Men moved easily between the Sects, and Christopher Hill suggests that a Quaker in the early 1650s had more in common with a Leveller, a Digger or a Ranter than with a modern member of the Society of Friends.[24] Anglicans and Presbyterians believed their clergy should be supported by tithes levied on the entire population. The Sects believed that a congregation should support its own chosen minister. These differing outlooks of "Church Type" and "Sect Type" are vital to understanding the dynamics of the religious history of the English Revolution.[25] The "Church Type" saw a role for government and the state in religious affairs, while the Sects saw no such role.

To Kill a King

The tension between the army and the majority in parliament increased, and not just about theological matters. Presbyterians in the House of Commons continued to negotiate with the defeated king during the time he was a prisoner. They hoped that he would agree to establish the Presbyterian Church. If the king had agreed, the Presbyterians would have restored the monarchy. The army and the Levellers were incensed by what they saw as the duplicity of the Presbyterians. Overton accused the Presbyterians of:

> Begging and entreating [the king] in such submissive language to return to kingly office... as if you were resolved to make us believe he were a god without whose presence we must fall to ruin, or as if it were impossible for any nation to be happy without a king.[26]

The New Model Army determined that rather than be restored to his throne, the king should face justice for his crimes against his people. Soldiers excluded the Presbyterian majority faction from parliament in a military coup known as "Colonel Pride's Purge". The colonel and his troops surrounded the House of Commons and expelled all members the soldiers deemed to be unsympathetic to their demands. It was the remaining "Independent" MPs, the so-called "Rump Parliament", who gave in to the army's demands and brought the king to trial and execution. When royalists used the term "king-killers" as a term of abuse, they were referring to the Rump Parliament, the Independents, the Sects or fanatics and the New Model Army.

The implication that the king was killed simply because he was king was misleading. Charles I was the first head of state to pay the ultimate price for making war on his own people. He was tried and found guilty and sentenced in a process that was public and transparent. Charles was charged with having drenched England in blood. He did not help his case by conspiring with Irish Protestant and Roman Catholic armies and the Scots up to the time of his trial, attempting to convince them to invade England and drench his English kingdom in blood yet again. The parliamentary army had intercepted his letters to the Duke of Ormond, the commander of the Protestant royalist forces in Ireland, instructing him to make peace with Irish Catholics in order that both could contribute soldiers to fight another war for the king on the British mainland. Cromwell had overcome a huge Scottish army at Preston in May 1648 which had invaded England at the invitation of Charles. Even in modern times, a man who would invite a foreign invader into his native country would face execution for treason.

In a recent re-evaluation of the trial, Geoffrey Robertson QC suggests that it was fair and just and could be defended on similar grounds to the trial and execution of the twentieth-century war criminals at Nuremburg.[27] At least one man directly involved in the affair had no doubt about the process of the trial or the outcome. Colonel Thomas Harrison, when he was charged with the king's murder, said, "It was not a thing done in a corner."

Cromwell's Campaign in Ireland

A few months after they had killed their king, Oliver Cromwell and his army came to Ireland. He landed at Ringsend in Dublin on 15 August 1649 with 12,000 soldiers. When Cromwell reached Dublin, the city was already under the control of forces loyal to him. Less than two weeks previously, on 2 August, the Parliamentary commander of Dublin, Michael Jones, had defeated the Duke of Ormond at Rathmines.

James Butler, Duke of Ormond, a member of Ireland's leading family and staunchly loyal to Charles I, had been reared in England and had led the Irish Protestant royalist forces since 1641. His army was smashed at Rathmines, and his munitions fell into the hands of his enemies.[28] Jones claimed that his forces killed 4,000 men and took more than 2,000 prisoners. Cromwell could land at Dublin without hindrance or molestation.[29]

Cromwell crossed the Irish Sea to subdue a country that had already endured eight years of civil war. The native Irish and Old English Roman Catholics had formed the Confederation of Kilkenny to fight Irish Protestants. Now after eight years of rebellion, civil war and chaos, a bewildering array of armies was in the field. At one point there were three armies in Ireland loyal to the English parliament: one at Dublin led by Jones, the others in Connaught and Munster led by Sir Charles Coote and Lord Inchiquin. Ormond's Irish Protestant army was loyal to the king. Since the outbreak of the rebellion in 1641, they had fought against the Old English and native Irish Catholics, who also claimed to be loyal to the king. From 1642, there was also a Roman Catholic army in Ulster under Eoghan Ruadh O'Neill (Owen Roe), the nephew of the "Great" Hugh O'Neill. Owen Roe had come from Flanders to fight for his Catholic religion and had no loyalty to the Protestant Charles I.

The execution of Charles and the fear that most Irish people felt in the face of the zealots and fanatics of the New Model Army insured that Ormond could unite all but the Parliamentary forces in an uneasy alliance to resist Cromwell. The outcome of Cromwell's war with Ormond would decide whether Ireland would fall under the rule of the parliament of England or form part of the kingdom of Charles II, the dead king's son.

In early September, Cromwell marched his army to Drogheda. After a short siege, his forces overran the town on 11 September. The behaviour of Cromwell and his army at Drogheda has been much disputed. It has been alleged that Cromwell's forces massacred the garrison and the civilian inhabitants of the town. Recent scholarship suggests that no contemporary documents support the allegation of a civilian massacre at Drogheda.[30] There is no disputing that many of the garrison at Drogheda were massacred.

Massacres were a common feature of warfare at the time. When a town refused the opportunity to surrender, no quarter was given. A besieging army forced to attack and capture a fortified garrison would kill all enemy combatants. Cromwell's offer of quarter in return for the surrender of Drogheda had been refused. Most of those butchered at Drogheda were soldiers and English and Irish Protestant royalists. The commander of the garrison at Drogheda, Aston, was an English Catholic royalist.

Some have claimed that those massacred were Irish Roman Catholics.[31] If Cromwell is best remembered in Ireland for his alleged massacre of Catholic civilians at Drogheda, he only has his own "blatant mendacity" to blame. He described the bloodshed as "a righteous judgement of God on barbarous wretches who had shed so much innocent blood".[32] He was therefore implying that the dead had been involved in the massacre of Protestants in 1641. Drogheda was a Protestant town which had suc-cessfully defended itself from a Catholic attack led by Phelim O'Neill in 1642. It is not clear why Cromwell would suggest that the Protestants killed at Drogheda were Catholics unless it was to make his victory more popular in England.

Cromwell marched his troops back to Dublin, and on or about 23 September, he headed south to attack Wexford. He finally appeared before Wexford with 7,000 foot and 2,000 horse on 1 October.[33] The garrison pro-ceeded to parley with Cromwell about surrender terms, but while the negotiations were continuing, the town was betrayed by an officer of the garrison, and Cromwell's sol-diers again set about a massacre. It was again alleged and contested that "hundreds of non-combatants were killed by rampaging troops".[34]

We have no doubt about the fate of the Roman Catholic priests at Wexford, for Cromwell himself appears to be boasting of murder as he tells us:

> some [priests] came holding forth crucifixes before them and conjuring our soldiers (for his sake that saved us all) to save their lives; yet our soldiers would not own their dead images for our living saviour; but struck them dead with their idols; many of their priests...were slain together by our soldiers about their altar.[35]

Cromwell next marched to New Ross, where the royal-ist garrison surrendered after a brief bombardment.[36] By mid November, Cromwell left New Ross to attack Waterford. The Waterford garrison refused to surrender, and Cromwell's forces laid siege to the city. However, the onset of winter and bad weather forced Cromwell to aban-don the siege and move to Dungarvan. In spite of the fail-ure at Waterford, Cromwell's good fortune continued when most of the Protestant garrisons in south Munster, includ-ing Cork, Bandon and Kinsale, declared for parliament.[37]

Cromwell rested his army at Cork and Youghal for the winter. He finally left winter quarters on 29 January to begin his spring campaign. He set about capturing the towns around Waterford and Kilkenny, and over the next few weeks Fethard, Callan, Cahir, Thomastown and Gowran fell to the New Model Army. After three days of assault by bombardment and infantry attacks, Kilkenny fell to Cromwell on 27 March 1650. Waterford clung on tenaciously but eventually fell to Ireton when the garrison began to quarrel amongst themselves.[38] However, Ireton did not take control of the city until August, by which time Cromwell himself had left Ireland for ever.

As defeat piled up on defeat, Ormond's position was becoming desperate. His Protestant troops were distrusted by their Catholic allies, and Cromwell managed to woo many of them away from their allegiance with generous surrender terms which allowed them to keep their estates. Ormond now only had Catholic troops on whom he could rely.[39]

Cromwell's last battle in Ireland was at Clonmel.[40] In early May, his troops moved on the town that was defended by Owen Roe with about 2,000 troops. On 9 May, after an effective bombardment, Cromwell's soldiers poured through a breach in the walls only to be stalled by secondary defences, and they had to retreat after taking terrible casualties. The defenders slipped away in the night. This was the nearest Cromwell had come to defeat in Ireland, or for that matter in his entire career.

The Westminster parliament ordered Cromwell to leave Ireland to deal with the deteriorating military position in Scotland, and he finally sailed away on 29 May 1650. He had been in the country for only nine months. In spite of his military success, he did not subdue Ireland. His subordinates such as Henry Ireton, Charles Fleetwood and Edmund Ludlow would continue the war, which dragged on for almost three years, finally ending in April 1653.[41] From the time of Cromwell's arrival to the end of hostilities three years later, Irish Roman Catholics had been treated with great cruelty.

Why did the New Model Army, fired by ideas of freedom of conscience, treat Roman Catholics with such sectarian brutality? Part of the answer has to be that the average English Protestant soldier and the preachers who accompanied them considered the native Irish racially and religiously inferior. The Irish spoke a barbarous tongue, dressed like savages, were steeped in Romanist superstition and were the dupes of the Antichrist. The Cromwellians on the other hand were the godly soldiers of the Lord who had cast down the tyrant. They had now come to the wilderness to deliver justice to the heathen to avenge the Irish Protestant dead of 1641.

Cromwell and his soldiers had been reared with stories of how bloody Mary Tudor had burnt hundreds of her Protestant subjects in the name of Roman Catholicism. Throughout the soldiers' lifetimes, the Thirty Year War had raged in Europe. This war involved the great European powers and was essentially a sectarian war in which Roman Catholic and Protestant armies matched each other in savagery. Thirty per cent of the civilian population of the German states died in the war. Englishmen believed that the forces of international Popery were bent on the destruction and extirpation of Protestantism. The English people lived in dread of Jesuit plots and invasion by "barbarous" Roman Catholic armies.

When the Irish Roman Catholics had risen in rebellion in 1641, their grievances were about usurped land, the oppressions of Black Tom Wentworth and their gradual exclusion from political influence.[42] They also were fighting for the freedom to practise their religion. The Protestants chose not to see it that way. For them, 1641 was a cowardly and unwarranted attack on godly Protestants who had lived in peace with their Roman Catholic neighbours for more than thirty years. Most English Protestants were convinced also that the rebellion in Ireland was part of the European war aimed at their destruction. The Pope sent his nuncio, Cardinal Rinuccini, to lead the revolt, and the Irish Catholics accepted his leadership. The Thirty Years War had come to Ireland. The English people were warned by alarmist pamphleteers that when the Irish Protestants were wiped out, the victorious forces of Popery in Ireland would turn their attention on England.

When Cromwell crossed the Irish Sea, he intended to prevent both Irish Catholics and Protestant royalists from invading England on behalf of Charles II. He also had vengeance on his mind for 1641.

Oliver Cromwell's time in Ireland was short, and it may be that both his military achievements and his fondness for atrocity have been exaggerated. It would be hard to exaggerate how the era of his rule changed Ireland for ever. His new regime embarked on a rigorous programme of land grabbing and expulsion of the native population. So although the war was about politics and land, it was also about religion.

The Rev. John Owen, who had stayed in Dublin preaching while the army fought, demanded that parliament recruit six preachers for pastoral work in the Dublin area. These persons "of pious life and conversation... qualified with gifts of preaching" began a crusade for "the advancement of religion and the propagation of the gospel... the suppression of idolatry, popery, and profaneness in that land".[43] The Dissenters and Wood Street and Saint Nicholas within the Walls were to be amongst the advanced guard in the war of religion.

The Cromwellians After the War in Ireland
The soldiers and settlers who came to Ireland between 1649 and 1660 were referred to as Cromwellians. Of a particular religious, political and social class, to their fellow Protestant neighbours, the Cromwellians were republicans, regicides and sectarian fanatics. They were "the

scum of England, a generation of mechanic bagmen who had come to power by conquest".[44] Edmund Burke, looking back over a century called, them "the mercenary soldiery of a regicide usurper".[45]

After subduing the country, they set about building a "true" Protestant reformation in a country in which the overwhelming majority of the population was Roman Catholic. They attempted to remove the native population of Ireland west across the Shannon to Connaught. They instigated a plantation of Protestants into the provinces of Leinster and Munster. They were only partially successful in their efforts to settle "godly" Protestants in the place of dispossessed Roman Catholics.

As far as Irish Roman Catholics were concerned, the Cromwellians were merciless butchers. Whatever about the truth or otherwise of the massacres at Drogheda and Wexford, there is no doubt that the Cromwellians and the New Model Army treated Irish Roman Catholics with harsh and cruel severity both during the war and its aftermath. Roman Catholic priests were ordered out of Ireland and often murdered on sight if they failed to comply. The Cromwellians' "to Hell or Connaught" policy would be recognised today as ethnic cleansing. Some of Cromwell's apologists suggest that he was unwell when in Ireland and that his behaviour was uncharacteristic. This is hardly credible, as the treatment meted out to the Irish Roman Catholics was not just down to Cromwell. The soldiers were enthusiastic participants in any cruelties inflicted, and parliament was supportive of the policy of expulsion. The Cromwellian expulsions continued for years after the war and were part of a calculated policy supported by most Englishmen, including those vehemently opposed to Oliver Cromwell.

"To Hell or Connaught" was applied mostly to the great Catholic landlords; the Catholic peasantry were not driven away because their labour was required by the new landowners. In the cities and towns, the dispossessed

Catholics were driven off, but many returned quickly because the regime was never able to encourage sufficient new settlers from England to take the place of the dispossessed.

Not all of the Cromwellians were ill-disposed to the native Irish. John Cooke, a lawyer who had prosecuted Charles I and defended John Lilburne, arrived in Ireland following the army's victory. He came with a mission to reform the legal system and to develop a new society on a "blank sheet of paper". Cooke foresaw a Protestant colony that could never again be challenged by an uprising or massacre such as he believed had taken place in 1641. Cooke had a great fondness for the native Irish, and he felt they could be civilised if they were exposed to the obvious truth of the Protestant religion. He believed that he had some success in Ireland and reformed the legal system in Munster to make it accessible to the poor. The rich Old English Protestants of Munster hated Cooke for siding with their poor tenants. At the Restoration, they were happy to give him up to the tender mercies of Charles II.[46] Because Cooke had been brave enough to step forward and prosecute the king, he was high up on the list of those who, when the time came, would be shown no mercy. He was executed as a regicide in 1660. Cooke's well-meaning and progressive reforms in Ireland did nothing to moderate the Roman Catholic folk memory regarding his fellow Cromwellians.

The Irish folk memory also exaggerated the crimes of Oliver Cromwell. Dr Maighréad Ni Mhurchadha has investigated the folk memory of Oliver Cromwell's four weeks in Dublin. She has recorded more than fifty allegations against him of attacks on property, desecration of religious sites, killing of individuals and destruction of houses and castles. He is alleged to have murdered nuns and monks and destroyed their religious houses as he moved from Dublin to Drogheda and Wexford.

Cromwell could not have been guilty of many of these alleged crimes. Some of the houses and castles were destroyed in the conflict, but many of the incidents happened before Cromwell arrived in Ireland. There were few, if any, monasteries or convents in Ireland at this time as they had been dissolved by Henry VIII in 1536. Dr Ni Mhurchadha makes a good point, that Thomas Cromwell oversaw the dissolution of the monasteries for Henry. There may have been a case of mistaken identity. She also observed that if Oliver Cromwell were responsible for all the destruction attributed to him on his way to Drogheda, he must have travelled there by three different roads.[47]

Oliver Cromwell brought a large number of radical republicans into Ireland as part of his invading army. Edmund Ludlow, Rev. John Owen, Rev. Hugh Peter and Colonel Robert Phayre had accompanied Cromwell across the Irish Sea. These men held radical political and religious views, as did many less well-known officers of the New Model Army. Some were Levellers and religious Independents. Some would later become Baptists and Quakers, and they opposed Cromwell's "rule by one man". At the time of the Cromwellian invasion, Baptists and Quakers were amongst the most enthusiastic of the army in Ireland, but later, because they objected to Cromwell becoming Lord Protector, they came to be seen as a challenge and a threat to the Cromwellian regime.

After the Cromwellian victory in Ireland, his officers became the local political rulers of the areas under their military control. When Cromwell left for England on 29 May 1650, never to return,[48] he left his son-in-law, Henry Ireton, in overall charge, but Ireton died of plague while besieging Limerick in 1651. Colonel John Hewson, a religious Independent, was military governor of Dublin.[49] Colonel Hewson's chaplain in Dublin was John Rodgers, who later became a Fifth Monarchist. Fifth Monarchists preached that the execution of Charles was a fulfilment of the prophesies of the Book of Revelation which heralded the fall of the Antichrist. Colonel Alexander Brayfield, governor of Athlone, was a Leveller. Colonel Thomas Sadler was governor of Galway and a Baptist, Colonel Phayre was governor of Cork, and Richard Hodden, a Quaker, was governor of Kinsale.[50] Ludlow was a republican and a Leveller sympathiser. He became commander of the army and was therefore in overall command of Ireland for a short time after the death of Ireton.

These revolutionary and republican soldiers founded "gathered" religious congregations where the "godly" could worship in accordance with their consciences. It was not easy to find godly ministers to abandon England and take up posts in Ireland, so Cromwell turned to the veterans of the New England Diaspora, and Rev. Nathaniel Weld and Rev. Samuel Mather obliged him by bringing their unique brand of militant Protestant dissent into Ireland.

Ludlow succeeded Ireton, but a short time later he was replaced by Charles Fleetwood, who married Ireton's widow. Fleetwood was a determined Independent, committed to religious tolerance. Ludlow had ensured that radical officers controlled the main towns and cities in Ireland. Some of these officers became Baptists while stationed in Ireland and refused to baptise their children, as they only believed in adult baptism. They alienated the Old English Protestants they had come to live amongst, and their rejection of child baptism also caused a breach with their fellow radicals and republicans, who continued to baptise their children.

The Baptists were also opposed to Cromwell's making himself Lord Protector. Charles Fleetwood did not move against them, holding fast to his view that these men were entitled to freedom of conscience, which for him was one of the main benefits of the Civil War.[51] The radicals' position was weakened by their reluctance to support the Lord Protector and by divisions amongst themselves. The Independents and the Baptists also clashed over the issue of military rule. The Baptists wanted military rule to continue as they were well placed in the army. The

Independents, who had supported the Rump Parliament, were in favour of civilian rule.[52]

Cromwell's son Henry replaced Fleetwood as lord lieutenant in 1657. Henry sidelined the radicals in favour of an alliance with the Old English Protestants. Oliver Cromwell was trying at this time to distance himself from his militant "godly" and Independent comrades in England. He was considering the offer from more conservative elements to become their king.

Henry has been credited with having broadened support for the Commonwealth in Ireland. Even the royalist historian Edward Hyde, first Earl of Clarendon, wrote kindly of Henry. Henry, who was particularly hostile to the Baptists and Quakers, purged and isolated the republicans. However, he was also suspicious of Samuel Winter's Independents. Although they had been Cromwell's most loyal supporters, they were no longer seen as trustworthy. Henry Cromwell undid the republican victory in Ireland and gave power back to the Old Protestant landed elite, many of whom were former royalists. He handed power to the class who later became known as the Protestant Ascendancy. The Cromwellian Protestants in southern Ireland and the Ulster Presbyterians were, from the very beginning, excluded from this "Ascendancy".

Some historians suggest that Henry Cromwell had no other choice but to ditch the republicans and court the Old English Protestant royalists because the republicans were divided and constituted too small an element of the population of Ireland for him to have relied on them. However, his decision most likely stemmed from the fact that he was a political conservative, and though he was an "Ironside" at the age of sixteen and a colonel at the age of twenty-two, he was suspicious of the radicalism of his fellow soldiers and officers.

Henry's new friends, the Protestant Ascendancy, handed Ireland back to Charles II as soon as the opportunity presented itself. After the death of Oliver Cromwell and the fall of Henry Cromwell in 1659, Ludlow returned to Ireland in an attempt to undo Henry's purges and save the republic, but by this time it was too late. The republicans in England and Ireland were in disarray, and Ludlow was not allowed to land at Dublin. The rule of the republicans was at an end, and Ireland and England were lost to the royalists.

Notes to Chapter One

1. Fraser 1997, p. 327
2. *Ibid.* p. 295
3. *Ibid.*
4. Holmes 2006, p. 1
5. *Ibid.*
6. *Ibid.*
7. Hill 2003, p. 14
8. Gregg, 2000, p. 113
9. Barnard 2004 B, p. 16
10. Reilly 1999, p. 19
11. Hibbert 2007, p. 207
12. Ashley 1959, p. 84
13. Robertson 2005, p. xvi
14. Gregg 2000, p. 160
15. As quoted in Manning 2003, p. 75
16. Gregg 2000, p. 160
17. Ashley 1959, p. 84
18. From a royalist ballad of 1643 denouncing the Puritans for banning Christmas festivities
19. Hunt 2002, p. 171
20. Gregg 2000, p. 220
21. 1646
22. Withers 1930, p. 154
23. Manning 2003, p. 18
24. Hill 1991, p. 14
25. Manning 2003, p. 22
26. Richard Overton, 'A Remonstrance of Many Thousand Citizens', 1646
27. Robertson 2005
28. McKeiver 2007, p. 59
29. S.J. Connolly 2008, p. 93
30. McKeiver 2007
31. *Ibid.* p. 63

32. S.J. Connolly 2008, p. 93
33. McKeiver 2007, p. 116
34. *Ibid.*
35. *Ibid.* p.122
36. S.J. Connolly 2002. p. 95
37. Esson 2009, p. 127
38. *Ibid.* p.135
39. *Ibid.* p.137
40. *Ibid.*
41. McKeiver 2007, p. 26
42. Of 256 MPs in 1634, 112 were Catholic; of 240 in 1640, 74 were Catholic (see Barnard 2000, p. 2)
43. Gribben 2007, p. 27
44. *Ibid.* p. 15
45. See O'Brien, C.C., ed., (2004), *Reflections on the Revolution in France*, p. 36
46. See Robertson 2005, p. 275
47. Lecture, "Cromwell's Four Weeks in Dublin", Dublin City Library, 9 March 2008 (Seacthain na Gaeilge)
48. McKeiver 2007, p. 25
49. Barnard 2000, p. 99
50. Manning 2003, p. 125
51. Barnard 2000, p. 100
52. *Ibid.*

Chapter Two

RESTORATION AND THE DISSENT

29 May 1660, London: the Monarchy Restored
His Majesty Charles II enters London after an exile of seventeen years. He leads an army of horse and foot reputed to be 20,000 strong. His soldiers brandish their swords and shout out in exultation. Church bells ring out and the fountains of London run with wine. Charles is determined to avenge the "murder" of his father. The regicides will now pay dearly for their crime or flee to the Continent in fear of the executioner's block. The newly restored king intends to break his promise to the Presbyterians and restore the position of the bishops in the Church of England. The bishops are determined to have their revenge on the "heretics and fanatics" who had displaced them during the Civil War.

Royalist Revenge and Reaction
Following the death of Cromwell, the republicans lost the initiative. Richard Cromwell succeeded his father as Lord Protector of England, but he lacked legitimacy, particularly within the ranks of the army, because of his lack of military experience. Although the parliament of England (the Rump Parliament), which by then consisted of only those members who had survived Pride's purge, was solidly republican, it also lacked legitimacy due to its unrepresentative nature. The election of a new parliament or the alternative of recalling the members excluded by Pride was certain to "produce a majority in favour of some kind of restoration of monarchy".[1]

Royalist agents went to work cajoling and bribing

important figures to plump for the restoration of Charles II. Their great breakthrough was to convince General Monck, who had a parliamentary army in Scotland, to march south. Ostensibly in favour of a more representative parliament, in reality he was overthrowing the republic, and just as a Dublin-based pamphleteer had warned: "and then comes in ding-dong bells King, Lords and Commons".[2]

The republican resistance was symbolic and somewhat pathetic. Colonel John Lambert, who had at one time been regarded as the man best placed to succeed Oliver Cromwell, went to the site of the battle at Edgehill to try to rally the army in defence of "the Good Old Cause". His followers had melted away, and all he could do was to fire a defiant shot before returning to London, where he was arrested and imprisoned in the Tower.

The republicans in Ireland were also in great difficulty. Sir Hardress Waller had settled in Ireland in 1629 and had been one of the regicides who had signed King Charles's death warrant.[3] Most Irish Protestants who had adapted to the Cromwellian regime did so because they wished to have the backing of a powerful English government in their conflict with Irish Roman Catholics. Their major concern now was to be seen to be on the winning side. Waller knew that he and his fellow republicans were in trouble. After an unsuccessful attempt to make his fellow army officers subscribe to a petition against the readmission of purged members of parliament, Waller was arrested by his own soldiers after a desperate bid to capture Dublin Castle.[4] It was now becoming clear that Charles II would rule in Ireland.

On 1 May 1650, a newly elected parliament of England declared Charles II king.[5] Crowds in London and other English cities who flocked out into the streets used the celebration to attack Dissenter meeting houses. Four days later, a Dublin crowd attacked a Baptist meeting house near Thomas Street, breaking up seats and tearing down the pulpit. On 14 May, the Dublin mob were marching in carnival mood. They carried:

> a hearse bedecked with candles... they carried an effi-
> gy of the Rump, a seeming carcass of a man st(uffed)
> with hay but without a head, followed by mourners
> with blackened faces. The people with their naked
> swords and staves hacked and battered at the Rump.

The scene was witnessed by a merchant who was delighted to declare that "the heretics and sectaries are deservedly laid aside".[6]

The Restoration of Charles II ushered in a new era. Almost the first act of the new authorities in Ireland was to arrest John Cooke and John Phayre and ship them in chains to London. Cooke was tortured to death in front of Hugh Peter (Cromwell's personal chaplain) in a terrifying preview of what was about to happen to Peter himself.[7] Peter was forced to look on while Cooke was taken down from the gallows; his bowels were cut out and burnt in front of him while he was still conscious. Peter cringed in terror at the sight. However, when his own turn came, Peter was suddenly transformed and displayed a calm and resolute demeanour. He looked to the sheriff and said, "You have slain one of the servants of God before my eyes so as to terrify me but God has given me strength." He then walked up to the scaffold unaided to face death brave-ly. He was slowly tortured to death in the same barbaric fashion as his friend.[8] All the while the crowd jeered him, calling out, "Where is your Good Old Cause now?"

The Irish-based regicide Hardress Waller escaped to France but eventually returned to England and was sen-tenced to death. His sentence was commuted and he died in prison in Jersey in 1666. John Phayre avoided execution by testifying against his friends. Ludlow escaped into exile on the Continent. Cromwell and Ireton were dead by this time, and Charles had to be content with desecrating their graves at Westminster Abbey and hanging their disinterred corpses.

The one-time preacher at Wood Street, Rev. John Owen, escaped the royalist vengeance due to friends in high places and his great reputation as a scholar. Owen has been described as "an intellectual and a physical giant".[9] He had returned to England after his time in Wood Street to become vice-chancellor of Oxford University. A strong defender of the Cromwellian regime, Owen had been in charge of the security of the city when a loyalist uprising was expected in 1654. He "was frequently seen riding at the head of a troop of horse. He was well mounted and armed with a pistol and sword."[10] Even though he was strong in the Cromwellian cause, Owen had remained on good terms with Edward Hyde, who became Charles II's chancellor. The inscription on a portrait of Owen preserved in the Dublin Unitarian Church records that Edward Hyde introduced Owen to Charles II. Hyde offered Owen the opportunity to keep his post at Oxford if he would conform to the Established Church. Owen, who was resolute in his religious principles, refused Hyde's offer. He was ejected from his university post, but his life was spared. Since he had once described the execution of Charles I as "the Lord's work", he must have considered himself a very fortunate man indeed.

The Restoration in Ireland gave rise to two immediate issues. What was to be done about the army, and what approach would the restored king take to the Cromwellian land confiscations? By 1662, James Butler, Duke of Ormond, was back in control of Irish affairs as lord lieutenant. After his defeat in Ireland, Ormond had gone into exile with Charles II, and his steadfast loyalty was finally rewarded. The Cromwellian army was now under the control of the man they had run out of Ireland a decade earlier.

Ormond purged this disaffected army, a Cromwellian creation which was regarded as a republican threat. Gradually it was reduced in numbers from 15,000 to 6,000, because "the inferior officers and common soldiers could not be relied upon".[11] But the army was not Ormond's most intractable problem; the Irish Roman

Rev. John Owen

Catholics who had been loyal to Charles I wanted their estates restored. However, this could only happen at the expense of Irish Protestants, royalists and Cromwellians. While the Catholic claimants pressed their petitions on Ormond, his Protestant royalist friends and allies who had supported Charles II were opposed to any reopening of the land question in favour of dispossessed Catholics.

The Cromwellian landowners and soldiers, who expected no support from the new regime, became involved in a series of plots and intrigues. In March 1662, Ormond revealed a plot by Dublin tradesmen, mostly former Cromwellian soldiers, to seize Dublin Castle. In May he revealed yet another plot, again involving serving and former soldiers.[12]

The plots were instigated by junior officers and religious radicals who intended to capture Dublin Castle and follow up with rebellion in Munster and Dublin. Colonel Alexander Jephson, MP for Trim, was executed following the failure of the second plot, and seven other members were expelled from the Irish House of Commons.[13] This plot is often referred to as Blood's Plot, as Colonel Blood, who later achieved fame for stealing the Crown jewels, was the best known of the conspirators. Ormond cracked down on religious dissent and political militants, and three army officers and a Presbyterian minister were executed.

For Ormond and his newly restored Anglican bishops, the former Cromwellian soldiers and religious militants in Dublin were not their only problem arising from turbulent Protestant Dissent. Nonconformism was growing in Ulster. Many Scottish Presbyterian ministers who had been ejected from their livelihoods in Scotland came to Ulster. There were several unsuccessful plots and rebellions in Scotland against the Restoration, and each failure led to a further flood of militant Scottish Presbyterians escaping to Ulster. Their Irish brethren (many of whom had themselves come from Scotland to escape persecution in the reign of James I) welcomed them and gave them shelter. Even some wealthy landowners such as Montgomery of Londonderry and Hamilton of Killyleagh were prepared to support their Scots cousins by giving them refuge in their substantial country houses. Hamilton of Killyleagh was an ancestor of the leader of the United Irishmen Archibald Hamilton Rowan. Robert Mossam, the Anglican Bishop of Derry, reported in alarm to Ormond that "fractious preachers run out of Scotland like wild boars hunted out of the forest and throw their foam of seditious doctrine among the people".[14]

By the middle of 1663, some Presbyterian ministers in counties Antrim and Down were in prison and some were on the run.[15] There had been no Ulster Presbyterian involvement in Blood's plot, but nevertheless Ormond used it as an excuse to crack down on the northerners. He ordered the imprisonment of all Presbyterian ministers in Ulster.

The Bishop of Derry complained that he did not have a suitable prison to hold all his arrested ministers securely. The Bishop of Raphoe had the same complaint but nonetheless kept some of them under lock and key until 1670.[16]

The Irish Dissenters resented the oppression by the Established Church and felt that they, as Protestants, were being treated more harshly than the Irish Roman Catholics, who were at this time confidently pressing their claims for the restoration of their estates.

Life also became difficult for Dissenters in England as Charles suppressed Dissenting congregations throughout the country. Blaming the Presbyterians and the Sects for starting the Civil War, the king regarded the Sects as fanatics who had been guilty of "overthrowing a Protestant Church and murdering a Protestant King". His restored Established Church insisted that Nonconformist views were heretical. Dissenters were banned from civil and military office. Chancellor Hyde introduced the Clarendon Code (1661–1665), which was designed to suppress religious dissent. It required all ministers to subscribe to the Book of Common Prayer and banned Nonconformist ministers from coming within five miles of a town where they had served. The Clarendon Code applied only in England and Scotland, but Ormond followed an equally oppressive policy in Ireland.

The Act of Uniformity (1662) had made it obligatory for a minister to be consecrated by a bishop of the Anglican Church. This led to 2,000 ministers throughout England and Ireland being ejected from their livings. In Dublin at least twelve ministers were forced to resign and leave their places of worship. Many of them were regarded as men of "distinguished piety, learning and eloquence who were manifestly suffering for conscience sake".[17] Many of their congregations stood by them; thus the number of Nonconformists in Dublin actually increased in this period. Rev. Samuel Winter and Rev. Samuel Mather were amongst those ejected. Their Independent congregation had to withdraw from St Nicholas within the Walls.[18] Winter was now expelled from his position in Trinity, and he and Mather had to leave Ireland. Rev. Mather, whose roots were in the New England Diaspora, had also come to Dublin at the behest of Cromwell. Their ejection from their livings was a great reversal of fortunes for a congregation which a few years before had enjoyed the support of the Cromwell regime.

Samuel Mather had demonstrated his commitment to religious tolerance when the influence of his congregation was at its highest. When Cromwell asked him to displace Anglican ministers, he had refused, saying he had come to Dublin to preach the gospel, not to hinder others from doing so.[19] Now, however, the Anglicans showed no reluctance to hinder Mather from preaching, and when given the opportunity, they drove him out of Ireland. He soon returned and re-established his congregation. Displaced from St Nicholas, he continued to preach in his house, expressing his disapproval of the restored episcopacy and the Book of Common Prayer.[20] He was arrested while preaching there and was sent to prison for a short time. Rev. Mather quickly learned that if he and his congregation were to enjoy any level of toleration, he needed to be careful about expressing opinions. He was released from prison in 1662 and preached in a new meeting house at New Row.

Mather had lived through the changes of fortunes of the Commonwealthmen. He had been through Archbishop Laud's persecution, the New England migration, the Civil War and the execution of the king. He had seen his prosperous and once well-connected congregation in Dublin suppressed. He returned to rebuild it, but this time he would be prudent. In spite of Mather's circumspection, a spark of the old Commonwealth militancy would sometimes flicker within the ranks of the congregation.

Rev. Jeremiah Marsden was an assistant minister to Mather at New Row in 1669. He had been chaplain to the

noted republican Colonel Robert Overton in 1659.
Marsden had raised a rebellion against Charles II in
Yorkshire in 1663, after the failure of which he fled to
Dublin. He declared openly in Dublin that he wanted to
"pull down the magistrates and preach the Fifth
Monarchy". The Fifth Monarchists were a radical sect
with roots in the New Model Army. They regarded the
Book of Revelation as prophetic, and they preached that
the execution of Charles I was the beginning of "the age of
virtue" which would lead to a thousand year rule of the
godly. The Fifth Monarchists had shared in the victory of
the Civil War and supported Oliver Cromwell until he
became Lord Protector. They could not accept Cromwell's
"rule by one man" and reluctantly withdrew their support
for his regime. Their leader Thomas Harrison, once a close
friend of Cromwell, was executed as a regicide at the
Restoration in 1660. A year later the Fifth Monarchists
were crushed utterly when they tried to stage a rebellion in
London.

Marsden had therefore tried to introduce the Dublin
New Row Dissenters to the most radical doctrine to
emerge from the English Revolution. Marsden very publicly refused to pray for the king and denounced Charles as
the ruler of Sodom and Gomorrah.[21] Such radicalism put
the Dublin New Row congregation in an increasingly pre-
carious situation in what were already very dangerous
times.

Samuel Mather understood the need for caution. He had
himself preached and refused to disown what he called
"the sober notion of the Fifth Monarchy". He had
opposed the Restoration, but he told his young assistant
that they had to accept current realities and not dream of
other times.[22] Mather had clearly learned to compromise in
order to ensure his survival and the survival of his congregation, but this was a lesson his assistant could not learn.
Jeremiah Marsden died in Dublin's Newgate prison in
1684, still holding his Fifth Monarchist views.[23] Despite the

fate of their assistant minister, the New Row congregation survived and prospered, due in no small measure to Samuel Mather's prudence.

The Wood Street and New Row Dissenters were described in time as English Presbyterian. The term "English Presbyterian" also came to be used in England to distinguish the more liberal and heterodox Dissenters from mainstream Presbyterian congregations. This has puzzled historians, but it may be that the term originated in Dublin to distinguish between the Scottish and English Nonconformists in the city and was then taken back to Britain as a description of the more liberal Independent congregations there.

From the Restoration in 1660 to the Glorious Revolution of 1688, the Sects maintained their congregations in spite of persecution and the hostility of government and the Established Church. They had to tread carefully lest they bring down the full rigour of the law on their heads, but government pressure did not succeed in closing them down, and they continued to demand religious toleration. The toleration they sought was freedom of worship and total civil liberty for all. It is not clear from the record whether this toleration was to be extended to Roman Catholics.

Dissenting ministers were much given to denunciations of Popery. This does not mean that they were necessarily prejudiced against Roman Catholics or supported the anti-Catholic penal laws. For Dissenters, Popery meant a system of political and religious hierarchy presided over by the Pope and bishops. Popery allegedly promoted superstition and idolatry and was thrust on a peasantry kept in ignorance and denied access to the scriptures. Popery denied any political or religious authority to a man's conscience or reason. Denouncing Popery did not mean that one supported political oppression of Roman Catholics in order to force them to change their opinions. Such oppression was exactly what Dissenters most resented about the

Established Church. Dissenters often pointed out that someone who changes their religion because of political oppression is not a convert but a hypocrite.

Within a few years of the ejections that followed the Restoration, the Dissenters gradually moved back into their meeting houses or built new ones. They were careful not to appear to be opposing the king or his government. However, the royalists and Tories had long memories, and the Dissenters were never allowed to forget who was now in charge. More than eighty years after their arrival in Ireland in the 1730s, some of their Irish Protestant neighbours would taunt them with doggerel which had more historical than poetic merit:

> Jack Presbyter blue tumbled down crown and mitre,
> Murdering the King, Wentworth and Laud.[24]

The Dublin Dissenters would not be allowed to forget their assocaition with those who had committed and justified the terrible crime of regicide.

Murder and Memory

The royalists were anxious to rewrite history in order that the British people would always remember with horror the republican anarchy of the Interregnum. Royalist propagandists transformed Charles I from a "Man of Blood" into an Anglican saint. The anniversary of his death, 30 January, was designated a church holiday, and Tory churchmen used it to praise passive obedience, to condemn rebellion and to attack religious dissent. The anniversary continued to be marked by royalists even after the Glorious Revolution and into the Hanoverian era. The Irish Tory churchman Jonathan Swift preached a sermon on the anniversary in 1710 to brand all those Protestants who were opposed to the Established Church as Dissenters, Socinians (meaning Unitarians) and deists.[25]

In parliamentary speeches, as well as pamphlets and sermons, Irish Tories condemned Presbyterian and Protestant

Dissenting communities in general as enemies of the establishment.[26] They would be reminded of their past involvement in rebellion, republicanism and regicide.[27] Tories
would often point out that those opposed to episcopacy
and the Established Church were by definition also the
enemies of monarchy. In this regard they loved to quote
James I's famous riposte to the Puritans when they asked
to be freed from the oppression of bishops. James replied,
"No bishop, no king."

One Tory churchman spelt out the relationship between
civil and church hierarchy in these terms: "Episcopacy and
Monarchy are, in their Frame and Constitution best suit-
ed to each other. Episcopacy can never thrive in a
Republican Government or republican principles in an
Episcopal Church."[28]

The royalists did not have it all their own way when it
came to remembering the past. While they marked 30
January to lament the murder of a saintly king, there is
evidence that some Dissenters discreetly celebrated the
event. There are lurid accounts published in 1703 and
1714 of republicans drinking toasts from a calf's skull and
singing an anniversary anthem in honour of the regicides.
It is likely that these stories are the invention of conservative propaganda.[29]

However, at the end of the eighteenth century, the
Dissenters in Belfast held an annual dinner at a club called
the Washington on 30 January to celebrate the execution
of Charles.[30] William Drennan, whose friends organised
this event, had signed a letter dated 30 January 1778 with,
"May tyrants tremble at the day."[31] He apparently regarded 30 January 1649 and the execution of Charles I as a
defining event in the evolution of human liberty.

Although the Restoration appeared at first to have been
carried out successfully, and the Stuart monarchy returned
to power without a rerun of the violence of the Civil War,
the deep divisions which existed in British society persisted.
The attempts to crush Protestant dissent did not succeed,

but they did make Dissenters more prudent in their actions and utterances, and the suspicions that the Stuarts were the allies of Popery were not assuaged. The monarch, his state and his bishops, by their continued attacks on Protestant dissent, strengthened the conviction that the state was no friend to true religion and that if a man is denied freedom of conscience by his monarch, he is oppressed by a tyrant.

Notes to Chapter Two
1. S.J. Connolly 2008, p. 124
2. *Ibid.*
3. *Ibid.*
4. *Ibid.*
5. *Ibid.*
6. *Ibid.* p. 128
7. Robertson 2005, p. 338
8. *Ibid.*
9. Stewart 1993, p. 102
10. *Ibid.*
11. Barnard 1997, p. 48
12. S.J. Connolly 2002, p. 135
13. Kilroy 1994, p. 24
14. *Ibid.* p. 231
15. *Ibid.* p. 229
16. *Ibid.*
17. Armstrong 1829, p. 55
18. Kilroy 1994, p. 63
19. *Ibid.* p. 61
20. *Ibid.*
21. *Ibid.* p. 67
22. *Ibid.* p. 67
23. *Ibid.* p. 68
24. Barnard 1997, p. 16
25. Fauske 2002, p. 48
26. Hayden, D.W., in Herlihy 1997, p. 53
27. *Ibid.*
28. See Fauske 2002, p. 44
29. Campion 2003, pp. 95–97
30. Agnew 1999, vol. 1, p. 475
31. Agnew 1998, vol. 1, p. 35

Chapter Three

PLOT, REBELLION AND GLORIOUS REVOLUTION

7 December 1688: Londonderry

The Protestant citizens of this walled city are gripped by fear and panic. James II, their lawful king, has absconded to the Roman Catholic court of Louis of France. Richard Talbot, the Catholic royalist Earl of Tyrconnell, is determined to hold Ireland for his master and help James to regain his British throne. Tyrconnell has terrified Irish Protestants by dismissing more than 7,000 soldiers from the Irish army, either because they were "Old Cromwellians" or just old Protestants.[1] An anonymous letter sent to Sir Hugh Montgomery at his house in Comber on the third of the month warned that on 9 December the (Catholic) "Irish" will commence a nationwide massacre of Protestants.

Within twenty-four hours, Dissenting ministers in Dublin are reading the "Comber Letter" from their pulpits.[2] Rev. Nathanial Weld of New Row and Rev. Daniel Williams of Wood Street are as terrified as some of their flocks and decide to flee. Thirty-three ships, packed mostly with Protestant women and children, sail from the port of Dublin bound for the safety of England between the seventh and ninth of December.[3]

Meanwhile an army of "dreadfully starved" Irish and Highlanders, commanded by the Catholic Earl of Antrim, marches towards Londonderry. The citizens of Londonderry fear that they are to be massacred. The Anglican bishop, Ezekiel Hopkins, warns that barring entry to the king's troops would be treason. Rev. Gordon, a Dissenting minister, urges the younger men to shut the city gates. Approximately a dozen young men of the lower classes draw their swords, seize the keys of the city and hoist the drawbridge. In defying the army of James II, the "Apprentice Boys of Londonderry" bring the Glorious Revolution to Ireland.

Tories and Whigs

Politically motivated citizens in England and Ireland in the late seventeenth and eighteenth centuries were either Tories or Whigs. Tories tended to be conservative supporters of monarchy. They believed that kings were above the law and that subjects should be passively obedient to their king. As loyal members of the Established Church, many of them regarded religious dissent as a crime and Dissenters as socially disruptive fanatics.

Tories gave their loyalty to any incumbent monarch, and many who had been loyal to James II were prepared to transfer that loyalty to William III when circumstance dictated. If God saw fit to replace James with William, then a God-fearing Tory held that all subjects should be obedient to the "powers that be". The Established Church and the king were seen as deriving their authority directly from God, and it was the Christian duty of all subjects to be loyal, regardless of the monarch's behaviour or actions.

Whigs held that the monarch's power was limited by law and parliament. The Whigs associated royal absolutism with Popery and tyranny. A Whig-dominated Protestant parliament had a duty to withhold the Crown from a Roman Catholic heir to the throne. They feared that kings, if unchecked, would dilute the authority of parliament. The Roman Catholic kingdoms of Europe were, in the view of the Whigs, ruled by tyrants who in turn were subject to the religious tyranny of the Pope in Rome. Whigs tended to be tolerant of religious dissent: not all Whigs were Dissenters, but all Dissenters were Whigs. They opposed any extension of royal power and stressed the rights and liberties of freeborn (Protestant)

Englishmen. With the exceptions of William III and George I, whom the Whigs regarded as the saviours of the Protestant succession, they believed that successive monarchs had conspired to deprive freeborn citizens of their liberties. The Whigs' much vaunted toleration did not extend to Roman Catholics. Roman Catholic kings were regarded as tyrants, and Roman Catholic commoners, including the majority of the Irish population, were the "willing slaves of despotism" and hence unsuitable for political liberty. [4]

The Protestant interest was paramount, and Whigs would not accept a Roman Catholic monarch, no matter how legitimate his or her claim to the throne. They feared that a Catholic monarch would accept the temporal authority of the Papacy and suppress Protestantism in England. Had not "Bloody Mary" Tudor tried to do as much in the mid 1550s? A Catholic monarch would be required by his religious convictions to rule as a despot with absolute and tyrannical power. Such a monarch would undo the Reformation and turn England into a Roman Catholic theocracy.

The Duke of York, the future James II, made public his Roman Catholicism in 1673. As a result the Whigs fought resolutely, but in vain, to prevent his ascending the throne in 1685. He and his older brother Charles had been reared as Protestants, but their mother, Henrietta Maria of France, was a Roman Catholic. She was suspected of covertly rearing her children in her faith, suspicions which had some foundation in reality. Both brothers would eventually avow their Roman Catholicism. In James' case, he did so as a young man, while Charles waited until he was on his deathbed. Some historians believe that Charles's deathbed conversion had more to do with the manipulation of a sick man by his unscrupulous brother than any particular religious convictions on the part of Charles himself. However, the suspicion that the Stuart monarchs since the accession of Charles I were in sympathy with Popery was to remain a destabilising aspect of his reign and that of his two sons, Charles II and James II.

Charles II having produced many children but no legitimate heir, James was next in line to the throne. By his avowal of Roman Catholicism, he galvanised Whig opposition to his accession. The Whigs tried to use their majority in parliament to pass an Exclusion Bill, preventing a Roman Catholic from ascending the British throne. On a number of occasions, Charles prevented the bill from passing into law by dissolving parliament.

Meanwhile, the Roman Catholics of Ireland were looking forward to a new Catholic Stuart king in the hope that he would ease their religious disabilities and restore the lands they had lost for the "crime" of serving James's father Charles I. The Irish Whigs and Protestants feared James for the very reason the Irish Roman Catholics would welcome him to the throne.

Algernon Sidney and the Rye House Plot

The Whigs were so determined to block the accession of James that they turned to a strategy of assassination. In 1683, they engaged in the conspiracy which became known as the Rye House Plot. The king and his brother were to be ambushed as they returned from the races at Newmarket.[5] The would-be assassins, reputed to be about one hundred in number, concealed themselves in a malting house belonging to Richard Rumbold, a one-time officer in the New Model Army. There was a fire at the king's house in Newmarket, and the royal party left the race meeting early, thereby avoiding the danger. The failure and exposure of the conspiracy led to a round-up of the Whig leaders. Richard Rumbold, John Wildman (a former Leveller) and Rev. Robert Ferguson (a Scottish clergyman) were implicated but escaped abroad. The exposure of the plot led to the execution of two of the Whig leaders, Algernon Sidney and William, Lord Russell.

Algernon Sidney (1623–1683) was a veteran of the Civil

War and had in fact been the first republican to come to Ireland. Sidney was a lieutenant colonel in the parliamentary army and governor of Dublin for a short time in 1646. He had fought heroically in the Civil War and was "dangerously wounded" at Marston Moor.[6] At some point Sidney wrote what later became a noted republican tract, *Discourses Concerning Government*. This work was not published until 1698, fifteen years after his death. Sidney was one of the first writers in early modern history to question hereditary kingship and suggest that a free people should choose its government.

Sidney had quarrelled with Cromwell over the execution of the king, and that is possibly why, unlike some of his republican comrades, he was not put to death at the Restoration. His luck did not hold, and he was executed at the age of sixty for his involvement in the Rye House Plot. At his trial, the views expressed in Sidney's unpublished *Discourses* and other private papers were used to prove the prosecution's case.

Lord Chief Justice George Jeffreys, the "Hanging Judge", presided at the trials of Sidney and his co-accused William Lord Russell and took great delight in sentencing them to death. As Sidney mounted the scaffold, he handed the sheriff a document protesting his innocence and outlining his principles. His first principle is the very essence of republicanism: "that God had left Nations unto the Liberty of setting up such Governments as best pleased themselves".[7]

Sidney "died stoutly and like a true republican", proclaiming his loyalty and lifelong commitment to the "Old Cause".[8] In death he became martyr for liberty and the foremost hero in the Whig pantheon. For a century and a half after his execution, his martyrdom would be recounted, his murderers excoriated and his reputation defended by Whig propagandists. During the American Revolution, both Thomas Jefferson and Benjamin Franklin acknowledged that they had been influenced by Sidney's posthumously published work. Thomas Jefferson described Sidney's writ-

ten work as "a rich treasure of republican principles".[9]
Sidney's status as a secular radical saint was probably the
most elevated and enduring of any figure in the history of
the English-speaking world.

More than 100 years after his execution, his memory
was still being toasted at Dissenter gatherings such as the
Birmingham dinner commemorating the fall of the Bastille
which led to the notorious Priestley riots in 1791. His most
well-known phrase was: "Where liberty is, there is my
country." In that same year of 1791, the Belfast United
Irishmen carried Sidney's famous slogan under a portrait of
Benjamin Franklin on 14 July as they commemorated the
fall of the Bastille.[10] When William Orr of Ferranshane
became the first United Irishmen to be judicially murdered
in 1797, the organisation published a list of toasts, including, "the cause for which Hampden[11] bled on the field,
Sidney on the scaffold and Orr on the gibbet".[12] It is clear
from the founder of the United Irishmen William
Drennan's letters to his sister in the 1780s and 1790s that
the trial and execution of Sidney and Russell formed an
important element of his Dissenter and republican mythology and identity. He referred to Sidney and Russell having
"sainted names", and when he used the pseudonym
"Sidney" for some of his early writings, it must have been
to honour his hero. The United Irish leader Robert Emmet
had also imbibed the mythology of the Whig martyrs
which is why, the night before his execution, he compared
his own martyrdom in 1803 with Sidney's in 1663.[13]

When Sidney was arrested, many prominent Dissenters,
including the philosopher John Locke and the plotters
Wildman, Rumbold and Ferguson, fled to Holland.
Rumbold unwisely returned to Britain and was captured
and executed in Scotland in 1685. Rumbold told the crowd
who witnessed his execution that "the mass of mankind
has not been born with saddles on their backs, nor a
favoured few men booted and spurred ready to ride them
legitimately".

In the last letter he ever wrote, Thomas Jefferson recalled these famous last words with approval more than 150 years later, on the occasion of the fiftieth anniversary of the American Declaration of Independence. The architect of the American Revolution hailed not just Algernon Sidney, but also Rumbold and his fellow Rye House Plotters as fighters for human liberty.

Two years after the Rye House Plot, Charles II died in his bed. His death was a calamity for the Exclusionists. They shed no tears for their king, who became known as the "Merry Monarch". Charles had butchered the regicides Hugh Peter, John Cooke, and Thomas Harrison in 1660. Later he executed Sidney, Russell and Rumbold. He had also restored episcopacy, reneged on promises of religious toleration and presided over the persecution of Dissenters. His death was a calamity because the heir to the throne was his brother, the avowed Roman Catholic James Stuart, Duke of York. James II became England's first Roman Catholic monarch since "Bloody Mary" Tudor. As the Roman Catholics of Ireland celebrated the accession of a king of Celtic lineage and of the old faith, the Protestant Dissenters in England and Ireland viewed the future with trepidation. The Whig philosophers sharpened their nibs, while Whig plotters sharpened their blades.

Monmouth's Rebellion

James set about promoting Roman Catholics to positions of influence in England and Ireland. He terrified the Protestants of Ireland, Anglican and Dissenter, by appointing Richard Talbot (later Viscount Tyrconnel), a Roman Catholic, as lord deputy. Talbot, noted for his foul temper, his violent language and his aggressive Catholicism,[14] seemed to have great influence with James. He injected new vigour into the controversy which had dogged Charles II and Ormond in relation to Ireland by pressing for the restoration of Catholic lands lost in the Cromwellian settlement. The Irish Protestants feared that the Roman

Catholics who had been dispossessed for supporting Charles I might now get their land back. Talbot purged the remaining Cromwellian element in the ranks of the Irish army. When the Protestants were replaced by Roman Catholics, the worst fears of the Exclusionist Whigs and the Protestant Irish appeared to be borne out.

The promotion of Roman Catholics such as Talbot in Ireland was justified on the basis that representatives of the majority population should be a natural part of any civilised government. However, the promotion of Roman Catholics to powerful posts in Protestant England was seen as the manoeuvrings of a tyrant. Many of the Catholics whom James promoted in England had come with him from exile in France. They were regarded as parvenus and upstarts, particularly by those who felt that they themselves had been denied the preferment they thought their due. The Jesuits were encouraging James to align himself with Louis XIV of France, the great absolutist monarch in Europe, who was despised and feared by all Protestant England. The rich and well-established Catholics of England, and even the Pope, thought James's links to the Jesuits and Louis ill-advised. The Catholics "who are closest to the court of Rome" were advising James that "if he join with the interest opposed to France, he would have the hearts of the people".[15]

The Dissenter exiles in Holland plotted a rebellion against the new king to be led by Charles's illegitimate son, the Duke of Monmouth (1649–1685). He had been implicated in the Rye House Plot, but had been pardoned by his father and had fled to Holland. When the time was adjudged right, Monmouth issued a proclamation drafted by Robert Ferguson which reflected the demands of the Levellers and other radical reformers of the 1640s and 1650s.[16] Under the influence of veteran republicans, Monmouth promised regular parliaments, a broadened franchise and religious toleration even for Roman Catholics. Monmouth's landing in England from Holland was to be the signal for uprisings by Dissenters in London and Scotland.

The plotters believed that Protestant England would rally to Monmouth when he landed with only eighty-two companions, and many Dissenters did rush to join the revolt. Thousands of poor, simple men flocked to join Monmouth's colours in what has been described as "the last popular rising of Old England and the last flash of the Good Old Cause".[17] Monmouth was easily defeated at the battle of Sedgemoor. He went to the scaffold at Tower Hill on 15 July 1685. It is said that the execution was a horribly botched affair. An intoxicated executioner, Jack Ketch, a local butcher, failed to sever Monmouth's head with five blows of his axe. He finished the job with a knife.

Not everyone agrees that Monmouth's rebellion was the last flash of the Good Old Cause. A twentieth-century historian has suggested that the rebellion and the Rye House conspiracy were part of the movement of opinion that brought King Charles I to the scaffold and which was to thrust King James II into exile for ever.[18] Robert Ferguson, the Rye House plotter and author of Monmouth's proclamation, had been a one-time friend of the former preacher at Wood Street, Dublin, Rev. John Owen. Rev. Owen may have been on the fringes of the Rye House Plot, but if he was, he escaped detection. He was most certainly aware of Monmouth's plans and may have helped to recruit soldiers for him.[19]

James wreaked a cruel and pitiless revenge. Judge Jeffreys instigated the "the Bloody Assizes" and imposed the death penalty on 1,000 Dissenters for their part in the revolt. Two hundred and fifty people, including two women, were executed, while the remainder had their sentences commuted and were shipped as slaves to the West Indies.[20]

Jeffreys' victims were beheaded and quartered and their mutilated bodies put on public display as befitted traitors and rebels. Thomas Babington Macaulay recounts how:

At every spot where two roads met, on every market place, on the green of every large village which had furnished Monmouth with soldiers, ironed corpses clattering in the wind, or heads and quarters stuck on poles, poisoned the air, and made the traveller sick with horror.

Jeffreys was often drunk, and he berated the accused before he pronounced the sentence of death. He sentenced Alice Lisle, a deaf and frail old woman in her seventies, to be burnt at the stake for the crime of feeding a starving rebel. Perhaps Alice Lisle's real crime was to have been the widow of John Lisle, who had assisted in the trial of Charles I. John Lisle had been murdered by the king's agents in Lausanne the previous year.[21] Instead of dying by fire as Jeffreys had decreed, old Alice Lisle was beheaded at Winchester or 2 September 1685.

Jeffreys made many insulting and foul-mouthed statements during the trials. Once he said, "There is not one of those lying snivelling Presbyterian rascals but one way or another had a hand in the late horrid conspiracy."[22] Jeffreys thereby earned for himself an infamous reputation as a judicial tyrant who was motivated by an aversion to Protestant Dissenters.

The Bloody Assizes and the murder of Alice Lisle would be long remembered. More than one hundred years later, Jeffreys would be recalled in a vengeful toast proposed by Henry Jackson at a meeting of the Pill Lane United Irishmen in Dublin in 1797.[23] Jackson had toasted "the fate of Jeffreys to Jeffreys". The then lord lieutenant of Ireland, Camden, was a Jeffreys and a descendant of the Hanging Judge.[24] At the height of his reign of terror, Jeffreys had boasted that he could "smell a Presbyterian at forty miles".[25] A few years later after the flight of James II, Jeffreys had also tried to flee England, but he was captured and died of kidney disease and drink in the Tower of London in 1689.

Henry Jackson's toast suggests that the Protestant

Dissenters of Dublin within the ranks of the United Irishmen had long memories of a blood- and drink-soaked tyrant more than a century after his death.

James II's reign lasted for only three years. His wholesale demotion of members of the Established Church and promotion of Roman Catholics, lately come from France, angered even the Tory bishops of the Church of England. Whigs and Tories alike began to search for an alternative sovereign. They fixed on James's daughter Mary, who was married to William of Orange. As James made one tactical error after another, he succeeded in alienating almost all of Protestant England before William and Mary made their move.

The Prince of Orange landed at Torbay with a huge army of Dutchmen. He was welcomed by Whigs and Tories alike, and James II abandoned his kingdom and fled to France without even fighting a battle. The flight of James and his replacement on the throne by William and Mary was ever after known as the Glorious Revolution of 1688. James later came to Ireland on a doomed mission to recover his kingdoms.

When James ran away, Talbot, his man in Ireland, by now Earl of Tyrconnel, considered doing a deal with William but decided to hold Ireland and help James regain his throne.[26] By this time Irish Catholic demands for admission to civil and military office had been well advanced by Tyrconnel. However, the resurgent Catholics were pressing their land claims ever harder. Tyrconnel now had 40,000 men under arms in his Catholic army.[27] On 12 March 1689, James arrived in Kinsale with some French officers and a shipment of arms and ammunition.[28]

The Irish Dissenters reacted with a mixture of faint-heartedness and extraordinary heroism in the face of the Jacobite threat. When the Comber Letter was circulated, Rev. Nathanial Weld of New Row decamped for the safety of England. Rev. Daniel Williams deserted his Wood Street flock and fled to London, never to return to Dublin.

Whatever dispensation the Anglican Protestants could hope for under Tyrconnel's Catholic regime, Cromwellians like Dr Williams and Rev. Weld could expect no mercy. The young apprentices of the city of Londonderry saved the Irish Dissenters from ignominy when they closed the gates of the city. The suffering and heroism of the beleaguered garrison was to become a central theme of Ulster Protestant identity in the centuries which followed.

Wherever the Protestants felt strong enough, they rose in local rebellion. The Dissenting townspeople of Bandon drove out the garrison, killing some of them and declaring their allegiance to William. Justin McCarthy, one of Tyrconnel's officers, put down the rebellion in Bandon.[29] Ireland descended rapidly into civil war between Catholics loyal to James and Protestants and Dissenters loyal to William. It was easier for Dissenters to declare for William as they had a history going back as far as Charles I of hostility to kings in general and to the Stuart kings in particular. It was much harder for Tories and Anglicans to oppose their lawful sovereign, and when James arrived in Dublin on 25 of March, he was welcomed by a delegation of Church of Ireland clergy who pledged their loyalty to him as king.[30]

James spent a frustrating time in Dublin. His Irish Catholic subjects demanded concessions, such as the restoration of their land and freedom of religion, but if James were to accede to these demands, his chances of rapprochement (if they had ever existed) with his Protestant subjects, English and Irish, would have evaporated for ever. In spite of their numerical superiority and their holding a vast amount of the territory of Ireland, the Jacobite armies did not manage to achieve much to advance James's cause. A reluctant William decided that the only way to break the deadlock was to come to Ireland in person.[31] He landed at Carrickfergus on 14 June 1690. He finally brought James to battle at the Boyne River on 1 July 1690. When facing defeat, James showed his character by leaving his soldiers and running away. He went to Dublin, and as quickly as he could thereafter he embarked from Kinsale for France, leaving Ireland for ever on 4 July 1690.

James left his Irish Catholic allies and his French forces behind to fight the Irish Protestants and Dissenters and their Dutch allies. James's Irish Catholic subjects sacrificed everything for a king whose English subjects wanted nothing as much as to be rid of him. The bloody and destructive war in Ireland left the country devastated when it finally ended in October 1691. The Roman Catholics were much worse off than they had been even under the so-called "curse of Cromwell".

James would never consent to release his defeated Irish Roman Catholic subjects from their pledges of loyalty. While he and his court accommodated themselves to their new circumstances in relatively comfortable exile, the Roman Catholics of Ireland suffered dispossession, penal laws and exclusion from civic life. The Catholic Irish suffered for their loyalty to a dynasty that regarded the Irish as at most expendable pawns in a game, the objective of which was to rule Britain. Ireland and the Irish figured in the Stuart calculations only as a back door or an afterthought.

Who Won the Glorious Revolution?
Though Ireland had suffered terribly in what came to be known as the Williamite War, the Glorious Revolution which saw James off had been a bloodless affair in England. James was replaced on the throne by William and Mary. The more radical Dissenters loyal to "the Good Old Cause" may not have wanted a new hereditary monarchy, but they supported William and Mary, because they hoped their new Protestant monarchs would respect parliament, restore the peoples' liberties and be tolerant of religious dissent.

The Whigs claimed that they had won the Glorious Revolution. William III had been offered the throne by parliament and would rule as a constitutional monarch. John Locke, the great Whig philosopher, published his *Treatise on Civil Government* as a justification of the Glorious Revolution. Locke, suggesting that there is a contract between the governor and the governed, argued that rebellion against tyrannical government is justified. This theory was deeply disturbing to those who believed a king should never be overthrown. Who then decided that the contract had been broken? If Locke's view was accepted, then no monarch could ever again be sure that they would reign until death. Locke's view that men had the right to resist tyranny had a profound influence on future radical thought. John Toland and Francis Hutcheson, Irish philosophers of the early eighteenth century, Thomas Jefferson, the architect of the American Revolution, Dr Richard Price, the great supporter of the American and French Revolutions in England, and William Drennan, the United Irishman, were all disciples of John Locke. The American colonists and the United Irishmen in their turn would justify their rebellions in Lockean terms.

Many Tories had supported the Glorious Revolution, but interpreted the events in a very different way from John Locke and the Whigs. The Tories claimed that James had abandoned his throne and his people, and God had provided a new monarch in the person of William III. It was a little more difficult for Irish Tories to rationalise their position, as James had been driven out of Ireland. Irish Protestants considered their physical survival and the possession of their property as much more important than political or theological consistency. They denied that they had rebelled against their legitimate king in spite of the clear evidence to the contrary. The Anglican Archbishop of Dublin William King justified the rebellion of Irish Protestants on novel grounds. He said that as it was the duty of the king to protect the property of his subjects and that as James threatened the property of Irish Protestants, they were entitled to resist him. If the bishop had thought this position through to its logical conclusion, he should have realised that he was giving Irish Roman Catholics justification for every rebellion they staged in their history. The British government was always threatening the property and land of Roman Catholics.

Tories believed that the king's authority came from God and that as the king was above the law, he had no contract with his people. Tories knew that the notion that a king could be cashiered by the people was a recipe for either continuous rebellion or a republic. If authority came from the consent of the people, they could remove a king who had broken his contract with them. If the king derived his authority from the people and not from God, then a question mark is placed over the role, the relevance and the existence of God. Was the king God's anointed or did God have any authority in earthly affairs? If God did not appoint the king, then God might as well not exist. For Tories, the Glorious Revolution was an act of God; for Whigs it was an act of the people.

In the wake of the Glorious Revolution and the defeat of James in Ireland, Irish Roman Catholics were subjected to an increasingly oppressive regime of penal laws. The Irish parliament passed a series of anti-Popery laws which removed the rights of Roman Catholic to bear arms, inherit property, practise their religion or participate in politics. The new laws were designed as a punishment for supporting James II. They were also designed to exclude them from political and economic life. Most countries in Europe had such penal laws against minority religions, but Ireland was unique in that it was the religion of the majority that was the target for suppression.

The Protestant Ascendancy in Ireland benefited from the confiscation of the land of Roman Catholics who had supported James. Not content with the fruits of victory, they pushed for ever harsher measures against Roman Catholics. They could cloak their sectarianism and greed in enthusiasm for the Williamite cause and anti-Jacobinism.

The Vatican made things worse for Irish Roman Catholics by allowing James, now in the court of France, the right to nominate Roman Catholic bishops in Ireland. In other words, the Roman Catholic Church was avowedly Jacobite and committed to the overthrow of the Glorious Revolution settlement.

The unshakeable loyalty of the Roman Catholic Church to the rightful king of England, now safely in France, added to the suffering of Roman Catholics in Ireland. Whether the great majority of poor Roman Catholics shared their Church's enthusiasm for James is hard to say. The Irish bards never tired of singing of when "the king over the water" would return "Agus na Gaeil a chur i gceart" (to restore the Gaels to their rightful place). To some less literary or musically minded Gaels, James was known as "Sheamus a caca" (Jimmy the shit).

After William's victory, the Dissenters enjoyed a period of relative religious freedom from the Act of Toleration 1689. The act allowed most Dissenters freedom of worship, but it did not suspend the other civil disabilities. This toleration did not extend to those with Unitarian views, nor did the era of tolerance last. When William died in 1702, his wife's sister, Anne, became Queen. Her reign began with a Tory campaign against the Dissenters' hard won toleration.

The Whig and Tory versions of the Glorious Revolution and their opposing views on the nature and the extent of kingly authority were still in dispute a hundred years later. This dispute was the very stuff of the Edmund Burke and Tom Paine debate at the end of the eighteenth century. Paine argued the Lockean principle that people had a right to cashier a tyrant, while Burke denied that the people either had or wished to have any such right.

The Tory–Whig debate ebbed and flowed throughout the eighteenth century. The questions were complex and the stakes were high. Did civil and religious authority reside in the persons of kings and bishops, or did civil authority reside in the people and religious authority in a man's conscience? The answer to these questions would determine whether England would become an enlightened democracy with a limited monarchy or an absolutist tyranny like pre-revolutionary France.

Notes to Chapter Three
1. Childs, J. 2007, p. 3
2. *Ibid.*
3. *Ibid.*
4. See James Connolly, 1987, p. 85
5. Harris 2006, p. 310
6. Houston 1991, p. 20
7. Houston 1991, p. 65
8. Ashley 1958, p. 150
9. Houston 1991, p. 8
10. Clifford 1989, p. 60
11. Whig hero who died in the Civil War
12. Paddy's Resource, 1798
13. Madden 1860, p. 462
14. S.J. Connolly 2008, p. 174
15. Pincus 2009, p. 141
16. Greaves 1992, p. 161
17. Ashley 1960, p. 168
18. *Ibid.*
19. Dilllon 2006, p. 16
20. Harris 2006, p. 88
21. Robertson, 2005, p. 346
22. *Ibid.* p. 59
23. Bartlett 2004, p. 144
24. *Ibid.*
25. Macaulay 1851, chapter V, 'The Monmouth Rebellion"
26. S.J. Connolly 2008, p. 179
27. *Ibid.*
28. *Ibid.*
29. *Ibid.*
30. *Ibid.*
31. *Ibid.*

Chapter Four

Atheist, Blasphemer, Preacher and Philosopher

1 March 1710, London: Burning Books

Six Dissenting meeting houses are in flames as the city is rocked by violence. The organised and well-directed mob, mobilised to save the Church of England, has targeted the homes of prominent Protestant Dissenters. Two people have been killed and fifty injured. Tory churchman Dr Henry Sacheverell has been suspended from office, and his pamphlet, The Church in Danger, *has been burnt by public decree. His crime is his denunciation of the Whig government's relative tolerance of Protestant Dissenters. It is surprising that the Whigs have stooped to the practice of book-burning and the persecution of an author. More surprising still is that the attacks on Dr Sacheverell are led by an Irish philosopher and champion of tolerance, John Toland. Toland has spent his adult life in the shadow of the book-burners and the persecutors.*

Dublin's New Parliament

The parliament which gathered in Dublin in 1692 at the end of the Williamite War set the pattern which was to last for more than a hundred years into the future, until it was abolished by the Act of Union of 1800. The membership was exclusively Protestant landed grandees and gentry. Previous parliaments had met very irregularly, but this parliament would meet for six months in every two years. The members of this parliament saw its role not as the orderly management of the affairs of all the people living on the island, but rather the protection of the Protestant interest.

73

This led them to pass a series of laws to exclude Roman Catholics from any share or influence in political life. Ownership of land was the key to entry into political affairs, and therefore many of the measures they enacted were designed to sabotage landholding by Roman Catholics.

Those who hoped that the new parliament would be grateful to their deliverer, King William, were to be disappointed. In spite of the crushing and overwhelming defeat which had been inflicted on the Roman Catholic Irish, the Irish Protestants felt insecure. They were aware that Cromwell's earlier suppression of the Catholics had not prevented their resurgence under Tyrconnell. No matter how weak the Roman Catholics were perceived to be, they outnumbered Protestants; and France remained strong and hostile.

The Dublin parliament prevented William from fulfilling his obligations under the Treaty of Limerick, which had ended the war. The terms allowing Jacobites still under arms at the surrender to keep their estates was deemed too lenient. The "broken treaty" would be added to the long list of legitimate Catholic grievances. This tension between the king and the new Irish parliament was to set the scene for many future controversies for the next century, as the Irish Protestants would sabotage any measure proposed by the government in England to alleviate the plight of Irish Roman Catholics.

Meanwhile in England, the Whig-Tory dispute was as bitter as ever. The Whigs believed they had won the Glorious Revolution and that the Tories had merely accepted the replacement of James by his daughter and her husband. There followed years of controversy where the Whigs accused the Tories of hoping to bring "the king over the water" back at the earliest opportunity. The Tories denied that they were Jacobite. They were, however, determined that the Established Church and its convocation of bishops were the only legitimate source of religious authority and that anyone who refused to accept this was a blasphemer, a heretic or worse. They disapproved of the limited toleration of Dissenters granted in the reign of William and were determined to go back to the old oppressions. Any challenge to the privileges of the Established Church was seen as an attack on the State as well as the Church.

John Toland

"Is dóigh gurb é an tÉireannach is cáiliúla é is lú a bhfuil eolas ag Éireannaigh air."[1] (Probably the most famous Irishman so little known by the Irish.)

By the late 1690s, as the Anglican Church and its Tory allies were gaining strength in both England and Ireland, the Dissenters and the Whigs found a new champion in the person of John Toland, a young Irishman. Toland was born in the Inishowen peninsula of Donegal in the year 1670, and he was destined, while still young, to become the most controversial and reviled figure in British and Irish public life. His early life is shrouded in mystery, but some say he was the illegitimate son of a Roman Catholic priest from the parish of Donagh, near Londonderry. He described himself as a restless spirit and claimed that from an early age he was a great searcher after religion. He said he "had tried all sorts and found the Presbyterian religion to be the best".[2] By the age of sixteen, he had embraced Dissenting Protestantism and had become, in his own words, "zealous against Popery". Ever afterwards he regarded the Roman Catholic faith as the grossest superstition and idolatry.

Toland spent some time in the universities of Glasgow and Edinburgh and thereafter migrated to London. Rev. Dr Daniel Williams, formerly of the Wood Street congregation, was living in London after fleeing his post at Dublin a few years previously in fear of the armies of James II. Williams was much impressed by Toland's talent and sponsored his education at the universities of Leiden and Oxford.

Toland was an erudite scholar, a linguist par excellence and an up-and-coming philosopher. He regarded himself as a follower and friend of that other great philosopher, John Locke. In his book, *The Reasonableness of Christianity* (1695), Locke had suggested that there was no need for church, priest or miracles, and that faith should be replaced by reason. Toland went even further in his own book, *Christianity not Mysterious,* published in the same year, in which he linked Locke's ideas explicitly to deism.[3] Deism means the belief in a single God who does not act to influence events, and whose existence has no connection with religions, religious buildings or religious books. If Toland was indeed a deist, he was an early adherent to a philosophy which was to gain ground throughout the eighteenth century.

Toland did not deny the existence of God, as his enemies alleged; rather he affirmed that he believed in a divine creator. He denied the existence of a god who interfered in the affairs of men. He also denied that priests have any special insight into scripture more than any other man. No person should believe anything that is clearly contrary to reason. Toland claimed that the purpose of his book was "to impeach corrupt clergymen who build an unjust authority upon the abused consciences of the laity".[4] He said his text was designed for the poor rather than philosophers.

Toland held that "religion has to be rational to have any authority". This was a radical idea in an age where scripture and church teaching were to be uncritically accepted by all Christians. The orthodox insisted that unlikely doctrines or teachings were not unreasonable but rather "mysterious". The insistence by Toland on the importance of human reason is said to have had a major influence on the German Enlightenment, Voltaire and other French philosophers.[5]

The fundamental point of Toland's book was that the Christian religion is simple to understand and that those who claim it to be "mysterious" are engaged in priestcraft and deceit. The problem with this suggestion was that while it could be interpreted as an attack on Popery, it could also be interpreted as an attack on the churchmen of the Established Church. Toland had exposed himself to charges of blasphemy. John Locke, who had no desire to be embroiled in Toland's fast approaching troubles, took fright and tried to distance himself from Toland.

In 1697 Toland came to Dublin to seek patronage and employment. The fame of his notorious book had preceded him to the city. He had arrived into a vibrant, if not a particularly tolerant, metropolis. In the course of the previous century, the city had changed from a small medieval city with a population of *circa* 10,000 people sheltering behind its ancient city walls to a sizeable expanding extramural city of 60,000 souls.[6] The proliferation of taverns and coffee houses provided venues for formal and informal gatherings. Toland loved coffee houses as they afforded him a ready audience for his erudition, his irreverent rhetoric and his controversial opinions.

Although Dublin had a small and growing Roman Catholic population, it was at this time a Protestant city. "A significant proportion of the population of the city were either English by birth or they were the sons and daughters of English parents who had arrived in the city in the late 17th century."[7] The Protestant Dissenters were an important if somewhat turbulent minority of the city's population. John Dunton, a visitor to Dublin in 1699, commented that the Dissenters were both numerous and wealthy. When Dunton met Rev. Joseph Boyse and Rev. Thomas Emlyn, both of the Wood Street congregation, he was greatly impressed by both of them, and he identified Boyse as chief of the Dublin Dissenters.[8]

Rev. Boyse was of New England descent and had succeeded Dr Williams at Wood Street in 1688. He was a prolific writer, always ready to defend the reputation of Protestant dissent. His work, *The Proper Office of a Christian Bishop,* was so unpopular with the Established

Church that the Irish parliament voted to burn the book.[9] Thomas Emlyn was an Englishman who would, within a few years, fall foul of the blasphemy courts of the Anglican Establishment and would be sent to prison in Dublin for expressing Unitarian opinions.

At this time, Anglicans controlled the Irish House of Lords and Commons but the Dissenters could wield some influence in Dublin Corporation, and indeed on occasion could fill the office of lord mayor.[10] Since Roman Catholics were excluded from all political influence in the city, civic political conflict was usually between Anglicans and Dissenters. The Anglicans could afford to ignore Roman Catholics, whom they had excluded from political life, but they were virulent in their attacks on Dissenters, who posed a challenge, or could at least be an irritant, to the Anglican hegemony.

Toland was by now a notorious Dissenter and was given a hostile reception from both the government and the city establishment. He found himself "harangued against out of the pulpit", and he found that the "Clergy were alarmed to a mighty degree against him".[11] Despite clerical hostility, Toland made many friends in Dublin, including Robert Molesworth (1656–1725), later Viscount Molesworth, whose father was a Cromwellian who had settled in Dublin. He became a lifelong patron and was to maintain his friendship with Toland and support him in many controversies until the death of Toland in 1722.

Despite his great capacity for making friends, the young Toland was even better at making enemies. He had a reputation already for loose talk in coffee houses, and his arrogant way of expressing his controversial views increased the number of his enemies and helped their efforts and plots against him.

The Irish House of Commons condemned his book as blasphemous and ordered it to be burnt. There was an interesting alliance between the national and municipal authorities in that the public hangman carried out the sentence, first outside the parliament house and then outside the city hall.[12] Toland claimed that one member of the committee that condemned the book sought to have him burnt with it.[13] When the government ordered the arrest of Toland, even his friends in Dublin felt he had brought his problems on himself by his incautious behaviour and making "a coffee house jest of the Trinity".[14] Two years earlier he came close to being expelled from Oxford on account of his coffee house antics. He was accused of "trampling on ye Common Prayer Book, talking against the Scriptures, commending commonwealths, justifying the murder of K(ing) C(harles) I and railing against priests in general".[15]

Now Toland had to flee Dublin to avoid standing trial. Had he not made himself scarce, he might have fallen into the hands of the hangman who had incinerated his book. In that same year (1697), Thomas Aikenhead, a young student, was hanged at Edinburgh. Aikenhead had said that the doctrine of the Trinity was not worth refutation and had declared religion to be a "Rhapsody of feigned and ill-invented nonsense". Unlike Toland, Aikenhead had not courted notoriety. He had said nothing publicly nor had he published his opinion; he had been overheard talking to friends. Aikenhead's fate is said to have haunted John Locke and led him to conceal his own Unitarian opinions.[16] It also helps to explain why Locke wanted no more to do with John Toland.

We shall never know what Toland's fate might have been had he delayed in Dublin. However belatedly, he showed judgement consistent with his great intellect, and he left the jurisdiction before he could be charged. Toland's enemies in Dublin were delighted by his flight, and the Archbishop of Dublin was congratulated "for making the kingdom too hot for Toland without the help of a faggot".[17]

Toland wrote a history of the Gaelic Druids. In it he portrays a clerical elite who shroud their doctrines in mystery, spells and incantations to exercise power and control over ordinary people who are denied the opportunity to judge things for themselves. Long after, William Blake would use Toland's work on the Druids to attack Christian priest-craft.[18]

Toland's native language was Gaelic, but he was fluent in more than ten languages. When he studied the oldest Gaelic manuscripts, he suggested that the early Christian church in Ireland was Unitarian. He asserted that there was no belief in a Trinity, no images in places of worship and no belief in transubstantiation.[19] In the mythology of Ireland, there is recognition that the man credited with the conversion of Ireland, St Patrick, had vigorously to defend the doctrine of the Trinity. He used the shamrock in doing so and gave Ireland its national symbol. If the fifth century Irish were polytheist pagans, as is usually suggested, then the idea of three Divine persons in the one God should not have been unduly difficult for them to grasp. However, if they were monotheist Christians, then the Trinity might have required explanation. Toland's claims of a Unitarian ancient Ireland should be treated with caution. Toland was a skilled propagandist who had a talent for doctoring the record to suit any argument he was trying to make.[20]

After his flight from Dublin in fear of his life, Toland never returned to Ireland, but he did maintain a correspondence with Molesworth. Ever afterwards, his direct influence in Irish affairs may have been limited, but he went on to become a major figure internationally. For the rest of his life, Toland played an important role in "both subversive and elite political circles both in England and the Continent".[21]

Toland settled in London but spent a considerable amount of time in the German province of Hanover. He enjoyed the confidence of the Electress of Hanover, who had been chosen to succeed Queen Anne to keep the Catholic Stuarts from the British throne. He worked hard and with some success in courting the affection of the Electress' daughter, Sophia Charlotte.[22] She particularly approved of Toland's views on the rights of women to engage in intellectual pursuits on the same basis as men.

The Hanoverians had good reason to be grateful to Toland, who helped to win public support for their succession to the British throne. However, the Electress died before Queen Anne, and it was her son, George I, who benefited from Toland's efforts. Toland was a republican, but he saw the house of Hanover as preferable to either Popery or absolutism (as personified by the Stuarts) and the High Anglican intolerance that had marked the reign of Queen Anne.

When Toland was on his deathbed in 1722, he wrote the following, in Latin, which he wanted to appear on his headstone:

> Here lies JOHN TOLAND, born in Ireland, near Londonderry who in his youth studied in Scotland, Ireland, and at Oxford; and having repeatedly visited Germany, spent his manhood about London. He was a cultivator of every kind of Learning; and skilled in more than ten languages: the champion of truth, and the assertor of Liberty but the follower or client of none; nor was he ever swayed by menaces or misfortunes, from pursuing the path, which he chalked out to himself, uniformly preferring his integrity to his interest. His Spirit is re-united to his heavenly Father, from whom it formerly proceeded. His Body, yielding to Nature, is also re-placed in the Bosom of the Earth. He himself will undoubtedly arise to Eternal Life, but will never be the same Toland. Born 30th November, 1670. Seek the rest from his Writings.[23]

These words are vintage Toland; his greatest admirer was himself. His remark about his resurrection was his last venture into controversy. His fair-weather friend John Locke had outraged orthodox Christian opinion by suggesting that the soul only, and not the body, rises for the final judgement. Toland wanted his Lockean views carved on his tombstone.

John Toland was Ireland's first Gaelic-speaking militant republican. He often described himself as a "Commonwealthman". Toland's first patron, Dr Williams, had been born during the Commonwealth and was for many years minister to the Wood Street congregation which had been frequented by Commonwealthmen. Toland did much to rescue the ideals of the Commonwealth and fashioned them so that they would be acceptable to a later generation.[24] He published and edited works by notable Commonwealth republicans such as John Milton, Edmund Ludlow and Algernon Sidney. Most notably he published the classic republican text *Oceana*, along with a biography of its author James Harrington, in 1702.[25]

Seventy years after his death, Toland's memory was invoked by Edmund Burke in *Reflections on the Revolution in France*. Burke did not honour John Toland as a fellow Irishman and a great scholar, but rather he denigrated him as "an atheist that nobody read anymore".[26] Burke was missing the point about the legacy and influence of John Toland. In his own time, Toland had immense influence, even if he was not universally popular. In fact, his unpopularity was a measure of his success. He once remarked that some Whigs, most Tories and all Jacobites hated him.[27] Someone who had little influence would hardly be well-known enough to be so hated. He had done much to secure the Hanoverian succession, and in that alone he made an immense contribution to the political history of Great Britain.

Toland's main contribution to radical thought was not in his own original works, although his work did have considerable merit, and much of it was far ahead of its time. He wrote in favour of emancipating the Jews, and he asserted the equal intellectual capacity of men and women. His lasting service to posterity though was to popularise the works of Milton, Ludlow, Harrington and Sidney. The radicals of Edmund Burke's era might not have been familiar with Toland's work, but it was through the efforts of John Toland, to some extent, that Thomas Jefferson, Benjamin Franklin, Dr Richard Price and William Drennan had read Milton, Ludlow and Sidney. It was also, to some extent, due to Toland that Sidney was revered as a republican martyr who was executed because he believed a free people should choose their government. In publishing the republican canon, Toland rehabilitated the "the Good Old Cause" and rescued the great authors of the Commonwealth from obscurity.

Twenty years later, in the safer reign of the first Hanoverian George, a group of like-minded republicans based amongst the congregation at Wood Street, Dublin, continued Toland's work. Harrington's *Oceana* was a great favourite of Dr Francis Hutcheson and his cousin William Bruce. Hutcheson was at this time teaching in a school established by the Wood Street Dissenters, and Bruce was a member of the congregation. They republished Toland's version of Harrington's *Oceana* in Dublin in 1727, five years after Toland's death in London. The members of the Wood Street circle were collaborators with his old friend Viscount Robert Molesworth.[28] They and Molesworth continued to champion the causes dear to Toland's heart: freedom of conscience, religious toleration and the abhorrence of all tyranny and arbitrary power.

John Toland was a major figure in the history of early modern republicanism. He honoured the Commonwealthmen of the English Civil War at a time when Tories condemned them as fanatics and king-killers. His links to the Wood Street congregation were at one remove. These consisted of his conversion to Protestant dissent in Ireland, the support he received from former Wood Street minister Dr Williams and the efforts of his admirers, Francis Hutcheson and William Bruce, to republish his work.

His ideological connections to the United Irishmen are undeniable. He championed the causes of freedom of conscience and civil and religious liberty. He opposed the tyranny of arbitrary power. He spent his life fighting against the Tories and the bishops of the Established Church. In their turn, the United Irishmen espoused the same causes and fought the same enemies.

Toland has been written out of the history of Irish republicanism perhaps because of his militant anti-Catholic radicalism. However, the Gaelic-speaking Roman Catholics of his native Donegal retain a warm affection for his memory even today where Gaelic remains the everyday language of the people. He has been described as *"trodaí ar son na fírinne agus moltóir na saoirse"* (a fighter for truth and an advocate of freedom) and is remembered in the folklore of his native county as *"Eoghan na leabhar"* (John of the books).[29]

The Blasphemy of Thomas Emlyn

A few years after Toland fled Dublin, the city was rocked by another religious persecution. The unfortunate man at the centre of this storm did not flee but stood his ground and faced the consequences. Thomas Emlyn was born in Lincolnshire in 1663. Nearly forty years later, he was the assistant minister in Wood Street. Rev. Emlyn was a troubled soul, and unlike Toland, the last thing he ever wanted was to court controversy. If Toland's probems in Dublin arose from his unwillingess to hold his tongue, Emlyn's arose because he stayed silent on a certain matter. His problems began in 1702 when a senior member of his congregation challenged him for never referring to the doctrine of the Trinity in his sermons. Much to the horror of his challenger, Emlyn confirmed that he did not subscribe to that doctrine. When his senior ministerial colleague, Rev. Joseph Boyse, was informed, his reaction was swift and severe. Emlyn was called before a meeting of the Dublin Presbytery, a coalition of Scottish Presbyterian, English Presbyterian and Independent ministers in Dublin.[30] Boyse was a great advocate of freedom of conscience for

Dissenters, but he was now ready to deny that very right to his assistant, and he and the Dublin Presbytery dismissed Emlyn. They gave him permission to leave Dublin for England but ordered him not to preach there. Emlyn reluctantly accepted their authority in Dublin but resented their claim to have authority over him in England. He suggested that they were behaving like the Pope.[31]

In London, he heard that he was being attacked from pulpits back in Dublin. He published a pamphlet explaining his position. His attempt to defend himself was his undoing. To hold heretical views was safe so long as one did not express them, but to publish them was to leave oneself open to a charge of heresy or blasphemy. Emlyn returned to Dublin to settle his affairs to discover the city was in uproar against him. He was promptly arrested. Rev. Boyse had rushed into print where he publicly accused Emlyn of denying "our Blessed Saviour to be one of that sacred three and as such the object of divine worship".[32]

The court he faced, though presided over by the lord chief justice, was attended by two archbishops who took the bench and five bishops of the Established Church. Emlyn was told he would not be permitted to speak at his trial and that he would be "run down like a Wolf without Law or Game".[33]

Rev. Boyse, his one-time friend and colleague, gave evidence against him, giving the court an account of Emlyn's opinions, which he had expressed to the ad hoc Dublin Presbytery. To those members of Wood Street congregation who supported Emlyn, it must have seemed like a dreadful betrayal for their senior minister to swear away a fellow minister in such a court. How could any Dissenting minister express himself freely in Presbytery if his words and opinions were liable to be betrayed by a colleague minister to the blasphemy courts of the Established Church?

Boyse's congregation revelled in its commitment to freedom of conscience. So why did he betray his friend and colleague and place him in the hands of his enemies? Surely

Boyse knew that Emlyn's persecutors would as happily have prosecuted Boyse himself. One explanation for the puzzling behaviour of Boyse may be the fear that gripped Dissenter congregations following the death of William III in that same year of 1702. Immediately, the limited tolera- tion enjoyed by the Dissenters came under strong attack by the High Church Tories, who saw the new Queen Anne's reign as an opportunity to suppress dissent. On both sides of the Irish Sea, Tories attempted to enact anti-Dissenter legislation. In many of the cities of England, Dissenter meeting houses were burning; any taint of heresy within Boyse's flock might be used as an excuse to eject the min- isters and disperse the congregation. Boyse perhaps felt that by throwing his friend to the wolves he was protect- ing his congregation. In the event, his tactic backfired, as the Tories used the climate of intolerance surrounding Emlyn's trial to introduce the Test Act 1704, which while it did not close down the congregation, barred Irish Dissenters from public office.

When enacting yet another piece of anti-Popery legisla- tion in that year, the Irish House of Commons was happy to use the occasion to attack the Dissenters by enacting an addendum to the effect that all public office holders must be members of the Established Church. This had the effect of banning Dissenters from corporations, civic offices and posts in the military. The Dissenters regarded this as a denial of the liberties they had won in the Glorious Revolution, and they made many attempts to have their liberties restored during the century that followed.

Although Emlyn was surprised by what Boyse had done, he took the somewhat benign view that had his friend been given more time to think about what he was doing, he would have tried to have himself excused.[34] The prosecution could not prove that Emlyn had written the pamphlet, but Boyse confirmed that his views were similar to those expressed in it. In an extraordinary perversion of the law, the chief justice told Emlyn and the jury that, "Presumption is as good as evidence." Emlyn was convicted, jailed for a year and fined £1,000.[35] He would have had to endure the pillory had the authorities not feared he would be torn to pieces by the mob.

The chief justice told Emlyn that if he lived in Roman Catholic France or Portugal, he would have been burnt at the stake. Emlyn observed that the chief justice himself would be likely to be burnt in such places for his orthodox Protestantism.[36]

As Emlyn had no prospect of paying the fine, the sentence amounted to imprisonment for an indefinite period. In the event, he spent two years and one month in prison. His time in the common jail was hard for him, and his Dublin clergymen circle, with the exception of Boyse, abandoned him. Emlyn recorded in his diary that:

> I thank God that he did not call me to this lot of suffering till I had arrived at maturity of judgement and firmness of resolution and that he did not desert me when my friends did. He never let me be so cast down as to renounce the truth or to waiver in my faith.[37]

Some tradesmen and several members of the "lower sort" within the congregation supported Emlyn, and they would come to the prison on the Sabbath to hear him preach.[38]

Rev. Boyse would eventually come to regret his actions, and he helped secure Emlyn's release by lobbying the lord lieutenant, the Duke of Ormond, in his favour.[39] The fine was reduced and Emlyn was eventually set free, after which Thomas Emlyn left Dublin for ever. He removed to London where it is said, "he carried on the Unitarian controversy with great spirit, effect and good temper until his death in 1743 in his 79th year".[40]

Rev. John Abernethy and the Irish Presbyterian Schism

As a victim of Established Church tyranny and the cowardice of his Dissenter colleagues, Thomas Emlyn's harsh imprisonment made him a symbol of freedom of conscience. His trial and conviction proved to be a major event in the struggle between Protestant Dissenters and the Established Church in Britain and Ireland, and it was to have the most profound implications for Presbyterianism in Ireland. The consequences of his persecution included the growth of liberal religion in Ulster and Dublin and the eventual separation of the liberals from the Presbyterian Church of Ireland.

It was in June 1705, as Emlyn served his last month in prison, that the Synod of Ulster imposed the Westminster Confession of Faith on all new ministers. No new minister, even if "called" by a congregation, was to be allowed to take up office until they had formally accepted the Westminster Confession in front of the Synod. The Confession is an unwieldy document in thirty-eight chapters which sought to capture all the essential truths of the Protestant religion. The general tone of this Confession is Calvinist, and its second chapter reasserted the doctrine of the Trinity. This innovation could not be imposed on existing ministers without provoking a Restoration-style ejection of unwilling ministers from their livings.

The attempt to impose the Westminster Confession provoked a reaction from some ministers. A number of young ministers, including Rev. John Abernethy (1680–1740), who was then ministering to a congregation in Antrim, founded the Belfast Society. The Society's members were mostly ministers but included a few lay people who studied philosophy and the scriptures. Abernethy had been in training for the ministry at Wood Street in 1702 when the Emlyn controversy rocked the congregation to its foundations. His exposure to the punishment of Emlyn convinced him that the persecution of a man for his opinions was wrong.[41] He and the members of the Belfast Society would accept no restriction on their consciences or any man-made confession as a test of orthodoxy.

John Abernethy was destined to become the most

Rev. William Bruce   Rev. John Abernethy

illustrious figure in the history of the liberal
Presbyterianism which is often referred to as New Light
Presbyterianism. He was born in Coleraine, County
Derry. As a child he had been sent to Scotland to escape
the Williamite War in Ireland, in which all his siblings
perished in the siege of Derry in 1689. He went to
Glasgow at the early age of thirteen to study for the min-
istry, and after finishing his training he ministered at
Antrim. His first brush with Presbyterian authority
occurred when he was instructed to take up duty in
Ussher's Quay in Dublin against his will. He refused to
leave Antrim and ministered there from 1703 until 1730.

Abernethy and his fellows in the Belfast Society were
suspected by their critics of espousing heresy. Some of these
ministers rejected the doctrine of the Trinity as having no
basis in scripture. Others accepted the Trinity but felt that
the issue was not particularly important. They were prepared to allow a place for anti-Trinitarians in their congregations and in Synods. Yet others felt that to be forced
to subscribe to the Westminster Confession or any man-
made test was an attack on their dearly held freedom of

conscience. The society argued that "it was only by being tolerant of different theological views within Presbyterianism, could the church plausibly petition for toleration from the Church of Ireland".[42]

Abernethy and the Belfast Society ministers regarded themselves as free to seek truth through the scriptures, scientific study and rational thought. Those who rejected the Trinity were, in effect, denying the deity of Jesus. It is hardly surprising that some less liberal Protestants regarded them as heretics. The drive to free themselves from theological constraints had political consequences as well. One historian observed that: "As the theological bonds of Presbyterianism came to be progressively loosened, dissenting ministers increasingly derived their character and cohesion from a passionate commitment to civil and religious liberty".[43]

The Presbyterian Synod of Ulster was clearly running scared of accusations of heresy when they tried to impose the Westminster Confession. In the previous year, the Irish House of Commons had enacted the Test Act, which cast out all Dissenter public office holders. Their anxiety to prove their orthodoxy suggests that they feared more government oppression. It should have been obvious to all concerned that Abernethy and others like him would never subscribe to any "Test". Abernethy preached a sermon, "Religious Obedience Founded on Personal Persuasion", which echoed the sentiments of the controversial English Bishop Benjamin Hoadly, who argued that the Gospels provided no basis for church authority. Abernethy suggested that espicopacy developed in the church because the early Christians were Jews who carried this "mistake" from their old traditions. He concluded his sermon with an assertion of personal religious freedom: "Let us stand fast in the liberty wherewith he hath made us free: Let us call no Man or Society of Men our Masters; for one is our Master even Christ, and all we are brethren."[44]

Abernethy and his fellow ministers who refused to subscribe came in time to be known as Non-subscribers but are often referred to as New Light Presbyterians. The New Light ministers wanted to remain within the Presbyterian mainstream. The controversy simmered for more than twenty years before the issue was finally forced. Eventually in 1726, John Abernethy and sixteen of his ministerial colleagues were ejected from the Synod of Ulster and driven into the Presbytery of Antrim. This was in effect a very Presbyterian schism.

Feeling isolated from the main body of Presbyterians in Ulster, Abernethy and his colleagues in the Presbytery of Antrim sought and were granted permission from the Dublin and Munster Dissenters "to form a warm coalition with them".[45] The sum of nearly £1,000 was raised by Presbyterian gentlemen in Dublin (the congregations of Wood Street and New Row) to help the Presbytery of Antrim.[46] The publisher William Bruce was the financial brain behind the schemes that paid the salaries and provided pensions for the minsters ejected from the Synod of Ulster. It might have been predicted that this alliance with the descendants of the English Presbyterians and Cromwellians would strengthen heterodoxy amongst the Non-subscribers, and so it proved.

When Rev. Boyse died in 1730, Abernethy replaced him at Wood Street. In some ways this seems a surprising succession. Boyse had shown in the Emlyn affair (more than a quarter of a century earlier) that he was at that stage an avowed Trinitarian and anti-Unitarian. Yet in 1726 Boyse and his congregation sided with the Non-subscribing ministers who were ejected from the Synod of Ulster. Boyse's congregation gave Abernethy "the call" to Dublin in the full knowledge that their new minister was not a Trinitarian. This is the type of development that makes it very difficult to trace the development of Unitarian opinions within individual congregations, or indeed within the consciences of individual ministers.

Abernethy was fifty years old when he came to Dublin and was by now regarded as the leader of Non-subscribing Presbyterianism in Ireland.[47] He had become a great preacher and his sermons were widely read and admired. He preached that moral and civil liberty were intimately connected, and he believed liberty was the equal right of all.[48] Abernethy preached that (religious) persecution violated the natural genius of man and that persuasion was the only proper weapon for Christians.[49]

John Abernethy died in 1740, and his friend Rev. John Mears said of him as part of his funeral oration: "He would never... submit to anything he judged to be wrong, or unreasonable, or to have the tendency to betray the cause of truth, virtue or liberty; in these things he was steady and inflexible, firm and as immovable as a rock."[50]

The Evolution of Unitarian Belief

The Emyln affair and the resultant non-subscription crisis led to many fundamental changes in belief within the non-subscribing clergy. They were aware that the Bible refers to a Father, a Son and Holy Spirit, but it does not say that they are three persons in one God, and it makes no mention of a Trinity. Unitarians therefore held that there is but one God who is the "Father". For them Jesus, whom they held to be the great teacher or master, is the son of man, and not the son of God.

The application of reason and science to scripture and church teachings often led to the rejection of other basic tenets of orthodox Christianity. If there is no Trinity and only one God, who is the Father, then Jesus the man could not be divine. If Jesus was not divine, the miracle stories, insofar as they defy science, may be fictions. If the world was created by God and was subject to the laws of science, then a miracle which defied science would suggest that God was contradicting himself.[51] The story of creation in Genesis could not be reconciled with science. Long before Charles Darwin developed his theory of evolution, fossil evidence had undermined the biblical account of creation. If the Garden of Eden and the Fall of Man is to be understood as allegorical, then all scripture might not represent literal truth. Today, some such conclusions would be regarded as reasonable for believers who regard themselves as orthodox. However, it was precisely because Unitarians used their reason to interpret scripture that they were regarded as heretics by High Church Protestants, Calvinists and Roman Catholics.

In the wake of the Emlyn affair, Unitarians in Ireland and Britain were careful about expressing their opinions. Even Abernethy himself, who was a vigorous defender of freedom of conscience, was careful to conceal some of his views. After his death, his friend Rev. Duchal (1696–1761) revealed that he had found "pretty amazing passages" in Abernethy's diary which he decided to keep secret.[52]

As the bonds of orthodoxy were loosened, the beliefs of Unitarians evolved gradually throughout the eighteenth century. Initially they held that the Bible was the one source of religious truth. By the end of the century, this had softened to a view that there was much in scripture that was useful for mankind. Thomas Jefferson used a scissors to cut out anything in the Gospels which was, in his opinion, contrary to reason. His work, which was not published until long after his death, is today known as the Jefferson Bible. For many years a copy of the Jefferson Bible was given to newly elected members of the US Congress. John Milton, John Locke, Isaac Newton, John Toland and later Richard Price and Joseph Priestley came to the view that many elements of accepted Christian church teaching which were in conflict with reason were unlikely and incredible. Whatever about the credence that could be given to Bible stories that appeared unreasonable, no credence whatever should be given to doctrines that were unscriptural.

In earlier centuries, in Roman Catholic countries, to claim an individual's right to interpret scripture would have led one to the Inquisition and the stake. In Protestant England, and for that matter Ireland under Anglican control, where some valued liberty and regarded themselves as tolerant, to deny the Trinity or to express doubt about the veracity of scripture or church teaching could end at the pillory or a prison cell. Since most Dissenter scholars knew the rules, and since Anglicans stressed ceremony and outward practice rather than doctrine as proof of orthodoxy, most philosophers and clergymen could sail close to the wind but maintain their personal liberty.

In spite of their rejection of the deity of Jesus, eighteenth-century Unitarians regarded themselves as Christians and were anxious to be so regarded by others. Non-subscribers regarded themselves as Christians and true Protestants. Modern-day Unitarians acknowledge their Christian and Protestant heritage. However, "some Unitarians even reject the label Christian", and one observer had described it as odd "that there are even atheist and agnostic sections of the Unitarian community".[53]

There was a spirit of free enquiry amongst Unitarians, and their opinions often changed over time or even altered completely. They could be at different stages of a trajectory which might start with Dissenting Protestantism and sometimes lead to deism or atheism.

William Godwin, the English radical of the late eighteenth century, was a Unitarian clergyman in his young manhood. In his later life he was an atheist. Samuel Taylor Coleridge was a Unitarian minister and a political radical in early manhood, but eventually became a Roman Catholic. The United Irishman, Oliver Bond, was the son of a Dissenting minister; a government spy alleged that Bond had no religion.[54] Bond's friend William Drennan claimed that in Dublin Unitarians were regarded by other Protestants as denying "that there is a God".[55] It is not clear whether the spy meant that Bond was an atheist or a Unitarian. Tom Paine commenced the *Age of Reason* by asserting, "I believe in one God and no more." In the same work, he asserted that Jesus was not God but a man. These are essentially Unitarian assertions. Paine's friends regarded him as a deist, while his enemies branded him an atheist and a Unitarian. For many Tories of the late eighteenth century, deists, atheists and Unitarians were all the same.

Tom Paine's *Age of Reason* has been seen as an attack on all "revealed" religion, but it has been recognised that "It contained nothing which would displease the advanced Unitarians".[56] William Drennan was himself a committed Unitarian and a great admirer of the famous Dr Joseph Priestley. Nonetheless, Drennan believed that the doubt and scepticisms engendered by Unitarian speculations paved the way for Paine and deism, or as he suggested, "Priestley lifts the latch for Paine to enter."[57]

A note of caution must be registered in relation to describing an individual or a congregation as Unitarian. Many Dissenting clergymen followed their personal quest for truth into full-blooded Unitarianism, but as E.P. Thompson observed, they sometimes "left their congregations behind".[58] If a clergyman wished to retain his congregation, his livelihood and his liberty, it was sometimes wise to be circumspect regarding his true opinions, and he might have been tempted to shy away from confrontation, particularly with his own congregation. Looking back at the period a hundred years later, Rev. William Lloyd observed: "The prohibition by law no doubt led to some evasion and concealment and probably the public profession of ministers was not always in harmony with their private opinions."[59]

Towards the end of the eighteenth century, Unitarians, particularly in England, were prepared to be more open about their beliefs. Such openness was not always prudent. In 1792 Dr Priestley and some friends formed what they called the "Unitarian Society" and petitioned parliament for a repeal of anti-Dissenters laws. They left themselves open to a stinging attack from Edmund Burke, who described them as a political faction trying to undermine the constitution of the state and destroy the Church of England.[60]

One thing that did not change amongst the Non-subscribers as their liberal beliefs evolved was their attitude of hostility to ecclesiastical establishments.

In 1787 the Bishop of Cloyne declared in his *Present State of the Church of Ireland*:

> Most of the leading Presbyterians in this kingdom (indeed all whose opinions the author has been able to collect) differ essentially from their brethren of Geneva, Switzerland, Holland, Germany and Scotland, as they reject the idea of any national church. If the Church of Scotland, to which they have a hereditary attachment, and to which they adhere, were established in this kingdom, they would still dissent. They are Independents in a civil view; though they are Presbyterians as to ecclesiastical discipline. Their principles do not, like those of the Roman Catholics, tend to set up, but merely to pull down, an ecclesiastical establishment.[61]

"Francis Hutcheson of Dublin"

Francis Hutcheson was "the Father of the Scottish Enlightenment". He was born near Saintfield in County Down in 1694, the second son of a Presbyterian minister. His grandfather had been born in England but was appointed as minister to Saintfield by the Cromwellian regime.[62]

The young Hutcheson had attended Glasgow, studying theology, and was expected to become a clergyman. However, he and his lifelong friend Rev. Thomas Drennan accepted an invitation from the Wood Street Dissenters to teach at their new academy located at Drumcondra Lane in Dublin in 1720. The school catered for the descendants of those who had arrived in the capital during the Commonwealth period — in other words the

"Cromwellians". Starting this school was a venture not without risk; such academies had once been prohibited by law, and it was still necessary for teachers to be licensed by a bishop of the Church of Ireland.[63] Of course, neither Hutcheson nor Drennan had a licence.

Hutcheson's time in Dublin was the happiest time of his life and his most creative period.[64] He met and fell in love with Mary Wilson and married her in 1725. His marriage was a very happy one, though blighted by the deaths of six of their seven children in childhood. It is clear from much of Hutcheson's writing that he spent much time observing and delighting in the actions of young children. It must have been a great source of sorrow to him that only his son Francis survived into adulthood.[65]

He wrote his first and most important work, *An Inquiry Concerning the Origins of our Ideas of Beauty and Virtue*, in Dublin. His book is a strong rebuttal of the theories of Thomas Hobbes, that man is by nature a selfish creature. Hutcheson argued that every person has a natural and disinterested benevolence which guides moral behaviour. In the book's most celebrated phrase, he asserted, "that which is good is what brings the greatest happiness to the greatest number". This work established him as one of the greatest philosophers of his generation.[66]

Besides Thomas Drennan, who came to the city with him, Hutcheson's best friend in Dublin was his cousin William Bruce. Bruce was at the centre of a circle of liberal Dissenters connected to Wood Street. This group numbered amongst its membership Rev. John Abernethy and James Duchal and the poet Samuel Boyse (son of Rev. Joseph Boyse). Another member of the circle was James Arbuckle, a graduate of Glasgow University and publisher of a newspaper, *The Dublin Weekly Journal*.[67]

William Bruce had a publishing business and a bookshop, the Philosopher's Head at Blind Quay. Bruce published Hutcheson's work and John Abernethy's sermons, which were widely read, and he also produced tracts and pamphlets on contemporary issues. This group often met in the Swords home of John Toland's old friend Viscount Robert Molesworth. They have been described as "Commonwealthmen" which was a term often equivalent to republican.[68] It is said of them that they, "handed to a second generation a patriotic spirit that included all Irishmen in its loyalties and diffused a liberal philosophy throughout more than one city or country".[69] In her *History of English Liberal Thought from the Restoration of Charles II to the War with the Thirteen Colonies,* Dr Caroline Robbins locates this Wood Street group as a link between the seventeenth-century luminaries such as Ludlow, Milton and Sidney and the great reformers of the later eighteenth century, Dr Richard Price and Dr Joseph Priestley.

When all the members of this Wood Street group were dead, Thomas Drennan's son William, the founder of the United Irishmen, when standing trial for sedition in 1794, acknowledged them as his main political influences when he wrote: "My father was a friend and associate of good and may I say great men. Of Abernethy of Bruce of Duchal and Hutcheson."[70] Dr Joseph Priestley, who was persecuted for his political opinions in that same year, also admitted to having been influenced by Hutcheson's Dublin circle.[71]

Hutcheson maintained friendships in Dublin amongst the ruling elites of church and state. He enjoyed the friendship of Lord Grenville (then lord lieutenant), Primate Boulter and Archbishop King. They tried unsuccessfully to woo him into the Established Church with promises "of great preferment".[72] When rumours of his good relations with these men reached Hutcheson's father, he wrote to his son seeking assurances that he would not desert his Presbyterian heritage. Hutcheson replied to his father that he had no intention of joining the Established Church.[73]

Since the school Hutcheson ran had no right to legal existence, he was threatened with prosecution for teaching Protestant youth "without subscribing to the ecclesiastical canons". He was protected from this by his friend Archbishop King.[74] King was responsible for the enforcement of religious law in Dublin, and he steadfastly refused to prosecute a man he regarded as a great scholar and a good friend. King assured Hutcheson that as long as he was Bishop of Dublin, Hutcheson had nothing to fear from the persecutors.

When the chair of moral philosophy at Glasgow fell vacant in 1730, Hutcheson was appointed to the post, which is an indication of the status of his reputation at the time. A brilliant and innovative teacher, he was one of the first university teachers to deliver his lectures in English rather than Latin. At Glasgow he taught David Hume (1711–1776) and Adam Smith (1723–1790), both of whom had significant influence over future generations of British, Irish and American radicals. David Hume is regarded as the greatest philosopher of the Scottish Enlightenment. Adam Smith, who himself taught at Glasgow, is best known for his book *An Inquiry into the Nature and Causes of the Wealth of Nations*, and he is regarded as the father of modern economics. Adam Smith referred to Hutcheson as "the never to be forgotten Hutcheson", and said that he was "undoubtedly and beyond all comparison the most acute the most distinct and the most philosophical of all my teachers".[75]

Hutcheson developed many advanced liberal opinions. In his work *A System of Moral Philosophy,* Hutcheson saw the civil power or government as founded on three acts of the whole people:

> The first requirement is an agreement or contract of each one with all the rest that they will unite into one society or body to be governed in all their common interest by one council. Secondly it requires a decree or designation made by the whole people of the form or plan of power, and the persons to be instructed with it. Finally there must be a mutual agreement or contract between the governors thus constituted and

the people, the former obliging themselves to a faithful administration of the powers vested in them for the common interest, and the latter obliging themselves to obedience.[76]

In a world where people were thought to have their social position conferred by birth and bloodline, Hutcheson held that all "human beings are born free and equal". He argued that society should be characterised by a roughly equal division of property. Rather than rulers having a divine right to their authority, Hutcheson believed that government should be both republican and broadly representative and education should be widespread. He believed that religious establishments (the system whereby a government decides that its citizens should conform to one religion) should be abolished. When the lower orders are liberated from poverty, tyranny, ignorance and superstition, the common citizen's moral sense would promote civic virtue and general happiness.[77]

Hutcheson attacked all forms of slavery.[78] He condemned slavery in 1742, decades before there was any significant abolitionist movement in either Britain or the Americas. Many of his students who later became clergymen in Britain, Ireland and the American colonies were champions of anti-slavery sentiment.

In 1776, Pennsylvania was the first of the American states to abolish slavery. Although Hutcheson never set foot in America and was thirty years dead at this time, he must be given some of the credit for the Pennsylvanian emancipation. Dublin-born George Bryan (1731–1791), "the champion of radical democracy", steered the anti-slavery legislation through the Pennsylvania state legislature.[79] Bryan's family had a long association with the Dublin Dissenters, and it is almost certain that Bryan attended Hutcheson's school at Drumcondra Lane, although he would not have been taught by Hutcheson himself, as he was born in 1731, the year after Hutcheson removed to Glasgow.

Bryan would have been brought up with the anti-slavery sentiments which Hutcheson bestowed on the New Light Presbyterians. Bryan's close collaborator in Pennsylvania was another Hutcheson disciple, Rev. Francis Alison (1705–1779). It is said that Alison helped to prepare the Irish Presbyterians of Pennsylvania for their prominent role in the American Revolution.[80] It is almost certain that Alison studied with Hutcheson at Glasgow.[81] Alison liked to quote Hutcheson to the effect that "the end of all civil power is the public happiness and any power not conducive to this is unjust and the people who gave it may justly abolish it".[82]

Alison's influence was not confined to Pennsylvania, and he preached to the Continental Congress during its revolutionary deliberations.[83] Thus Hutcheson, through his writings and his students, had a profound influence on the American Revolution and particularly on Thomas Jefferson, the main author of the American Declaration of Independence. Thomas Jefferson was more influenced by Hutcheson than he was by John Locke.[84]

Hutcheson thought that governments should be created by popularly elected assemblies, that elections should be by ballot and should be held regularly. He held that public office should not be bought or inherited but should be awarded on merit.[85] People had a right to resist public and private tyranny. A community or nation should protect itself with a citizens' army. He regarded standing armies as potential agents of tyranny. A generation after his death, during the American Revolution, his Irish Presbyterian countrymen founded just such a citizens' army, the Volunteers.

Hutcheson was "the link between the Enlightenment taught in the Scottish universities and the tradition of liberal Presbyterianism which flourished in the Society of United Irishmen".[86] His phrase, "an action is best when it produces the greatest happiness for the greatest number", became a slogan of liberal reformers and democrats and was used by William Drennan when he first proposed the formation of the United Irishmen.

Hutcheson loved Dublin, and died while on a visit to that city in 1746.[87] He is buried in the churchyard of Saint Mary's, which is also the final resting place of his cousin William Bruce. Today Saint Mary's is a public park located in what is now Wolfe Tone Street. Many United Irishmen would have revered the memory of Francis Hutcheson. Some of the leaders of the Dublin United Irishmen are remembered in the street and place names of the city. While most Dubliners can direct a visitor to Wolfe Tone Street, Oliver Bond Street, Russell Street, Lord Edward Street and Emmet Road, "Never to be forgotten Hutcheson" lies in what is now an unmarked grave in the Dublin he loved and "where his best work was done".[88]

If the citizens of his beloved adopted city have consigned the memory of their most eminent scholar and philosopher to oblivion, the citizens of his home town have been more generous. In 2003, the people of Saintfield, County Down, unveiled a plaque to Hutcheson, very appropriately on the wall of the First Presbyterian Church where his grandfather had been minister and where the young Francis would have first imbibed his Dissenting Protestant principles.

Hutcheson's influence was immense in his lifetime but probably even greater after his death; his principles informed the demands of reformers throughout the eighteenth century and beyond. They provided a template for generations of radicals and are the foundation stones of modern democracy. When Major Cartwright published *Take Your Choice* in England in 1776, he called for manhood suffrage, annual parliaments, secret ballots and payment for MPs. Hutcheson's influence on Cartwright is obvious. The major is regarded as having, in turn, "refined the claims of advanced political reformers from 1776 to the Chartists and beyond".[89]

Hutcheson's principles were repeated in the pages of the

102

Northern Star, the paper of the Belfast United Irishmen, sixty years after he first published them.[90] These were the principles that propelled the United Irishmen into rebellion in 1798 and again in 1803.

A historian from Hutcheson's native County Down elegantly observed that:

> When local cleric, Rev. Thomas Ledlie Birch, preached to a large army of Presbyterian rebels in the town of Saintfield in 1798, history had turned a full circle. The town where the young Francis Hutcheson had his first schooling now witnessed the presence of an insurgent dissenter army, fired by the Enlightenment values that Hutcheson himself had done so much to kindle.[91]

Notes to Chapter Four
1. Ní Mhurchú agus Breathnach, 2001, p. 182
2. Campion 2003, p. 215
3. Dillon, 2006, p. 337
4. Campion 1999, p. 83
5. Stewart 1993, p. 104
6. Twomey 2009, p. 10
7. *Ibid.*
8. Dutton 2000, p.175
9. *Ibid.*
10. *Ibid.*
11. Campion 2003, p. 74
12. Campion 2003, p. 77
13. *Ibid.*
14. Barnard B 2004, p. 166
15. *Ibid.* p. 93
16. Paulin 1998, p. 8
17. Toland , J., p. 14
18. Campion 1999, p. 226
19. Campion 1999, pp. 205–25
20. Worden 2002
21. Campion 2003
22. *Ibid.* p. 52
23. I am indebted to Marius Harkin, The Ulster American Folk Park, for this information.
24. Campion 2003, p. 97

25. Robbins 1987, p. 169
26. Burke 2003, p. 186
27. Campion 2003, p. 56
28. Brown 2002, p. 30
29. Harrison 1994
30. Emlyn 1731, p. 47
31. *Ibid.* p. 48
32. Brown 2002, p. 83
33. Emlyn 1731, p. 48
34. *Ibid.*
35. Stewart 1993, p. 110
36. Emlyn 1731, p. xxviii
37. *Ibid.*
38. *Ibid.* p. xiv
39. *Ibid.* p. 111
40. Armstrong 1829, p. 71
41. *Ibid.*
42. Brown 2002, p. 84
43. McBride 1993, p. 53
44. Ferguson 2008, p. 56
45. See Armstrong 1829.
46. *Ibid.* p. 63
47. Robbins 1987, p. 165
48. Armstrong 1829, p. 84
49. *Ibid.*
50. Brown 2002, p.84
51. Agnew, 1998,1999, vol II, p. 209
52. *Ibid.* p. 53
53. Grayling 2001, p. 6
54. Bartlett 2004, p. 98
55. Agnew 1998, 1999, vol. II, p. 5
56. Thompson, E.P., (1963), p. 105
57. Agnew 1998, 1999, vol. II, p. 207
58. *Ibid.* p. 29
59. Lloyd 1899, p. 175
60. 'Speech on the Petition of the Unitarians', 11 May 1792
61. Published in Dublin 1787.
62. Stewart 1993, p. 71
63. Brown 2002, p. 80
64. *Ibid.* p. 25
65. *Ibid.* p. 27
66. Orr 2000
67. Brown 2002, p. 99
68. *Ibid.*

69. Robbins 1987, p. 163
70. Stewart 1993, p. 71
71. Paulin 1998, p. 85
72. Armstrong 1829, p. 60
73. Brown , in Herlihy, ed 1998, p. 94
74. Armstrong 1829, p. 60
75. Orr 2000
76. Ferguson 2008, p. 67
77. Miller et al 2003, p. 488
78. Ibid.
79. Ibid. p. 484
80. Ibid. p. 510
81. Ibid. p. 511
82. Ibid.
83. Ibid.
84. Paulin 1998, p. 60
85. Stewart 1993, p. 71
86. McFarland 1994, p. 15
87. Brown 2002, p. 74
88. Ibid.
89. Thompson 1964, p. 92
90. Stewart 1993, p. 101
91. Orr 2000

Chapter Five

CHARLES LUCAS AND
THE DUBLIN WORKING CLASS

16 October 1749: The Irish House of Commons
*The Earl of Harrington, the lord lieutenant of Ireland, has
summoned Dr Charles Lucas to the House, accusing him
of "an audacious attempt to create a jealousy between the
two kingdoms". Lucas, who has come accompanied by a
large crowd of supporters, maintains defiantly that the
Irish Catholic rebels of 1641 were defending themselves
and that both sides in that war were guilty of atrocities. He
stands over his claim that Ireland is a distinct kingdom.
The House orders him out and votes that he is guilty of
sedition, that he has promoted insurrection, that he has
justified past rebellions, and that he is an enemy to his
country and should be imprisoned in Newgate. Fearing
that his angry followers will attempt an uprising, Lucas
decides to flee Ireland.*[1]

The Indefatigable Tribune
When Francis Hutcheson died in Dublin in 1746, he had
been visiting his republican friends of the Wood Street
circle. One of these was his cousin, the publisher William
Bruce. Bruce and his group were at this time enthusiastic
supporters of a new and exciting figure in the radical
politics of Dublin. Charles Lucas (1713–1771), an emerging pamphleteer and politician, was of Cromwellian stock.
His great-grandfather, Lieutenant Colonel Benjamin Lucas,
had settled in County Clare after the Cromwellian War in
Ireland. Apprenticed to an apothecary in Dublin about
1730, Charles was elected to Dublin Corporation

sometime in the 1740s, as a member of the Apothecaries' Guild.

Dublin was by now the premier city of Ireland. It was the seat of government, the main port of the country, and contained the only universities in Ireland, Trinity College and the College of Physicians.[2] On the northern edge of the city stood the Linen Hall, which exported linen manufactured in the north and west of Ireland. The north and south walls of the Liffey now stretched to the east as far as Ringsend. New fashionable streets – Henrietta Street and Gardiner's Mall north of the Liffey, and Kildare Street and Grafton Street on the south[3] – had been laid out, and Dublin merchants dominated Irish overseas trade. Ships tied up against the Liffey walls from Ringsend up to the Custom House on Essex Quay.

The Custom House and the Exchange building were regarded as handsome. However, when John Wesley visited Dublin in 1747, he observed that there were scarcely any public buildings in any way remarkable except the parliament in College Green.[4] The parliament house was "the greatest of all physical monuments to the [Irish Protestant] ascendency class".[5]

The Irish Houses of Lords and Commons sat for half a year every two years. As the landed aristocracy and gentry dominated these institutions, earls, viscounts, squires and MPs had to build elegant town houses in reasonable proximity to the parliament. Dublin's artisan class of coach-builders, gold and silversmiths and furniture makers produced luxury goods to satisfy the extravagant tastes of this metropolitan elite.[6] It was to these artisans, their guilds and the other "Freemen of Dublin" that Charles Lucas would look for support in his campaign to democratise the government of Dublin City.

Dublin had enjoyed a substantial growth in population, but the increased population of the city (120,000 by 1740) had made it a divided city.[7] There were 3,000 "Freeman of Dublin" by 1749.[8] The Freemen were members of trade guilds who could elect ninety-six representatives to the Common Council of Dublin Corporation. These Freemen were becoming more literate, better off and were inclined to resent the subservience of their Common Council to the unelected and self-selecting Board of Aldermen of Dublin.[9] The twenty-five aldermen were drawn from the city's wealthiest Protestant merchants and held office for life.[10]

As soon as Lucas was elected, he commenced a campaign to increase the influence of the Common Council at the expense of the Board of Aldermen. He soon broadened his campaign to include "an aggressive assertion of Irish constitutional rights and an insistence on the primacy of representative institutions over monarchy and aristocracy".[11]

Although nominally a member of the Established Church, Lucas let it be known that he was conformist merely as a legal duty and that there was "no tenet necessary for salvation in which he differed from the Presbyterians".[12] He sought to build a reform movement based on the "new men" of the Protestant urban class and from descendants of Cromwellian settlers, and he secured the support of the Dublin Dissenters for his campaign.[13] While Lucas's supporters were all Protestants, he complained that many Roman Catholics regarded him as a Cromwellian.[14]

When the Dissenters sided with Lucas, his opponents accused him and his followers of trying to pull down the Established Church. Lucas's political opponents and their faithful allies, the Dublin Anglican clergy, suggested that many of Lucas's supporters were "king-killers". They reminded the citizens of Dublin that "such people had been responsible for the execution of Charles I".[15] Charles had been dead for a hundred years at this point, but the Anglicans still felt that there was political advantage in pinning his death on the Dublin Dissenters.

Even James Digges La Touche, Lucas's friend and political ally, who was no Tory, felt the need to warn the City Commons to "Beware of those who pretended to love liberty, but claimed a right to dissent from the Established Church, who constantly Drink in Public the Rights and Liberties of the City of Dublin and in private the memory of Oliver Cromwell".[16] One historian has suggested that this may have been an attempt to embarras Lucas or might have been an effort by La Touche, who was of Huguenot stock, to protect himself from such charges.[17]

Lucas's enemies claimed that he drew support from another quarter even more obnoxious than the Cromwellian Dissenters. They alleged he got himself elected "by cajoling the very scum of the people".[18] If this is true, Lucas was the first Dublin-based politician to mobilise the common people of the city in pursuit of political ends. La Touche later claimed that since Lucas' time:

> you might hear the lowest tradesmen call themselves free citizens with more than Roman arrogance... Our Dublin citizens since that memorable year [1749] have been so wrong headed as to talk of national rights and liberty... they now read newspapers and even the votes of the Commons, and have been more than once audacious enough to crowd the streets around the parliament House.[19]

Lucas gained the enmity of the Irish government when he published his *Address to the Free Citizens of Dublin* in 1749. In it he questioned the right of the king to legislate for Ireland. Members of the Irish House of Commons and Dublin Corporation, pleased that Lucas had pushed his luck too far, pounced. Declaring that his pamphlet was treasonable, they denounced Lucas as an enemy to his country. The citizens of Dublin, however, supported Lucas, and there were public demonstrations in his favour, and both he and La Touche were granted honorary membership of several of the city's guilds. However, the support of the people could not protect him from the vengeance of the law. He had to make himself scarce and leave the kingdom to avoid prosecution. When he fled, he was replaced on the

Corporation by his ally, Thomas Read.[20] Read was a prominent member of the Wood Street congregation and a part of William Bruce's circle. The replacement of Lucas by a prominent Dissenter raised further alarm amongst the Dublin Anglican bishops, who claimed that the New Light Presbyterians were attempting to take over the management of the city and tear down the Church.[21]

Lucas fled to Leiden in Holland, the traditional "refugee city" for radical Protestants. Long before, Leiden had given refuge to Freeborn John Lilburne, John Locke and the Rye House plotters. Lucas qualified as a doctor there.

Lucas returned to Dublin on the accession of George III in 1761. Since the cause of his flight had been his alleged insult to George II and George II was now dead, Lucas had no case to answer. His homecoming was a massive personal triumph. The sitting MP for Dublin City, James Dunn, the candidate of the Dublin Dissenters, generously stood aside for Lucas, who scored a stunning victory.[22] He held the seat until his death in 1771. His efforts in parliament were directed at the long-held objective of the reformers to reduce the pension list, whereby the members of the House of Commons were bribed into placing their own interests before the interest of their country or its citizens. He established a pro-reform and anti-government paper, the *Freeman's Journal*.

Charles Lucas "helped to develop a lively lower class political culture in Dublin".[23] In 1759, when serious rioting broke out in Dublin as a result of rumours of an Act of Union, it was claimed that the riot began in the Earl of Meath's liberty (the Liberties) and involved "Protestant weavers and New Light Presbyterians". The rioters were, it was claimed, "a sect amongst the Protestant descendants of Cromwellian settlers who exhibited a dislike of monarchy and the Established Church".[24] Lucas was ten years in exile at this point, but he was seen as having contributed to the radicalisation of the Protestant lower orders of Dublin.

Lucas had clearly a lasting influence on the artisans of Dublin. Although his reputation and his influence were high amongst the Dissenters and "the very scum of the people", he also had an international reputation. Shortly before Lucas died in 1771, Benjamin Franklin came to Dublin to visit him and other Irish "Friends of America".[25] Three years later, when Thomas Jefferson was penning the Declaration of Independence, it is claimed that he was influenced by the writings of "the Irish revolutionist Charles Lucas".[26]

Much later still, when Wolfe Tone, in exile in Paris, mused on a Pantheon for heroes of Ireland, he included Charles Lucas alongside Jonathan Swift.[27] Tone was somewhat carried away in his enthusiasm; Lucas was a radical Whig while Swift was a staunch Tory. Had Swift not been dead by the time Lucas burst on to the Dublin scene, the likelihood is that they would have been implacable enemies.

There is a marble statue of Charles Lucas in City Hall in Dublin. The man Wolfe Tone knew to be a hero worthy of an Irish Pantheon is almost unknown in the city he served faithfully and from whence he was exiled for questioning the authority of the king. He had returned from exile in triumph as the champion of the Dublin working class. Lucas was once described as "the foremost figure in Ireland's dash for liberty". In 1840, Rev. William Drummond of Great Strand Street, in his biography of Archibald Hamilton Rowan, described Lucas as an "indefatigable Tribune in whose writings the first dawning of a national and Irish feeling are to be found".[28]

At the time of his death in 1771, Lucas was an MP and a radical celebrity. He was laid to rest in Saint Michan's after a massive civic funeral attended by many thousands of his devoted Dublin constituents. They inscribed as his epitaph:

> Lucas, Hibernia's friend her joy and pride
> Her powerful bulwark and her faithful guide
> Firm in the Senate steady in his trust
> Unmoved by fear and obstinately just.

Notes to Chapter Five
1. Murphy 2009, p. 24
2. J. Hill 1999, p. 20
3. Moody and Vaughan 2009, p. 45
4. *Ibid.*
5. McBride 2009, p. 114
6. J. Hill 1999, p. 22
7. *Ibid.* 1999, p. 91
8. *Ibid.*
9. *Ibid.*
10. *Ibid.*
11. S.J. Connolly 2008, p. 240
12. J. Hill 1999, p. 33
13. See H. Burke in Donlon 2006, p. 32
14. *Ibid.* p. 31
15. *Ibid.* p. 102
16. *Ibid.*
17. *Ibid.* p. 101
18. Smyth 1992, p. 126
19. *Ibid.*
20. Smyth 1992, p. 226
21. Hill [, J.] 1997, p. 102
22. Herlihy 1997, p. 35
23. *Ibid*, p. 126
24. *Ibid.* p. 130
25. S.J. Connolly 2008, p. 402
26. Aptheker 1960, p. 102
27. Bartlett 1998, p. 490
28. Drummond 1840, p. 75

Chapter Six

WAR AND SERMON

19 April 1776, Eustace Street, Dublin
George III has ordered a fast day so that his subjects can pray for the victory of British arms against the rebellious American colonists. Rev. Isaac Weld (1710–1778) ascends the pulpit at Eustace Street, Dublin, and addresses his congregation. Rev. Weld tells them that the British Empire is in imminent danger of falling into dissolution. He warns that it is not external enemies but the internal corruptions and weakness of the empire that will be the cause of its collapse. He will not pray for victory in a war he regards as essentially a civil war. He concludes with rueful passion: "When brother lifts his hand against brother then every life that falls is an irreparable loss to the state. When kindred blood is shed victory is ruin."[1]

George III and the Dissenters

The relationship between George III, who ascended the throne in 1760, and his Protestant Dissenter subjects would always be difficult. This was despite the fact that from the beginning the Dissenters had been loyal to his ancestral House of Hanover. Before the death of the heirless Queen Anne in 1714, the parliament of England had agreed that the Protestant House of Hanover should inherit the throne of Great Britain and Ireland. Dissenters welcomed George I, Elector of Hanover, when he succeeded Anne. The Hanoverian succession resulted in the end of the rule of the hated Stuarts and provided England, Ireland and Scotland with a new Protestant dynasty.

While the Hanoverian Succession was peaceful, it was

not universally regarded as secure. Throughout the first half of the seventeenth century, the Dissenters and indeed most of Protestant England feared the return of the Roman Catholic Stuarts from the French court. The Roman Catholic powers of Europe and the Pope refused to recognise the Hanoverians and supported the claims of James III, "the Old Pretender", as the lawful king of England. As long as the Jacobite threat remained, Dissenters could not afford to indulge in republican flights of fancy. They had an interest in the stability of the Hanoverian monarchy and they knew it. Their oft-repeated protestations of loyalty to the Hanoverians were genuine, but their loyalty did not mean that they would be content to allow a Hanoverian monarch to exceed his authority or deny them freedom of conscience. The Dissenters continued to fight in vain against the Test Act. They also continued to demand religious toleration throughout the reign of the Hanoverians.

The Old Pretender never ceased conniving and conspiring with his Jacobite supporters to foment rebellions in favour of the House of Stuart. However, fourteen years before the accession of George III, the Jacobite military threat had been extinguished once and for all at Culloden Moor in Scotland in 1746. The Old Pretender's son, Charles Stuart, known to his supporters as "Bonny Prince Charlie" and to his enemies as the "Young Pretender", had led his feudal army of Scottish clansmen to the slaughter.

The Highlanders fought the Duke of Cumberland, George III's uncle, armed with broadswords, dirks and shields, while Cumberland commanded a modern army equipped with cavalry, cannon, musket and grapeshot. The Highlanders were slaughtered during the battle and in the aftermath as they tried to flee. After Culloden when "Butcher Cumberland" had done with the Highlanders, there remained no serious Jacobite threat to the House of Hanover.

The absence of the Jacobite threat was not the only factor which militated against George III enjoying the whole-hearted loyalty of his Dissenter subjects. Other issues served to highlight the king's reactionary impulses. Firstly, he sponsored the harassment and imprisonment of John Wilkes, the reforming MP for Middlesex. Secondly, the king let it be known that any form of religious toleration was anathema to him and that he would defend the privileges of the Established Church. Thirdly, he resisted all demands for reform of corrupt, oligarchic and unrepresentative parliaments at Westminster and Dublin.

John Wilkes (1725–1797) criticised the Earl of Bute, the king's chosen prime minister, in 1768, suggesting that as Bute was a relation of the Stuarts, he was most likely a Jacobite. Wilkes' main problem with Bute was that he came into office, not because he had support of the House of Commons, but because he was the king's favourite. The king had Wilkes arrested, imprisoned and deprived of his parliamentary seat. When a London crowd gathered round the prison shouting, "Wilkes and Liberty. Damn the King," they were fired on by troops. Seven people were killed in what became known as the St George's Field massacre.

The general body of Dissenters in England were vigorous supporters of Wilkes. The famous Dr Johnson was no doubt referring to this when he claimed that Wilkes' supporters were "the sectaries and the natural fomenters of sedition". Johnson also said they were "a rabble of whose religion little now remains but a hatred of all establishments". In spite of many unconstitutional manoeuvres to deprive Wilkes of his parliamentary seat, his loyal voters of Middlesex re-elected him time and again, and it was as an MP that he castigated government policy before and during the American Revolution.

While the Wilkes agitation attracted the support of Dissenters, it was events in America that galvanised them into opposition to the king and his government. From very early in his reign, George III's policies created tension with his American subjects.

The American Revolutionary War had its origins in a

grievance which was familiar to all Englishmen: the king's right to introduce new taxes without the consent of the people's representatives in parliament. This principle, which had been argued about and fought over in England for generations, had led to the execution of Charles I and was one of the reasons why James II was forced into exile. Believing that he had a prerogative to impose taxes in America, George III's early attempt to do so in the Stamp Act of 1765 created opposition and defiance which worsened over the years and eventually led to war.

George III decided that he would tax his American subjects so that they might pay the cost of the armies and the navy needed for the defence of the colonies. However, George could only introduce such taxes on his English subjects with the consent of the British House of Commons. While a majority in the House of Commons supported the king's proposals, the Americans argued that since they did not elect the members of that assembly, the king's proposals amounted to "taxation without representation", a principle to which no freeborn Englishman, no Whig and, as it turned out, few Americans would accept. The king could either retreat or use his considerable armed forces to bring the rebellious colonists to heel. He opted for armed force.

Even before the shooting started (the first shots of the American Revolution were fired at Lexington on 18 April 1775), the Irish and British Dissenters instinctively sided with the colonists. When hostilities began in earnest, some of the most enthusiastic soldiers in the new American army were natives of Ulster, from where there had been massive migration to America. It is estimated that between 1717 and 1776, more than a quarter of a million Irish Dissenters made the journey. There was scarcely a family in the north of Ireland that did not have a relative in the American colonies.[2] There were economic, political and religious aspects to this migration.

Economic recession, rent increases, land disputes and a succession of droughts were some of the reasons for the greatest mass migration of people from Ireland to the New World during the eighteenth century, but there were religious issues as well. The Established Church was determined to make Ireland a cold place for Dissenters. They could not set up new congregations, their clergy could not perform legal weddings, nor could they bury their dead according to their own principles. One minister said that he and his congregation went to America to avoid oppression, to shun persecution and to worship God according to their consciences.[3] The Ulster migrants arrived in the New World with a strong sense of grievance towards the Established Church, the king and Tories in general.

John Lewis may not have been a typical migrant from Ulster, but he would have shared the political outlook of his fellow Irish Presbyterians. Of Huguenot descent, he was born in Donegal in 1678. He fled to America in 1730 after killing a landlord who had threatened to dispossess a number of his tenants.[4] His tombstone in the Shenandoah Valley of Virginia bears the inscription:

> Here lie the remains of John Lewis, who slew the
> Irish lord, settled in Augusta county, located the town
> of Staunton and furnished five sons to fight the bat-
> tles of the American Revolution.

Many Ulstermen in America fought with distinction. It was militia from Ballymena and Ballmoney in Antrim who defeated the king's troops at King's Mountain and Hannah's Cowpens, the two major battles in the southern states. Gerard Brandon, a Donegal man, led the American cavalry charge at King's Mountain, and the Americans at Hannah's Cowpens were led by Daniel Morgan of Draperstown, County Londonderry.[5]

A compositor from Strabane, John Dunlap, printed the Declaration of Independence, and the *Belfast Newsletter* was the first newspaper outside of America to print the Declaration in full for readers.[6] George Washington was commander-in-chief of the American forces, and such was his confidence in his Scots-Irish troops that he said, if necessary, he "would take his last stand for liberty with the Scots-Irish Presbyterians of my native Virginia" .[7] One Hessian officer said, "Call this war by whatever name you may, only call it not an American rebellion; it is nothing more or less than a Scotch Irish Presbyterian rebellion."[8]

The Dissenters in Ireland regarded the king and his ministers as the aggressors in the conflict, believing the war was an unjust attack on the liberties of the colonists. The war was seen as having a negative economic impact on Ireland, which was being left vulnerable to invasion by France or Spain, two much-feared absolutist Popish governments.

In an attempt to boost support for the war, the government announced "fast days" when the clergy were expected to preach about the evils of rebellion and the importance of loyalty to the monarch. Rev. William Steel Dickson was a non-subscribing minster and former pupil of Adam Smith at Glasgow and later a leading United Irishman. He believed the war was "an unprincipled mad crusade", and he took the opportunity provided by the fast days to give vent to that opinion.[9] In a sermon delivered to his congregation in Ballyhalbert on 13 December 1776, Dickson bemoaned the fact that "brother points the fatal minister of death against brother", and he declared that "if the contest should be prolonged America must be ruined and in its ruins we must suffer".[10] He said that even if the king won the war, the cost of keeping the defeated Americans in subjection would be more than Britain and Ireland could bear.

Similar sentiments were being expressed in Dissenting meeting houses throughout Ireland. Isaac Weld's sermon, dated 19 April 1776 (as quoted above), is typical of the genre. Weld's sermon was not as strident in its anti-war sentiment as Dickson's, but regretted the war in a way that would have given little comfort to the king and his ministers.

Major General Richard Montgomery

Just three months before Rev. Weld's sermon was composed, the Montgomery family of Swords, Dublin, lost a much loved son, and America gained its first hero of the war. Major General Richard Montgomery fell, leading his men in the deep winter snows of 31 December 1775. He was the highest ranking officer to die in the conflict. He had given the Americans a much needed early victory when he captured Montreal shortly before his death.

Montgomery was born in Dublin in 1738, the son of Captain Thomas Montgomery, who held a seat in the Irish House of Commons representing County Donegal. Richard's elder brother, Alexander, would later hold that seat for thirty years. Richard graduated from Trinity College Dublin in 1756. He had then pursued a career as an officer in the British army, seeing action in the Seven Years War against the French in America and Cuba.

Montgomery was sympathetic to the political radicals of his day and, when he returned to England, threatened to resign rather that suppress the "Wilkes and Liberty" campaign. He felt that a soldier's role was to fight on the battlefield, not to suppress civil unrest. Montgomery's refusal to attack civilians may have contributed to the end of his career in the British army. In the event, he sold his officer's commission and left the army after he was passed over for promotion. He went to America in 1772, where he married Janet Livingston, a daughter of a judge of the New York Supreme Court, in 1773. He bought a farm in New York State and settled down.

The outbreak of war changed everything for Montgomery. George Washington appealed for experienced soldiers to lead his new army. Montgomery was reluctant to fight his old comrades and to leave his new wife, but he felt he had a duty to defend the new American republic. He commanded an army which was ordered to attack Canada. From September to December 1775, he overran an immense expanse of Canadian territory, capturing two British forts and the city of Montreal. His gamble to try to take Quebec proved a step too far.

Having failed to force the surrender of Quebec by means of several artillery barrages, he chose to lead his men in a night attack which took place in a terrible blizzard in the last hours of 1775. As he drew his sword to encourage his men to charge an enemy fortification, he was cut down in a hail of grapeshot and mortally wounded. When his body was found by the British the next morning, they afforded him a dignified funeral, something which they would rarely afford to traitors and rebels. Richard Montgomery was, of course, known to the British and respected by them as an honourable man and a fine soldier.

A year after Montgomery's death, in his pamphlet, *A Dialogue Between the Ghost of Montgomery and an American Delegate in a Wood near Philadelphia*, Tom Paine invoked Montgomery and Algernon Sidney to warn would-be American backsliders that there should be no compromise short of a full republic. At one point the delegate asks, "Should you distinguish between the King and his minister?" Montgomery's ghost replies,

> I live in a world where all political superstition is done away. The king is the author of all the measures carried on against America. The influence of bad ministers is no better apology for these measures, than the influences of bad company is for a murderer, who expiates his crimes under a gallows.[11]

Montgomery may have left Dublin to avoid marrying a women he had made pregnant. The Great Strand Street baptismal register records that a Richard Montgomery baptised a daughter, Catherine Sophia, there in 1769. The Montgomery family were members of the Great Strand Street congregation, and Richard's brother Alexander paid a pew rent there for many years. Richard's biographer tells us that he was in Dublin in 1769 where he had a delicate personal problem with a woman who wanted him to marry her. He suggests that this was one reason why Richard left Dublin to make a new life in America.[12]

Richard's status as a martyr for liberty helped to boost his brother Alexander's political career in Ireland. Alexander was first elected to the Irish House of Commons in 1768 and held the seat for more than thirty years. His kinship with the hero of Quebec increased his popularity, and he held the rank of colonel in the Irish Volunteers. His career of "flamboyant extremism" resulted in his holding his seat in the election of 1797 with the support of the United Irishmen.[13] Alexander was asked by his good friend and one-time fellow MP, Lord Edward FitzGerald, to take command of the Ulster United Irishmen in 1798. Alexander declined because he was in poor health at the time and because he was seventy-seven years old.[14]

Richard Montgomery has been forgotten in his native city of Dublin, but there are no less than sixteen counties in various American states called Montgomery County in his honour. After his death, the war dragged on for many years and would not finally end until the American victory at the Battle of Yorktown in October 1781.

As the war continued relentlessly, the reverses for the British forces and the victories of the Americans were greeted with joy in Ulster. William Drennan wrote to his sister, "It is probable that future historians will date the fall of the British Empire from 16th October 1777 [the American victory at Saratoga]... to see this great empire fall into its political dotage, was it for this Hampden bled and [Algernon] Sidney suffered?"[15]

As the American Revolution triumphed, Thomas Jefferson and Benjamin Franklin and the other Founding Fathers could draw on the canon of Commonwealth literature and authors such as Algernon Sidney, John Locke, Francis Hutcheson and Charles Lucas to justify their rebellion in terms comprehensible to all "freeborn men". The Revolution produced a new philosopher and apostle of republicanism who spoke to the common man, Thomas Paine. Paine, who was born in Norfolk in England in 1737, arrived in America in 1774 in search of a new career, having previously been a stay-maker, a privateer and a customs official. Almost on arrival, Paine discovered his true calling; he became the philosopher and propagandist *par excellence* of the American Revolution.

Paine could write in a simple style which appealed to the American working man and farmer. He could challenge Tory hypocrisy and cant and put heart and courage into the common soldier. As General Washington's army endured the cold and hardship of their camp at Valley Forge in the winter of 1776, Paine rallied their courage with his immortal phrase: "These are times that try men's souls." Paine could mix eloquently expressed profound truth with crude propaganda. Once he observed:

> What is a Tory? Good God! What is he? I should not
> be afraid to go with a hundred Whigs against a thou-
> sand Tories… Every Tory is a coward; for servile,
> slavish, self-interested fear is the foundation of
> Toryism; and a man under such influence, though he
> may be cruel, never can be brave.[16]

Paine produced his pamphlet *Common Sense* (1775) in the style of a sermon of a Dissenting minister. It was full of both scriptural references and political insights. Paine told his readers that "Government by kings was first intro-duced into the world by the heathens, from whom the children of Israel copied the custom. It was the most pre-posterous invention the Devil ever set on foot for the pro-motion of idolatry."

The Fifth Monarchists of the English Civil War held there was no legitimate king but God. Paine asked, "But where says some is the King of America? I'll tell you Friend, he reigns above, and doth not make havoc of mankind like the Royal Brute of Britain… let it be brought forth placed on the divine law, the word of God; let a crown be placed thereon, by which the world may know, that so far as we approve of monarchy, that in America THE LAW IS KING."

After the American victory at Yorktown and the surrender of the British forces, Benjamin Franklin signed the Treaty of Paris on 30 November 1782. The new America had no king, no aristocracy, no Established Chuch and no hereditary power. Universal male suffrage was introduced, though only for whites. Black slaves and women of any colour and station were not to be treated as full citizens. White male citizens of all ranks and religions had the right to bear arms. The separation of church and state achieved in the new American republic was regarded by the Dissenters as being very much to their advantage.

Although slavery continued, the Americans proceeded to build the first political democracy on earth. The (white) American people ceased to be subjects and became citizens. They became the sole source of political authority. The government was the people's servant rather than their master.[17]

Those in Britain and Ireland who supported the king's war against his American subjects blamed the Dissenters, both English and Irish, for the loss of America. Horace Walpole observed, "I see our American cousin has eloped with a Scots Irish Parson."[18]

Not everyone shared Walpole's light-hearted view of the matter, and the pro-American Dissenters were often branded as traitors. The traitor term did not greatly damage the Dissenters at this time as there had been considerable opposition to the war and pro-American sentiment amongst all sections of the British and Irish public. There was also opposition within the British House of Commons, which included Charles James Fox, leader of the opposition. Even Edmund Burke opposed the war for pragmatic reasons, though he supported the king's right to impose taxation without representation on America.

The Americans had cast off the rule of the "Royal Brute of Britain" and established their republic. The Dissenters in

Ireland and Britain observed developments in America with delight and were given an example to follow.[19]

The American War and the Irish Volunteers

In 1760, as the Seven Years' War between Britain and France raged around the globe, a small party of French troops had landed at Carrickfergus and held its castle for three days. They intended to stage a raid on Belfast. As there were few regular troops available to defend the city, the citizens of Belfast and its environs mustered an impromptu volunteer army and marched to confront the enemy. The small French force abandoned their plans to attack Belfast, re-embarked and were engaged by Royal Navy frigates. The lesson was learnt that in times of necessity, Ireland should not rely on British regular troops but should look to itself for defence.

Fifteen years later, the American war left Ireland denuded of the British troops who usually garrisoned the country. Companies of Volunteers sprang up all over Ireland, with as many as 40,000 men enlisting. At first the authorities were pleased with the loyalty of the citizens, but it quickly became clear that many Volunteer companies, particularly those in Ulster and Dublin, were far more radical than the government would have wished. Rev. Steel Dickson described the popular enthusiasm for Volunteering in Ulster:

> Physician, surgeon and apothecary; lawyer and attorney all were soldiers. Even the Presbyterian Ministers were so inspired with the patriotism of the day that in several places the rusty black was exchanged for the glowing scarlet and the title of "Reverend" for that of "Captain'; a self-created, self-arrayed, and self-supported army presented itself which strangers contemplated with wonder, enemies with fear and friends with pride, exultation and confidence.[20]

Volunteering quickly spread throughout Ireland. Everywhere they marched, displaying the most resplendent uniforms the individual could afford. The Volunteers staged mock battles and manoeuvres, sometimes of epic proportions. They had social gatherings with convivial drinking, toasting and the passing of political resolutions. Their main tactic for influencing government was to hold conventions such as the one held in Dungannon in 1782. The objective of this convention was to root out corruption and court influence in the legislative body. Such gatherings of armed propertied citizens demanding reform brought pressure on government. Britain was vulnerable to this kind of pressure while the American war lasted. They were even more vulnerable in the immediate aftermath of defeat in America.

The Volunteers were determined to resist foreign aggression. They asserted their independence from government control and demanded political and economic concessions from government. The Dungannon Convention of the Volunteers met in February 1782 in an atmosphere of high enthusiasm. The Americans had accepted the surrender of Cornwallis at Yorktown the previous October. The threat of invasion of Ireland had receded, and the Volunteers, most of whom had supported the Americans, were now determined to drive home what they perceived to be their advantage over the British government.

The Volunteers corresponded with the best-known British and American reformers of the day. They wrote to Benjamin Franklin, who was in Paris to negotiate the independence of the new United States of America. They also made contact with Dr Richard Price, John Jebb, Major Cartwright and others in England, "most distinguished for their talents and their zeal in the cause of liberty". Franklin, Price, Jebb and Cartwright were Unitarian in their theology. The purpose of this correspondence was to seek advice on their reform programme.[21]

The programme the Volunteers eventually adopted called for a redistribution of seats in parliament, shorter parliaments and an extension of the franchise to leaseholders, the ballot, registration of voters and a total exclusion (from parliament) of placemen and pensioners.[22] Placemen and pensioners were those MPs who, when elected, accepted jobs, pensions or other bribes from government in return for their support. At this point the Volunteers had little interest in the plight of Roman Catholics. Catholics who tried to join the Volunteers were almost universally rejected and "often not without insult".[23] Catholics were forbidden to bear arms, and many Protestants were anxious that this should remain the position.

In March 1779, Rev. Steel Dickson preached a sermon to the Eichlin Ville Volunteers calling for the admission of Catholics to the corps. This sermon marks a turning point in the history of Ireland. Rev. Steel Dickson's sermon was the first step in what eventually developed into a democratic project to modernise Irish society on a non-sectarian basis. The Dissenters regarded the Irish House of Commons as corrupt, oligarchic and unrepresentative.[24] The Volunteers, on the other hand, were seen as the nation's citizens-in-arms. They were an expression of the public will expressed by "citizen soldiers" who had no allegiance to tyrants and were committed to the good of the nation. The Volunteers at this point were the Protestant nation.

Steel Dickson would have Roman Catholics admitted as members of the Volunteers and hence part of the nation. This implied recognition that Roman Catholics could be trusted to play a full and virtuous role as free citizens in defending their country.

Rev. Steel Dickson was telling his fellow Dissenters that the Penal Laws, which had been used by Irish Protestants to oppress their Catholic fellow countrymen since the end of the Williamite War, were unjustified. Unitarian clergymen who were known to hold this view had only ever expressed it to their congregations. Dickson was now moving non-sectarianism on to the political agenda. He was the first Irish Protestant publicly to acknowledge that the

treatment of Roman Catholics was unjust and unwarranted. He was also prepared to make common cause with
Roman Catholics in the fight for reform of the legislature.

Catholic and Protestant would be united to oppose foreign aggression and to win concessions from government.
Steel Dickson urged the Volunteers to show, "it is only
against the enemies of your country, liberty and peace, be
their religion what it may be that your arms are pointed –
and that whoever is a friend of these is your friend and the
object of your protection".[25]

Five years were to elapse before Dickson's call was heed-
ed, and it was not until 1784 that the policy of excluding
Catholics was changed. Catholics then joined in great
numbers.[26] Dickson's call for unity between Roman
Catholic and Dissenter anticipated Wolfe Tone and the
United Irishmen by more than a decade. Dickson delivered
this sermon ten years before the fall of the Bastille and
before the Roman Catholics of France had shown the
world that they could make a revolution.

The Volunteers won free trade in 1780 and nominal
independence for the Irish parliament in 1782. These gains
were quickly seen to be illusory. The British government
retained control of the armed forces and the judiciary and
retained the power to bribe enough place-chasers and
pension-hunters in the Irish Lords and Commons to ensure
it always got its way. There was no broadening of the franchise, and the oligarchic landed interest still controlled the
Irish parliament in College Green. There was no lifting of
the penal tariffs against Irish goods on the British market.

A national Volunteer convention was held in Dublin in
1783 which drew up a plan for reform for presentation to
parliament. Lord Charlemont, the Volunteer leader, fear-
ful that government might now suppress the movement,
worked to dampen the political agitation. The movement
ran out of steam, lost much of its prestige, and the cause
of reform went into a decline that continued to the end of
the decade.

In July 1789, the demoralised Dublin, Ulster and British reformers heard news that gladdened their hearts and lifted their spirits. The Bastille, that fortress of oppression which had for four centuries stood as the symbol of the absolute power of tyrant kings, had fallen to the people of Paris. William Wordsworth captured the mood of the British reformers when he wrote, "Bliss was it in that dawn to be alive but to be young was very heaven." The Irish reformers would soon react by forming the first avowedly non-sectarian democratic organisation in the country's history: the Society of United Irishmen.

An Irish Unitarian Minister's American War

Amongst the warm supporters of the American cause in Ireland, none was as passionate as Rev. William Hazlitt, minister to the Dissenting congregation in Bandon, County Cork. Bandon had been a haven of Protestant Dissent from its foundation in the early seventeenth century. In 1649, as Oliver Cromwell invaded Ireland, the townspeople of Bandon attempted to rise against their royalist garrison and declare the town for parliament and Cromwell. When James II landed in Ireland in 1689, the people of Bandon were amongst the first to declare for William of Orange. On this occasion, they hoisted a flag which has become a watchword of Ulster loyalism in the nineteenth and twentieth centuries. "*Ne cede*" has been translated as "No surrender".[27]

Hazlitt's time in the town of Bandon, "where even the pigs are Protestant", was fertile ground for recruitment into the Volunteers. Arthur O'Connor, later leader of the United Irishmen, and his mentor, Acropolis Morris, had been members of the Bandon Volunteers. This corps was "particularly advanced in its political opinions and was amongst the first in Ireland to declare for legislative independence".[28]

In the late 1770s the Dissenting congregation in Bandon was seeking a minister. Their needs could not be met by their New Light brethren in the Southern Association, so they wrote to the best-known Unitarian minister in England, Dr Richard Price. He recommended his friend Rev. William Hazlitt for the position.

Hazlitt was father of William Hazlitt, the famous writer and essayist. William senior had been a long-time friend of Dr Price and Dr Priestley. He was a graduate of Glasgow University, a former pupil of Adam Smith.

William Hazlitt senior was the son of a County Antrim minister[29] who had moved his family to Shrone Hill, County Tipperary, before his son was born in 1730. It is likely that Rev. Hazlitt's family were amongst settlers invited to the area by Joseph Damer, the largest local landowner. Damer had enticed a colony of Ulster Presbyterian weavers to relocate to Shrone Hill to develop a textile industry. Damer was a very wealthy descendant of a Cromwellian cavalry officer who fled to Ireland at the Restoration in 1660. The Damer family were long-term patrons of New Light Presbyterianism in Dublin, particularly of the Wood Street/Great Strand Street congregation.

Having graduated from Glasgow, Hazlitt got the call to a congregation in the south of England. He was happily ministering in Maidstone in Kent until the outbreak of war in America. Hazlitt's enthusiasm for the American cause was such that he provoked a split in his congregation which became so bitter that he had to resign his ministry.[30] Finding himself unemployed, he accepted the Bandon post.

There was a British prison camp housing American rebels a few miles distant from Bandon at Kinsale. Most of the inmates of this so-called "French Prison" camp had been seized at sea by the British navy, so the prisoners were the officers, crew and passengers of men-of-war, privateers and merchant vessels.[31] Hazlitt befriended the prisoners who were being held in appalling conditions and were being abused by their guards, the 14th Regiment of Light Dragoons. The British authorities did not regard their captives as prisoners of war but as rebels for whom no level of punishment was too harsh. Hazlitt wrote to the Cork newspapers relating that amongst 260 prisoners, 60 had died due to the hardships they had suffered. He said that 57 were now in hospital in a dying condition, some of them with their legs rotting off for want of proper care.[32] He said that a great number of the prisoners were naked, without a shoe, a stocking, or a shirt or anything else to cover their shivering bodies.[33] The Dragoon officers would amuse themselves by running their swords into the hammocks of the sick.[34]

Not only did Hazlitt publicly campaign on behalf of the abused prisoners, he helped three of them to escape,[35] sheltering them for a long time amongst his friends in the Bandon area. Hazlitt and his friends were in great alarm when one of the escapees fell ill with a fever and appeared to be dying. It was easier to hide a living man than a dead one; they had no safe way to dispose of the body. In the event the man recovered and the danger was averted.

The soldiers harassed Hazlitt, but their ill-tempered cruelty was not confined to the Bandon Dissenters or their minister. A group of army officers forced some Roman Catholics to eat pork off the streets of Bandon on Good Friday at sword point, killing a man in the process. Hazlitt ensured that the offenders were prosecuted, though they were acquitted. The officers, having murdered once with impunity, next threatened to murder Hazlitt. He reported them to the War Office. An enquiry was held, and the only witness for Hazlitt was Miss Rolt, a member of his congregation. When some of them tried to put her out by sneeringly asking what her religion was, she replied, "Gentlemen, I am a Protestant Dissenter and I am not ashamed of my religion."[36] Hazlitt won his case but asked for leniency for the accused. He managed through his contact with Dr Price to have the 14th Dragoons removed from Kinsale.

Hazlitt did not enjoy the full support of his congregation, as the following attests:

> One Sunday morning he was more than usually vehement in advocating the right of our Transatlantic cousins to govern themselves, when up started one of his hearers, and hurriedly pulling his plug of tobacco out of his mouth said, "I didn't come here to listen to treason", said he, addressing the preacher; then taking up his hat and cane, he indignantly walked out.[37]

Hazlitt suffered so much harassment that, very much against the advice of Dr Price, he left Bandon for America, but he did not find a welcome in the country for whom he had sacrificed so much. His unorthodox beliefs, and his determination never to compromise them, meant that a number of potentially rewarding positions in the ministry were lost to him. After three years he arrived back in Britain in penury. He eventually secured a congregation in Wem, Shropshire, where his son, the young William Hazlitt, spent most of his youth.

A minute of the Southern Association in the records of the Dublin Unitarian Church dated 1 December 1799 contains a list of twelve Dissenting ministers who were members of their Association. The name of William Hazlitt of Bandon is crossed out and the words "gone to America" are written in the margin.[38] He left Ireland for ever on 3 April 1783. Hazlitt was described by a fellow clergyman as an ultra dissenter in religion and in politics a republican.

The Society of United Irishmen was established eight years after Hazlitt left Bandon. His daughter Margaret observed that, had he remained in Cork, he would not have survived the 1798 rebellion as his zeal for liberty would have led to him being "sacrificed to party rage".[39] Margaret may well have been right as at least four Unitarian ministers were sacrificed in the rebellion, and several more were lucky to escape the gallows.

William Hazlitt remained a friend to human liberty, and in 1805 he helped Kitty Emmet, the last surviving member of Dublin's pre-eminent republican family left on the Irish side of the Atlantic. After the execution of her uncle Robert and the early death of her guardian, Mary Ann Emmet, Kitty was broken in health and spirit and in need of a place of refuge and recuperation. At the request of William and Sarah Drennan, Rev. William Hazlitt opened his family home in Wem to Kitty Emmet.[40] She remained with the Hazlitt family until her death in 1824.

Hazlitt's son William held his father in great affection, and in his essay entitled "Coffee House Politicians" paints an amusing image of his father and his fellow radical clergy:

> It is not a very long time ago that I saw two dissenting ministers... stuffing their pipes with dried currant leaves, calling it radical tobacco, lighting it with a lens in the sun and after every puff fancying that they undermined the borough mongers... These same old dissenting ministers throughout the country (I mean the descendants of the old Puritans) are to this hour a sort of Fifth monarchy; very turbulent fellows, in my opinion altogether incorrigible and according to the suggestions of others should be hanged out of the way without judge or jury, for the safety of church and state.[41]

Notes to Chapter Six

1. RIA DUC SER 3
2. Curtin 1998, p. 17
3. Hume 1998, p. 13
4. *Ulster Scot*, June 2007
5. Hume 1998, p. 13
6. Kennedy 1995, p. 96
7. *Ibid*. p. 29
8. *Ibid*. p. 30
9. Clifford 1991, p. 15
10. *Ibid*.
11. Gabriel 2002, p. 177
12. *Ibid*. p. 49
13. Mansergh, 2005, p. 229
14. *Ibid*.
15. Agnew 1998, vol. 1, p. 29
16. Paine, 1986, p. 63

17. Bonwick 1991, p. 5
18. Kennedy 1995, p. 29
19. *Ibid.*
20. *Ibid.*
21. McNeill 1960, p. 60
22. *Ibid.*
23. *Ibid.* p. 16
24. Stewart 1993, p. 22
25. *Ibid.*
26. *Ibid.* p. 21
27. Haddick-Flynn, K., p. 77
28. Livesey, J., p. 4
29. Stewart 1993, p. 185
30. Grayling 2001, p. 2
31. Moyne 1964, pp. 288–97
32. *Ibid.*
33. *Ibid.* p. 292
34. *Ibid.* p. 289
35. *Ibid.*
36. *Ibid.* p. 296
37. *Ibid.*
38. RIA DUC EUS
39. Paulin 1998, p. 2
40. Elliot 2003, p. 126
41. Stewart 1993, p. 187

Chapter Seven

A CABAL OF INSECTS

4 November 1789, Old Jewry Meeting House, London
Rev. Dr Richard Price, at sixty-seven, appears feeble as he ascends his pulpit to address the "Society for the Commemoration of the Revolution" (the Glorious Revolution of 1688). The occasion is a celebration of the birthday of William III. His audience have come to hear Dr Price's reaction to the news from Paris. Just a few short weeks ago, the citizens of that city had stormed the Bastille, the grim symbol of oppression and despotism. They have overthrown a most abominable tyranny and declared the sacred and inalienable Rights of Man.

Dr Price reflects the delight of his listeners and suggests that their struggle for universal liberty has not been wasted. He concludes: "Be encouraged, all ye friends of freedom, and writers in its defence! The times are auspicious. Your labours have not been in vain. Behold kingdoms, admonished by you, starting from sleep, breaking their fetters, and claiming justice from their oppressors! Behold, the light you have struck out, after setting America free, reflected to France, and there kindled into a blaze that lays despotism in ashes and warms and illuminates Europe."[1]

Dinner and Treason
Joseph Johnson, the publisher, held weekly dinner parties over his bookshop in St Paul's Churchyard in London. Beginning in the 1780s, he continued this practice for over two decades. The food was usually simple: roast meat, vegetables and rice pudding.[2] His guests in the early years included Benjamin Franklin, Dr Joseph Priestley and Dr

Richard Price. By the early 1790s, Tom Paine (now back in England following his taste of revolution in America) would debate the unfolding situation in France with William Godwin the philosopher, the enigmatic William Blake and Mary Wollstonecraft, the writer and soon to be notorious feminist.

It might seem strange that William Blake, who was one of England's greatest poets and artists, should be in such political company, but he was the author of the great Dissenter anthem, "Jerusalem" and "an ardent member of the new school, a vehement republican, a sympathiser with the Revolution, a hater and condemner of kings and kingcraft".[3]

Johnson's dinner parties, where Dissenters drank wine, toasted, talked "treason" and heresy, were in effect meetings of the intellectual leadership of the radical reformers. Price, Priestley, Wollstonecraft, Godwin and Paine were prolific writers, and Johnson published them with a will. Democrats, radicals and indeed reactionaries throughout the Anglophonic world read their books avidly.

One of the Best-Hearted of Men or a Black-Hearted Bigot?

Dr Richard Price, born in Glamorgan in South Wales in 1723, was educated at a Dissenting academy in London. In 1756 he wrote *Review of the Principal Questions of Morals,* in which he argued that individual conscience and reason should be used when making moral choices. This idea would be taken as a given today, but in a world where laws came from God and were interpreted by church and state hierarchies, such ideas could be politically subversive as well as religious heresy.

In 1776 Dr Price published *Observations on the Nature of Civil Liberty,* which supported the American cause and sold a stunning 60,000 copies.[4] This pamphlet made him one of the most widely known men in England and America.[5] He was offered American citizenship by Congress as a reward for his support, but he declined the offer. John Adams, the second President of the United States, acknowledges the American debt to Price as follows:

> Our friend Dr Price has distinguished very well, con-
> cerning physical, moral, religious, and civil liberty...
> In every free state, every man is his own legislator.
> Legitimate government consists only in the dominion
> of equal laws, made with common consent, and not
> in the dominion of any men over other men.

Dr Price's support for America was popular in London and won him the Freedom of the City. A much beloved figure in his own locality of Newington, whenever he rode into town on his old horse, the local artisans and dealing women would shout, "There goes Doctor Price. Make way for Doctor Price."[6]

He was not, however, universally popular in England. One man in particular despised Dr Price and everything he stood for. In 1776, Edmund Burke (soon to be the best-known Irish member of the British House of Commons) wrote to his constituents, the Sheriffs of Bristol, to criticise Dr Price's views on the origins of government. Burke hated Price's idea that sovereignty came from the people.

Burke, who had been born in Dublin and educated at Trinity College, was at this point an up-and-coming MP for the city of Bristol and was to spend the rest of his life building a formidable reputation as a politician and writer. Fifteen years after his first attack, Burke would attack Price again with much more vigour but on the same grounds in *Reflections on the Revolution in France*.

This early attack on Dr Price was not the first manifestation of Burke's reactionary politics. Nearly thirty years earlier, when Burke was a student in Trinity College Dublin, Charles Lucas had been leading his campaign to reform Dublin Corporation. Burke's attitude to Lucas and his campaign has been the subject of controversy. Burke's first biographer, Robert Bisset (1800), suggested that Burke began his political career by writing essays which mocked Lucas and his "levelling principles".[7] However, William O'Brien (1928) did not believe this charge against his hero. O'Brien took an unfortunate hostage to fortune when he declared that "Had Burke been guilty of such a poisoned assassin's thrust against the foremost figure in Ireland's dash for liberty, no-one could claim he [Burke] was a friend to Ireland".[8]

O'Brien was relying on Samuel & Son (1923), who constructed a theory that Burke had not attacked Lucas but had written to support him. We now know that the Samuels' theory is wrong. It is clear from the work of modern historians, including Dr Helen Burke, that Edmund Burke played a prominent covert and disingenuous part in the attacks on Lucas. The young Burke worked closely with Dr Hiffernan, a satirist who hated Lucas and all he stood for. Hiffernan echoed the charges of Lucas's Anglican opponents when he claimed that Oliver Cromwell was the hero of those who supported Lucas and his campaign.[9]

Edmund Burke's attitude to Charles Lucas reveals something about Burke himself. From early adulthood until his death, he was a consistent opponent of reform and reformers. The culmination of Edmund Burke's life's work was his attack on Dr Price in *Reflections on the Revolution in France* in 1791. Helen Burke has suggested that for Burke, Lucas was in many ways the forerunner of Dr Richard Price.[10]

When Burke set about building his political career in England, he would have become familiar with Dr Price's writings in favour of America and general reform. From the outbreak of the American war until his death in 1790, Dr Price enjoyed an immense reputation throughout England, America and in Ireland. In 1783, the Ulster convention of the Volunteers had written to him and to other prominent reformers such as John Jebb and Benjamin Franklin, seeking their advice on their reform programme.

Price responded to the Volunteers by suggesting that Papists of property should be admitted to the franchise. In other words, Roman Catholics should be treated the same as Protestants. He felt that any danger from the Catholics was more likely to result from alienating penal laws than from their religion.[11]

As the most eminent Dissenting minster of his time, Dr Price was chosen by the Society for the Commemoration of the Revolution to preach at Old Jewry to celebrate the birthday of William III in November 1789. In his *tour de force* from the pulpit, Dr Price reflected the delight of all liberal opinion in Britain and Ireland at the recent events in France which had transferred power from an absolutist monarch to an assembly of representatives of the people.

However, Dr Price's sentiments were deplored by Edmund Burke and provoked him to write his *Reflections*. Dr Price's friends had prevailed on him to publish his sermon, and when Edmund Burke read it he was infuriated, or at least feigned fury. Until the publication of his *Reflections,* many, including Tom Paine, thought of Burke as a Whig. They were as surprised as they were angry when he revealed himself as the champion of the Tories. Burke's response to Dr Price's sermon is a classic exposition of reactionary thought, a polemic defending hereditary kingship, the aristocracy and the Established Church. It is an eloquent attack on democracy.

Burke in his *Reflections* condemns those who brought about the new order in France and fortells that it will end in blood and tears. Burke was very early with this attack on the French revolutionaries, before the September Massacres or the execution of the Royal Family, or indeed "before there was anything serious to react against".[12]

It was not only the Jacobins or the *sans-culottes* that concerned Burke. Burke's invective was directed at those in Britain who saw the early phase of the Revolution as a triumph of human liberty over what they had believed to be an abominable tyranny.

Although Burke's admirers imply that he feared that the Revolution would descend into bloodshed, he was not at all squeamish about bloodshed. In fact, one of his objectives in writing his *Reflections* was to start a war between Britain and France. When there was hope that the war might cease after years of conflict, he wrote *Letters on a Regicide Peace* in an attempt to keep the hostilities going and the blood flowing.

Burke observed of Price's sermon that, "Few harangues from the pulpit have ever breathed less the spirit of moderation than this lecture in old Jewry", and went on to say:

> I find, upon inquiry, that on the anniversary of the Revolution in 1688, a club of Dissenters, but of what denomination I know not, have long had the custom of hearing a sermon in one of their churches; and that afterwards they spent the day cheerfully, as other clubs do, at the tavern. For my part, I looked on that sermon as the public declaration of a man much connected with literary caballers and intriguing philosophers, with political theologians and theological politicians both at home and abroad. I know they set him up as a sort of oracle, because, with the best intentions in the world, he naturally phillipizes[‡] and chants his prophetic song in exact unison with their designs.[13]

Burke claimed ignorance of Price's denomination, but his ignorance is obviously feigned. Later in *Reflections* he goes on to sneer at Nonconformists, their "well-assorted warehouses" and their practice of establishing new congregations according to their "own particular principles". Price was well known and popular, and his Unitarianism was no secret. Burke was in no doubt whatever about Dr Price's denomination.

---

‡ This may be a reference to Phillip of Macedonia, who liked seers to tell him what he wanted to hear.

Burke goes on to identify Hugh Peter (Oliver Cromwell's chaplain, executed in 1660) as a predecessor of Dr Price, in a clear attempt to brand Dr Price as an extremist. If Burke meant that both Peter and Price were Dissenting clergymen and talented preachers of the tradition that resolutely opposed arbitrary power, then his comparison is fair enough. Both Peter and Price stood for individual choice in religion and wanted to keep the government's hands off the individual conscience. However, for one hundred and thirty years after the judicial murder of Peter, royalist propagandists had portrayed him as an extremist who had cruelly murdered his king out of religious fanaticism. Burke would not directly label Price a "king-killer" and a fanatic, but by associating him with Hugh Peter, as vilified in royalist propaganda, this is precisely what he was doing.

Burke thought that clergymen knew little of politics and suggested that, "no sound ought to be heard in the church but the healing voice of Christian charity. The cause of civil liberty and civil government gains as little as that of religion by this confusion of duties." Modern liberals who stress the need for a separation of church and state, or between religion and politics, would be grievously mistaken to sympathise with what Burke is suggesting here. Burke said elsewhere that "In a Christian commonwealth the Church and the State are one and the same thing, being different integral parts of the same whole".

When Burke denied the appropriateness of clergymen dabbling in politics, he was thinking only of Dissenters. He stoutly defended the "religious national establishment" which he considered "the foundation of the whole [British] constitution". He also revelled in the fact that the English universities were under Anglican control when he declared, "Our education is in a manner wholly in the hands of ecclesiastics". He had no problem with the Church of England standing full square behind king and status quo. If he objected to the temporal and political claims of the Roman Catholic Church, he never said so.

Dr Price was a clergyman renowned for the quality of his sermons, and he was one of the best known political writers of his era. Price linked religion and politics but not as a fundamentalist who would use the political system to impose his ideas on others. Rather he would reform the political system as he would reform religion. He would allow all citizens to express their political and religious views as they saw fit. He believed that the state had no role in imposing belief or opinion, either religious or political.

Burke accepts that Price had a significant international reputation and then disparages Price's admirers by describing some of them as "intriguing philosophers". He also accuses Dr Price of working with atheists to subvert the monarchy and the Christian religion. Whether Burke has a poor opinion of philosophers in general or just of those who admired Dr Price remains unclear. Burke may have had in mind Thomas Jefferson and Benjamin Franklin, who had helped to create the first society in the history of the world to separate church and state on a permanent basis. In their era, Jefferson and Franklin would have been regarded as second-tier philosophers, and on at least one occasion, Burke referred to Franklin, who had engaged in intrigue to make his American homeland a democracy, as a philosopher. Jefferson and Franklin openly avowed their admiration for Dr Price.

The well-known Irish writer, the late Dr Conor Cruise O'Brien suggested that the reason for the strength of Burke's reaction to the sermon is its tone of anti-Popery, which O'Brien equates with anti-Catholicism.[14] He goes on to suggest that Burke suspected Price of association with the Gordon Riots of 1780, which arose from opposition to a bill relaxing penal laws against Roman Catholics. A Protestant mob controlled central London for three days, and many Roman Catholics' homes and businesses were destroyed.

Price was well known for religious tolerance and for his support for extending the franchise to Catholics. His good friend and colleague Dr Priestley had angered those who led the Gordon Riots by publishing a pamphlet supporting the toleration of Catholics.[15] Dr Priestley had called for "a complete and limitless toleration which included Catholics".[16] Nor were such calls novel amongst Unitarian clergymen. Rev. Thomas Emlyn had attacked the penal laws against Catholics as early as 1705.[17] Throughout the eighteenth century, generation after generation of the Unitarian clergymen had preached religious tolerance and civil liberty for all, including Roman Catholics.[18] If Burke suspected Price of involvement in the Gordon Riots, it seems an extraordinary suspicion for him to have harboured.

Burke's alleged suspicions may just have been a convenient excuse for his defence of French and British tyranny and his attack on the reformers. Price's sermon contains a number of anti-Popery references, but it is unfair to suggest it is anti-Catholic. When Price attacks Popery, it is from the traditional Whig perspective with which Burke would have been familiar. The Roman Catholic Church establishment had just been destroyed in France. Dissenters regarded the Roman Catholic establishment as representing "all the illiberal forces of arbitrary despotism". They believed the Roman Church "promoted ignorance and superstition which retarded the progress of rational and virtuous government".[19] This is a very different matter from whether individual Roman Catholics should be persecuted for their religious opinions. Burke would have been aware that both Drs Price and Priestley supported political rights for Catholics and would never have countenanced a rampage by a sectarian mob like the Gordon Riots.

Burke's contempt was not confined to Dr Price and his admiring, intriguing philosophers; his greatest contempt was reserved for working people when they asserted their rights in political action. He despised, in particular, ordinary women who were audacious enough to intervene in the public arena. Burke branded the male working class as "the swinish multitude". Much of Burke's prose in

Reflections borders on the hysterical, but his contempt for the female poor is as if "he was possessed by a daemon of the nether regions". Burke described the women who took the French royal family back from Versailles as "unutterable abominations of the furies of hell, in the abused shape of the vilest of women". Mary Wollstonecraft responded, saying, "Probably you mean women who gained a livelihood selling vegetables and fish, who never had any advantages of education".[20]

In spite of Dr Price's euphoria at the fall of the Bastille, his address was a temperate exposition of constitutional republicanism informed by religious tolerance. It was delivered by a man who was almost universally regarded as erudite and liberal. If the anti-Popery rhetoric of Whigs and Dissenters constituted anti-Catholic sectarianism, there were few who had done more than Dr Price to discourage it. Price told the Dissenters that their principles of religious toleration must apply to all mankind, as well as themselves.

Dr Price advocated liberty of conscience in religious matters, the right to resist tyranny and the right of people to choose their own government.[21] No modern democrat or liberal could argue with these principles. Dr Conor Cruise O'Brien in his own time was a liberal politician who did much to protect democracy in Ireland from those who would have fractured it by promoting religious sectarianism and extremism. He owed more of his values to Dr Price, whom he denigrates, than to his hero Burke.

Burke displays not a little religious bigotry of his own by sniping at Price's Nonconformity. Later Burke's naked sectarianism was made clear. During a debate in Parliament in May 1792, Burke had this to say of Unitarians and the London Corresponding Society:

> These insect reptiles, whilst they go on only caballing and toasting, only fill us with disgust; if they go above their natural size and increase the quantity, whilst they keep the quality, of their venom, they

become objects of greatest terror. A spider in his natural size is only a spider, ugly and loathsome, and his
flimsy net is only fit for catching flies. But, good God!
Suppose a spider as large as an ox, and that he spread
cables about us; all the wilds of Africa would not produce anything so dreadful.[22]

This statement is from a man who criticised Dr Price for
lacking "the spirit of moderation" in his public utterances.
Wolfe Tone described Burke's *Reflections* as his "famous
invective", and the Belfast United Irishmen described it as
"perverted eloquence".[23] William Drennan described Burke
as being as coarse and vulgar as one of Robespierre's
hirelings.[24] Burke, it is said, hated the French Revolution
because it reminded him of the Gordon Riots, which we
are told appalled him. Yet the anti-Dissenter riots in
Birmingham, which led to the destruction of Priestley's
home and chapel, delighted him. It was not the actions of
the "swinish multitude" or the "mob" which concerned
him so much as their motives.

Edmund Burke was targeting Joseph Johnson and his
circle when he declared:

A literary cabal had some years ago formed something like a regular plan for the destruction of the
Christian religion.... To command opinion, the first
step is to establish a dominion over those who direct
it. They contrived to possess themselves, with great
method and perseverance, of all the avenues to literary fame. Many of them indeed stood high in the
ranks of literature and science.

Burke was right to claim that Johnson and his group
were trying to influence opinion. That he would regard
that as somehow reprehensible suggests that Burke was no
democrat. Indeed, Burke made no secret of his detestation
of democracy. Yet he circulated his *Reflections* widely, hoping to rouse public opinion in defence of the Christian religion. He would have known that the only outlet for the

rage of a disenfranchised public was mob violence. The Christian religion in danger was an effective slogan for war-mongering against the people of France. Dissenters, who wished the French Revolution well, could be branded as the public enemy.

To this day Burke is credited with having Whig instincts. Although he associated with Whig politicians, there is little to suggest he shared their world view. His covert attacks on Charles Lucas's reform campaign in Dublin in 1748–1749 and his support for the Dublin oligarchy while still a student suggest an anti-Whig attitude even in young adulthood. While he opposed the American war on pragmatic grounds, he supported the Crown's right to impose taxation without representation.

Burke held ordinary people in utter contempt. He used the term "Leveller" as a term of abuse for political reformers and clearly regarded reformers of his own era as the inheritors of the mantle of the Sectaries of the English Civil War. His enthusiasm for monarchy and his intolerance of Nonconformism and support for the Established Church suggest that, rather than being a Whig, Burke was always a Tory.

When Charles Fox tried to move a bill in the House of Commons to repeal the penalties against Unitarians in 1791, Burke described the Unitarians as allies of the French Jacobins and warned the House not to wait:

> until the conspirators, met to commemorate the 14th July, shall seize on the Tower of London and the magazines it contains, murder the Governor, and the Mayor of London, siree upon the King's person, drive out the house of Lords, occupy your gallery, and thence, as from an high tribunal dictate to you.[25]

Here Burke is whipping up hysteria of a conspiracy. It was just this sort of hysteria for the enemy within which led the unfortunate Colonel Despard and his followers to the scaffold a decade later. Burke was no fool. He saw that both the Unitarians and the London Corresponding Society were seeking to bring about a society based on democracy, egalitarianism and religious tolerance – principles he loathed.

Burke's success with his *Reflections* succeeded in turning up the heat on Johnson's group. Dr Price was denounced as a dangerous extremist, and Dr Priestley and Paine were driven into permanent exile by government pressure and the "Church and King Mob". Joseph Johnson and William Godwin were jailed for sedition. Blake was charged with sedition but acquitted. Wollstonecraft was never charged, but after her early death in 1797, her reputation lay in tatters as a result of her husband Godwin writing an account of her life and loves that was too frank for the respectable tastes of the age.

Proving the axiom that history is written by the winners, of Johnson's circle, only Franklin avoided prosecution, preserved his personal liberty and was heralded as a hero in his own country. Franklin's fame and reputation remains unassailable. His British friends deserved as much, but the defeat of British republicanism ensured that if they are remembered it is only because they were too talented to be forgotten.

In his lifetime Burke was seen as the winner of the debate, at least in England. Burke wanted Britain to wage a counter-revolutionary war with France, and he got his wish. The English and Scottish reform movements were smashed by treason trials as Burke acted as a cheerleader for coercion. Burke ensured that the Unitarians' campaign to repeal the Test Act would be defeated in the House of Commons. His tactic in that debate was to brand Dr Priestley a subversive and Dr Price a revolutionary who were determined to destroy the Established Church. The incitement to hatred he engaged in by his *Reflections* and his Commons' speeches helped to push a reluctant William Pitt to wage war on France. It led to the Church and King Mob reaction, the Birmingham riots and the exile of Priestley and Tom Paine.

Burke, who died in 1797, did not live to see liberal democracy and universal suffrage become the norm. Democracy, equality, universal suffrage, freedom of conscience in religious matters were principles which appalled him. He would have seen individual choice in religion or, indeed, irreligion and the separation of church and state as the destruction of civilisation. Yet there is no shortage of historians and scholars who are prepared to defend him and suggest that he made a contribution to modern liberal democratic thought.

Dr O'Brien has correctly identified Burke's family links to Irish Roman Catholicism and his support for Catholic emancipation as the key to understanding his career. Burke hoped that the emancipation of Catholics would result in the rupture of the relationship between the Roman Catholics and Dissenters, which was what the Society of the United Irishmen was all about. The conservative forces, in the two kingdoms, would have been stronger if Burke had been successful.

In spite of Burke's failure to unite them, he gained the undying gratitude of English Tories and Irish Roman Catholic conservatives alike. He played a pivotal role in the foundation of Maynooth College in 1795 so that aspiring Roman Catholic priests could train in Ireland where they could not be seduced by French principles. Burke thereby helped to ensure that Irish Roman Catholicism would be dominated by a group of churchmen who would see to it that never again would their flocks flirt with radical Protestant democrats. Religious division and sectarian hatred, rather than unity, would define political relationships in Ireland thereafter.

Dr O'Brien was right to point out that Burke was very conscious of his Jacobite ancestors. Burke felt Catholic Ireland had suffered greatly for the loyalty they had shown to the House of Stuart. An ancestor of Burke was mayor of Limerick in 1646, and he tried unsuccessfully to join the Catholic Gaelic forces with Old English conservatives to defeat the parliamentary forces in the interest of Charles I.[26] Like his ancestor, Burke had envisaged an alliance of landed Irish Roman Catholics and the British Tory establishment in order to defeat the Dissenters. Burke never doubted that the Dissenters, Unitarians and those he chose to call "levellers" were attempting to bring down both church and king. He felt that Roman Catholics, once satisfied with emancipation, would be as loyal defenders of George III as their ancestors had been of Charles Stuart.

If Burke was the winner in the great debate, he did not get it all his own way. Two of Dr Price's close friends were quick to come to his defence and rebut Burke. Mary Wollstonecraft was first with *A Vindication of the Rights of Man*. In March 1791, Tom Paine published *Rights of Man*, which quickly became a best-seller. Such was the power of Paine's pamphlet that the Price-Burke debate was transformed into the Burke-Paine controversy and proved to be "the most crucial ideological debate ever carried on in English".[27]

The Dissenters and reformers in Britain and Ireland were delighted with Paine's defence of their hero Dr Price. They saw clearly that Burke's target was not only the French Revolution but the British reform movement. Paine did more than just defend Dr Price. Using the simple yet stylish prose he had honed during the American Revolution, Paine directed a blistering attack on Burke's notions of kingship, aristocracy and hereditary power.

Paine contrasts Burke's sympathy for the plight of the Queen of France with his total lack of concern for the inmates of the Bastille, "those who lingered out the most wretched of lives... in the most miserable of prisons... He [Burke] pities the plumage but forgets the dying bird."[28] Paine further suggests that Burke is "sorry the Bastille were pulled down and wished it were built up again".[29]

In one colourful passage, Paine denounces kings and monarchy as the fomenters of war and the collectors of plunder:

Those bands of robbers having parcelled out the world, and divided it into dominions, began, as is naturally the case, to quarrel with each other. What at first was obtained by violence was considered by others as lawful to be taken, and a second plunderer succeeded the first. They alternately invaded the dominions which each had assigned to himself, and the brutality with which they treated each other explains the original character of monarchy. It was ruffian torturing ruffian. The conqueror considered the conquered, not as his prisoner, but his property. He led him in triumph rattling in chains, and doomed him, at pleasure, to slavery or death.[30]

This highly entertaining prose had broad appeal, and the success of the *Rights of Man* was astounding. Craig Nelson writes:

At a time when the British population numbered 10 million (with a 40 per cent literacy rate) and most English novels sold 1,250 (while non-fiction averaged 750), in its first three months of sale *Rights* sold 50,000 copies in its official edition, with anyone's guess as to the number of pirated, serialised and excerpted versions.[31]

Cheap editions of the pamphlet were distributed throughout England and Ireland. Thomas Paine was a celebrity. Joseph Johnson had been afraid to publish the book, believing that he would be putting himself in grave danger, and Paine was helped by Thomas Rickman, another radical publisher. One useful insight Rickman gives us into Paine at this period is that he made a short list of Paine's friends. Apparently Paine confined his friend-ships to a very "select few", all of whom were part of the Johnson circle. Rickman recorded the names of William Godwin, Major Cartwright, John Jebb, Dr Joseph Priestley, Horne Tooke and William Blake.[32] All of them were Dissenters, and with the exception of Horne Tooke and Blake, the rest were or had been Unitarians. Rickman's list contained the name of only one aristocrat, Lord Edward FitzGerald.[33] Edward FitzGerald, the younger brother of Ireland's premier peer, the Duke of Leinster, was soon to become the most charismatic, romantic and ultimately tragic leader of the United Irishmen.

Joseph Johnson was not a man to scare easily when it came to publishing controversial material. His prudence, which in the light of the popularity of the work proved a bad business decision, was justified because Paine brought down the wrath of the government and the mob upon himself. The book would eventually be banned, and Paine would have to flee England.

Throughout 1791, the French Revolution and the Burke-Paine debate inflamed passions in Britain and Ireland. Men were adopting their positions as democrat or aristocrat. *Rights of Man* was embraced by the democrats and denounced as sedition and treason by the aristocrats.

Rights of Man was in demand throughout Ireland and particularly in Ulster; Wolfe Tone referred to it as the Koran of Belfast.[34] All those who gathered together in Belfast and Dublin towards the latter end of 1791 to create the Society of United Irishmen would have followed the Burke-Paine debate and would have sided with Paine. However, *Rights of Man* had not introduced the Belfast republicans to new ideas; rather, as Nancy Curtin observed, it merely "confirmed rather than inspired the educated middle-class founders of the Irish republican movement in their adherence to their radical agenda".[35]

In this era, pamphlets on political subjects would have been directed at an educated upper-class and middle-class audience. The gentlemen of the Dublin and Belfast Societies of United Irishmen were a typical target audience of the pamphleteers. Now though, something unprecedented was afoot, and working men in cities all over England, Ireland and Scotland began to take an interest in matters which heretofore had been considered the concerns of their "betters". Workers suddenly found that constitutional reform and democracy were matters in which they had a stake and a point of view. This was the first period in history that working tradesmen began to be organised on a mass basis to achieve national political objectives. Whether Paine was the inspiration for this or whether it was the events in France which captured the imagination of "the men of no property", these artisans embraced Paine's work as a Bible.

The usual selling price of *Rights of Man* was 3 shillings, well beyond the means of ordinary working folk. The United Irishmen realised that *Rights of Man* could be fashioned into a tool for recruiting working men to the republican cause, so they produced cheap editions in Dublin and Belfast and sold them for as little as 1 penny or 2 pennies.[36] Workers in Dublin, Belfast and in many cities throughout Britain began forming reading clubs.

In January 1792 a group of tradesmen met in London's Bell tavern, near the Strand, to form the London Corresponding Society (LCS). Very soon they could boast a membership of more than 2,000.[37] Similar clubs to the LCS, which has been described as the first working-class democratic party in history, sprang up all over England and Scotland. In Scotland, Rev. Thomas Fyshe Palmer, a Unitarian minister, had introduced *Rights of Man* to "low weavers" in Dundee in 1793. For this "crime", Palmer was sent to the penal colonies and he never again saw his native land.

Paine's work was the centrepiece of the LCS's campaign for universal male suffrage. It was also at the centre of the United Irishmen's political education campaign as they tried, "to turn every man into a politician".[38] Thomas Hardy was a radical Scottish shoemaker based in London and was the founder of the LCS The LCS initially sought only democratic reform. However, according to Hardy, "Paine's bible seemed to electrify the nation, and terrified the imbecile government into the most unjustifiable measures."[39]

Eventually both the LCS and the United Irishmen were suppressed and driven underground. Reformers were forced into a similar strategy in Scotland. Yet these now secret and illegal organisations still remained attractive to workers and many from the "lower orders" were sworn into the new revolutionary cells.

Two London-based United Irishmen and LCS members, John Binns and Colonel Edward Marcus Despard, took to the new conspiratorial structure like ducks to water. Binns was born in Dublin, but in the mid 1790s he was based in London. He and Despard, a former British war hero, used Paine's work to develop a revolutionary movement with a high level of plebeian involvement in London and Leeds, Sheffield and Manchester.

The radicalisation of workers begun by Paine in 1791 outlived the suppression of the British radical movement and the failure of the 1798 rebellion in Ireland. When the final desperate attempts at revolution collapsed in Dublin and London in 1802 and 1803, it was working men inspired by Paine's *Rights of Man* who stood with Robert Emmet and Colonel Despard to the end.

Notes to Chapter Seven
1. Price, 'Discourse on the Love of our Country', 1789
2. Ackroyd 1995, p. 89
3. Gilchrist 1863
4. Porter 2001, p. 402
5. Aptheker 1960, p. 147
6. Gordan 2005, p. 49
7. See H. Burke in Donlon 2007, p. 29
8. W. O'Brien 1926, p. 38
9. See H. Burke, in Donlon 2007, p. 30
10. *Ibid.* p. 30
11. Small 2002, p. 144
12. Williams 1968, p. 7
13. E. Burke, p. 94
14. C.C. O'Brien 1992, p. 395
15. Eshet 2001, p. 154
16. Priestley 1780, pp. 499–516
17. Emlyn, 'A Letter to Dr Willis Dean of Lincoln', 1731, p. 231

18. Armstrong 1829
19. Curtin 1998, p. 36
20. Taylor 2003, p. 218
21. Morgan 2003, p. 83
22. Speech to House of Commons, 11 May 1792, on the Petition of the Unitarians
23. Clifford 1989, p. 63
24. Agnew 1998, 1999, vol. II, p. 210
25. Andrews 2003, p. 8
26. O'Donnell in Donlan, 2007, p. 21
27. Thomas W. Copeland
28. Nelson 2006, p. 200
29. *Ibid.*
30. Paine in Foot, Kramnick 1987, p. 271
31. Nelson 2006, p. 202
32. Byrne 1955, p. 93
33. Tillyard 1997, p. 116
34. Bartlett 1998, p. 119
35. Curtin 2004, p. 22
36. *Ibid.* p.179
37. Nelson 2006, p. 221
38. O'Donnell 2003A, p. 37
39. Nelson 2006, p. 221

Chapter Eight

THE GIANT AND THE HELOT

1788, Barristers' Dinner Club, Dublin
Twenty young barristers are dining with their usual good cheer. Their hilarity is fuelled by the best of French claret. A servant tells them there is a gentlemen at the door who wishes to address them. Into the room steps a well-dressed giant of a man. This "apparition of Herculean frame" is endowed with gigantic limbs that suggest supernatural strength. By his side he has a shaggy Newfoundland dog of corresponding magnitude. The giant holds a large, yellow, knotted club. He has a sword by his side. The dog looks to his master and back at the company as if asking whom he should first attack and devour. The giant stares at each individual.

"Gentlemen," he says menacingly, "I have heard that some members of this club have been so indiscreet as to take the character of a young woman whose part I have taken. Who avows it?" The dog looks at his master again and back at the company. Nobody replies, but one or two knives are clutched under the table. Some know they cannot reply to the satisfaction of the giant and at the same time tell the truth. In a louder voice, the giant repeats his question: "Does any gentleman here avow it?" The only answer he receives is the faint buzz of fear which circulates the room. At length the giant says, "Any man of courage would admit it, so I must conclude my information was erroneous. I regret having alarmed your society." He bows three times very low. All the barristers rise to their feet and return the salute. The giant and the dog both back slowly out of the room. Two barristers rush to the windows to

154

make certain the danger is over. When they give the all-
clear, the room rocks with uproarious relieved laughter.[1]
The barristers will remember their interview with
Archibald Hamilton Rowan.

Archibald Hamilton Rowan

Archibald Hamilton was born in London in 1751. His
Scottish ancestor, James Hamilton, was made Viscount
Clandeboye in 1622 on the accession of James VI of
Scotland to the English throne. Hamilton was given pos-
session of Killyleagh castle in County Down. The viscount
is known to have been the patron of at least seven Scots
Nonconformist clergymen who settled in Down and
Connor.[2] In times of persecution, he was willing to shelter
Nonconformist clergy in his own home.[3]

Archibald Hamilton took the name Rowan to benefit
from his maternal grandfather's will. The terms of the will
stipulated that Rowan be educated in Cambridge and was
not to come to Ireland until he had attained the age of
twenty-five. His mother's ancestor, William Rowan, had
raised a company of men who fought for William III at the
Boyne in 1690. Rowan's paternal grandfather, having finished his studies at Trinity College Dublin, was elected a
fellow of the university but would not take the necessary
oaths due to his Dissenter views. He was later made a lay
fellow of Trinity, but shortly thereafter he left Ireland to
live in England.

In his youth, Rowan lived with his father in Brooke
Street, London, "a favourite meeting place for English radicals".[4] His father introduced him to his circle of radical
friends, which included some celebrated figures such as
John Wilkes of "Wilkes and Liberty" fame. He also met
the redoubtable Charles Lucas of Dublin. Rowan
remarked that Wilkes and Lucas had an influence on his
early sentiments.[5]

At Cambridge, Rowan came under the influence of his
father's friend, John Jebb. Jebb later resigned his teaching

post at Cambridge when he left the Church of England, due to his Unitarianism, and qualified as a medical doctor. Jebb was "the leading mainstream radical of the 1770s and early 1780s who came closest to advocating popular sovereignty."[6] Jebb maintained a cordial relationship with Rowan throughout his life. Another Unitarian at Cambridge who was under Jebb's tuition was Thomas Fyshe Palmer, later a leader of the Scottish radicals.

Rowan earned no degree at Cambridge. His biographer, Rev. William Drummond, suggests that Rowan was rusticated for "high-spirited behaviour", the euphemism for aristocratic hooliganism. He subsequently attended Warrington, "the most liberal Dissenter Academy in England", where Dr Joseph Priestley was a tutor for a time.

At least one modern scholar made the error of classifying Rowan as an Anglican.[7] Stephen Small of Harvard, in his *Political Thought in Ireland, 1776–1798*, tells us that both Rowan and Arthur O'Connor were Anglicans. Mr Small was wrong about both Rowan and O'Connor, and his error is compounded by the fact that he was citing Rowan's and O'Connor's alleged Anglicanism to deny undue influence of Dissenters in the leadership of the United Irishman. Rowan was a lifelong Unitarian from a Unitarian family. When living in Dublin, he was attached to the Great Strand Street congregation. Arthur O'Connor, who was born in Cork, was a member of the Irish House of Commons who joined the United Irishmen in 1795. He was reared as an Anglican, but it is clear that his religious outlook was influenced by his Protestant Dissenter mother, and that by adulthood he had abandoned Anglicanism in favour of a more liberal Protestantism.

Rowan came to Ireland in 1784 and built a house at Rathcoffey, County Kildare. He employed Michael Quigley, a young bricklayer, who was influenced by Rowan's "left-wing" politics and joined the United Irishmen a few years later.[8]

Rowan, Mary Neale and Lord Carhampton

Rowan had a town house at Dominick Street, Dublin. He made himself popular with the working people of Dublin by involving himself in a number of controversies on the side of the poor of the city. He took up the case of Mary Neale, a young girl who had been lured into a brothel and raped. Lord Carhampton, formerly Colonel Lutteral, was the alleged perpetrator of this crime. Mary Neale's father charged one Mrs Llewellyn, the brothel keeper, with the attack on his daughter. The Neale family was arraigned on trumped-up charges of burglary to blacken their names and to discredit their claims. Both Llewellyn and Carhampton were close friends of Francis Higgins, also known as the "the Sham Squire", who was deeply involved in this dirty business.

When Rowan took the part of Mary Neale, he would already have known Carhampton to be "vile and infamous". He knew there was a "strain of prostitution in his character" which showed as much in his behaviour in politics as in the brothel.[9] Lutteral had stood for a seat in the British parliament against John Wilkes. He received only 296 votes as against 1,143 for Wilkes. The cabinet tried to unseat Wilkes and force Lutteral on the people of Middlesex as their representative.[10] The Middlesex/Clerkenwell district was renowned from the fourteenth to the twentieth century as a hotbed of dissent. Lollardy, Nonconformism, republicanism and communism flourished there in different centuries. It is hardly surprising that the people of Middlesex resisted this unconstitutional manoeuvre. Lutteral was "unpopular to the point of loathing in England, and was hooted from its shores".[11] As Rowan was a friend and an admirer of John Wilkes, he may therefore have had the motive of political antagonism for taking up Mary Neale's case. Rowan saved Neale's reputation, but Carhampton was never asked to answer for raping this young woman.

Many years later, Carhampton's vile and infamous

character would again assert itself. When he arrived in Ireland he had aligned himself with Beresford, Foster and Fitzgibbon, the troika who controlled Ireland from Dublin Castle. These men saw their role as managing the Irish parliament on behalf of the government in London and cutting off all possibilities of reform or progress in Ireland. John Beresford was a head of the Revenue, John Foster was speaker of the House and John Fitzgibbon was lord chancellor. Carhampton worked closely with the troika and was thus part of the junta who would set out to destroy the United Irishmen and provoke the rebellion of 1798.

As commander-in-chief of the British forces in Ireland, he played a notorious role in smashing the United Irishmen and the Defender organisations in Connaught. To supplement his use of house-burnings, rape, pitch-capping, half-hangings and floggings, Carhampton invented a new and illegal tactic for dealing with rebels and the disaffected. He pressed men into the British fleet.[12] Carhampton swelled the ranks of the navy by sending thousands of Irish revolutionaries (and indeed many innocent men) into the fleet. He may have been indirectly responsible for the mutiny on the Nore in 1797, the most serious mutiny in British naval history.

By successfully defending Mary Neale, Rowan had become a great champion of the Dublin working class. The families of a number of tradesmen who had been killed by the military while engaged in bull-baiting in Dublin on St Stephen's Day 1789 asked Rowan to help them. Although Rowan was able to establish that the dead had been guilty of no crime, the city sheriff who had ordered the shooting was cleared of wrongdoing.

In common with most radicals and reformers of his day, Rowan was delighted by the French Revolution. On 14 July 1790, the first anniversary of the fall of the Bastille, John Binns, an eighteen year-old soap-boiler's apprentice, watched the Volunteers from around Dublin march through the city centre. Binns described how Archibald

Hamilton Rowan led a group of one hundred armed and uniformed Independent Dublin Volunteers. They carried a transparency depicting "a globe which showed America shedding a blaze of light on the old world".[13]

Binns related how a group of ruffians grabbed Rowan's banner and ran for the safety of the gatehouse of Dublin Castle yard. This led to a confrontation between Rowan's men and a large contingent of soldiers who were guarding the castle. In spite of both sides confronting each other with loaded weapons, the incident passed off peacefully.[14] Binns was also present in Pardon's Fencing Academy in Fownes Street, Dublin, in 1793 when Rowan distributed a printed address to the Volunteers which led to himself and the author of the address, William Drennan, facing charges of seditious libel.

William Drennan and the United Irishmen

William Drennan was born in the manse of the First Presbyterian Church, Rosemary Street, in Belfast in 1754. As a youth in Belfast, he had been an ardent supporter of the American cause and, like most of his Belfast fellow citizens, an enthusiastic member of the Volunteers. Disillusioned by the failure of the Volunteer movement and the Whigs to achieve parliamentary reform, he first mooted the idea in 1784 and again in 1785 of a secret society of republicans when he suggested an "entire scheme for a secret inner circle of dedicated radical reformers".[15] Nothing came of this suggestion at the time, but he would return to it a few years later when times were more auspicious.

Drennan had qualified as a medical doctor at Glasgow in 1778 and initially practised in Newry. He took lodgings with Rev. Boyle Moody, a first cousin to his friend Rev. William Bruce. Rev. Bruce was at this time ministering at Great Strand Street, Dublin. Boyle Moody and Drennan worked together with limited success to make their local MP, Isaac Corry, support the progressive wing of the faltering Volunteers. Drennan could not attract enough patients in Newry to make a living, so he moved to Dublin in 1789.

Drennan set up as a physician in Dublin, where his reputation as a writer and a poet had preceded him. (He is credited with first calling Ireland the Emerald Isle.) Drennan had come to national attention with the publication in 1784 and 1785 of his *Letters of Orellana, an Irish Helot*, the earliest expressions of his support for radical constitutional reform, Catholic emancipation and civil rights.

The young doctor associated with both the Eustace Street and Great Strand Street Unitarian congregations in Dublin, thereby gaining entry into a respectable circle. The Great Strand Street congregation were regarded as being "wealthy and of rank".[16] Many of them were businessmen, lawyers or doctors, and there were two members of parliament on the vestry committee, Travers Hartley and Alexander Montgomery. Alexander was a brother of Major General Richard Montgomery, the hero of Quebec. The membership of the congregation tended to be as radical in their politics as they were liberal in religion.

Drennan seems to have had the habit of attending Sunday services in both meeting houses, but he eventually served on the vestry committee at Great Strand Street. His late father Rev. Thomas Drennan would have been well known to the older members of both congregations from his time working as a teacher for Francis Hutcheson's Dublin school in the 1720s and 1730s. Drennan senior was eventually "called" as minister to First Presbyterian, Rosemary Street, Belfast, in 1736, where he served until his death in 1768. Rev. Drennan ensured that his Belfast congregation remained closely aligned to their brethren in Dublin.

The close connection continued after Thomas Drennan's death, and Rev. Dr William Bruce, a friend of the younger Drennan, spent twenty years at Great Strand Street before moving to Rosemary Street in 1790. The congregations cooperated in printing sermons, training ministers and providing pensions for the widows of ministers.

William Drennan and his sister, Martha McTier, kept up a regular correspondence throughout their adult lives, including the twelve years William spent in Dublin. The copious letters of his Dublin years provide a mine of information on an exciting and eventful era.

Drennan's letters to Martha and her husband Sam McTier often refer to the Bruces, the Huttons, the Dunns, the Welds, the Moodys, the Taylors and the Mercers. These were genteel Dublin Unitarian families who were to be both his social circle and his patients.[17] All these families, like the Drennans, had produced clergymen over the generations and were in some cases related to each other through marriage. Martha clearly loved to hear news of these people, because those she did not know personally, she knew by reputation.

William Drennan finally made progress with his proposal for a secret society in the atmosphere of enthusiasm and excitement in Ireland which followed the fall of the Bastille and the publication of Tom Paine's *Rights of Man*.

In May 1791, Drennan wrote from Dublin to Sam McTier in Belfast proposing: "a benevolent conspiracy – a plot of the people... – the Brotherhood its name – the Rights of Man and the Greatest Happiness of the Greatest Number its end – its general end real independence to Ireland, and republicanism its particular purpose".[18]

Sam McTier responded in July that the Belfast radicals warmly approved, and said "if your Brotherhood takes place we will immediately follow your example".[19]

Just one month later, in August 1791, Theobald Wolfe Tone, a Dublin barrister, published a pamphlet addressed to the Presbyterians, arguing they would never attain the liberty they sought if they did not make common cause with their Roman Catholic fellow countrymen. Tone had recently struck up a friendship with Thomas Russell when they met in the public gallery of the Irish House of Commons. Russell was a Cork-born army officer who had seen service in India. They were now seeking to convince reformers of the need for a pro-reform organisation which would bridge the religious divide in Ireland. Tone's pamphlet, *An Argument on Behalf of the Catholics of Ireland*, built on Rev. Steel Dickson's work and sought to encourage the evolving enlightened Dissenter attitudes to their Roman Catholic fellow countrymen. Tone's argument was helped by the events unfolding in Europe. The French Revolution had shown that Catholics were capable of overthrowing a despot and disestablishing their church. The Catholics of France put their duty as citizens above their religious inclinations, so Irish Catholics might do the same.

When Drennan made his suggestion for a benevolent conspiracy, he knew that there was already a secret committee in existence in Belfast of which his brother-in-law, Sam McTier, was a member. Samuel Neilson, a successful woollen draper and the son of a Unitarian minster, was the leader of a group of Dissenters who formed an advanced democratic party in radical Belfast. Of the eleven members of this party's committee, he, McTier, William Tennant, Robert Simms (a wealthy tanner) and William Sinclair were to become the best-known. Even amongst these Belfast radicals, Neilson was regarded as a hothead. In accepting Drennan's proposal, Neilson and his group were not founding a new organisation, but they were opening up their existing organisation to Roman Catholics, Anglicans and freethinkers.

Neilson invited Wolfe Tone and Thomas Russell to come to Belfast, and they were present on 18 October 1791 when he broadened his secret committee to membership beyond the Presbyterians. Tone and Russell were so impressed by Neilson's radicalism that they nicknamed him "the Jacobin".[20] Tone believed Neilson's committee "directed the town's [Belfast's] affairs".[21] One of the first decisions of the new society was to launch a newspaper. The first edition of the *Northern Star* appeared on 1 January 1792 with Samuel Neilson as editor.

Soon the society in Ulster was to grow spectacularly. Hamilton Rowan's biographer, one-time Great Strand Street minister Rev. Drummond, captured the mood of optimism engendered by the new society:

> The union passed through every class of society lighting on the bench and the pulpit on the desk and on the anvil shooting like an electric shock through the ranks of the militia, animating the breast of women with heroic daring, and infusing courage into the hearts and vigour into the arms, even of boys and children.[22]

Not all the Belfast Dissenters were at one with Neilson and his group in their enthusiasm for immediate Catholic emancipation. During his stay in Belfast, Wolfe Tone had a bitter encounter with William Drennan's friend Dr William Bruce. Dr Bruce, who was born in Dublin and educated at Dr Priestley's academy at Warrington and Trinity College Dublin, was the sixth generation of an uninterrupted line of Presbyterian ministers which ran from the Reformation until the early nineteenth century.[23] Rev. Bruce's father was a cousin of Francis Hutcheson. Like so many more of the liberal Dissenting clergy, William Bruce had been active in the Volunteers. He had once preached from his pulpit to the Volunteers in the uniform of the Lisburn True Blues.[24] He also attended the Volunteer convention held in the Rotunda in Dublin in November 1783. For twenty years he ministered to the Dublin Great Strand Street congregation.

Bruce had only recently arrived in Belfast after resigning his post as minister to Great Strand Street, Dublin to accept a "call" to Thomas Drennan's one-time congregation at Rosemary Street, Belfast. He also took up a post at the Belfast Academy, the newly established Dissenter school. Tone and Bruce quarrelled as to whether the time was right for Catholic emancipation and universal male suffrage. Tone and the United Irishmen were for immediate emancipation. Bruce was concerned that to move too quickly in this direction might be dangerous, as illiterate and uneducated voters could be manipulated by landowners or priests. Tone conceded that the argument was fuelled by alcohol. Nonetheless, in his diary Tone branded Bruce as an intolerant high priest.[25] This was unfair, if not untypical, of Tone who was often caustic in his comments regarding those who disagreed with him.

Bruce, who was a moderate Whig, had been prepared to work with Roman Catholics as far back as 1782. In that year, Dr Bruce, Napper Tandy, John Binns senior (the uncle of John of the LCS) and members of the Catholic Committee came together in Dublin to form a Dublin Chamber of Commerce (DCC). One historian described the DCC as the first national political movement which was "non-gentry, urban, part-Catholic, part-Dissenter".[26] It is also significant that the prominent liberal Presbyterian Henry Joy, in later life a very close friend of Dr Bruce, followed the example of the "worthy and highly respected merchants of Dublin" and established the Belfast Chamber of Commerce in 1783.[27]

Had Bruce known that Tone had branded him an intolerant high priest, he would most likely have been deeply offended. There is little a non-subscribing Presbyterian abhors more than intolerance and high-priestcraft. Many of the Presbyterians who agreed with Tone on the Catholic question were members of the congregations that Bruce ministered to both in Belfast and Dublin, and neither of these liberal congregations would have accepted an intolerant high priest as their minister.

In his refusal to support the United Irishmen, Dr Bruce differed with many of his friends on this issue. In 1798, he joined the yeomanry in defending Belfast to suppress the rebel threat. William Drennan and Dr Bruce were dear friends in youth, but their relationship never recovered from this quarrel. Dr Bruce also quarrelled with William Tennant, a leading United Irishman and member of his Belfast congregation, over Bruce's support for the yeomanry. Bruce was a moderate reformer and not a militant republican, like Drennan or Tennant. In branding him a high priest, Tone who was being intolerant and not a little unfair.

The foundation of the Society of United Irishmen split Belfast Presbyterianism, but not between the tolerant and the intolerant. A contemporary scholar of Non-subscription in Ireland, Rev. John Nelson, has pointed out that neither was the split between revolutionaries and conservatives: the split was between revolutionaries and moderate reformers.

Bruce and Tennant must have re-established their friendship after Tennant's release from his long imprisonment in Fort George after the rebellion. In the library of the Dublin Unitarian Church, there is a copy of Dr Bruce's sermons published in 1805 and signed with the following inscription: "This book is the property of Mr William Tennant of Belfast and has been donated to the Great Strand Street lending library." There are plaques in memory of Dr Bruce and William Tennant in First Presbyterian Church, Rosemary Street, Belfast, and there is a portrait of Dr Bruce in the vestry of the Dublin Unitarian Church today. William Drennan is commemorated by a plaque outside the Rosemary Street Meeting House.

The Dublin United Irishmen

The Dublin Society was formed in November 1791, with the first meeting taking place in the Eagle Tavern in Eustace Street. Eustace Street was also the location of meeting houses of the Quakers and the Unitarians. A contemporary song, "The Dublin Jack of all Trades", which associates the various trades in Dublin with the streets where they were practised, contains the following verse:

On George's Quay I first began, I there became a porter
Me and my master soon fell out which cut my 'quaintance
    shorter
In Sackville Street a pastry cook, in James's Street a baker
In Cook Street I did coffins make, in Eustace Street a
    preacher.

Amongst those who attended the first Dublin meeting of the United Irishmen with Tone and Russell were William Drennan, Archibald Hamilton Rowan, Henry Jackson and Oliver Bond. Henry Jackson was a successful Presbyterian businessman, the owner of an iron foundry in Dublin. His son-in-law Oliver Bond, the son of a Presbyterian minister, had made a fortune in the woollen business since coming to Dublin from Donegal in 1782.

As the room at the Eagle could no longer accommodate the growing numbers, the later meetings of the Dublin United Irishmen were held in the Tailors' Guild Hall in Back Lane, near Cornmarket. A young Trinity undergraduate walked into a meeting and "There he saw Wolfe Tone, Napper Tandy and Hamilton Rowan sitting together. He was not impressed by Tone or Tandy: Tone was "a flimsy man in whom there was no harm"; Tandy was the ugliest man the student had ever gazed on. Rowan, however, was the most handsome and the largest man he had ever seen. Tone and Tandy seemed like pygmies beside him".[28]

In Belfast and Dublin, the Unitarian congregations provided many illustrious and prominent members of the new society. William Drennan and Archibald Hamilton Rowan were members of the Great Strand Street congregation. It is likely, though not certain, that Oliver Bond and Henry Jackson were also associated with Great Strand Street. Samuel Neilson, William Tennant and Sam McTier were all three attached to Rosemary Street, Belfast.

The long coach journey between the two cities was no barrier to family ties, close friendships, business connections and political comradeship. Many of the businessmen in both congregations lodged with each other when they visited their respective cities. William Tennant and Samuel Neilson of Belfast, when visiting Dublin, often lodged with Oliver Bond. Tennant, Bond and Jackson were related through marriage. Samuel Neilson's wife would deliver parcels from Martha McTier in Belfast to her brother, William Drennan in Dublin. On the Neilsons' frequent visits to Dublin, they lodged with their dear friends the Bonds.

It is clear therefore that the Bonds, the Jacksons, the Tennants, the Neilsons and the Drennans were all friends and/or relations who had significant mutual connections in Belfast and Dublin. These liberal Presbyterians were republicans and supporters of full political and religious rights for Roman Catholics.

However, in spite of links in terms of personnel and religious affiliation, the Dublin and Belfast United Irish societies differed in social composition, structure and activity. The Dublin society in its early days was a middle-class body which discussed political issues, corresponded with radicals around Ireland and throughout Britain, including Scotland. They corresponded with Dr Priestley, Tom Paine and Thomas Muir, the Scottish radical, as well as with other prominent reformers throughout Britain. They published pamphlets and addresses to the citizens of Dublin. The society was a debating and propaganda club, "with a membership that fluctuated from about a hundred during the first half of its existence down to about forty in 1794 when the open organisation was suppressed".[29]

In Belfast things were different. Neilson's secret committee was building a mass revolutionary movement. Neilson came to Dublin in January 1794 to try to convince the Dublin Society to adopt the northerners' approach. He shocked some of the Dublin members with this suggestion. Neilson told them (correctly) that their organisation was infiltrated by informers.[30] The Dublin membership were not disposed, at this point, to move from demanding reform to preparing for revolution.

Both the Belfast and Dublin organisations were anxious to revive the Volunteers. The principle that an armed citizenry provided the best guarantee for liberty and freedom was a notion shared by both reformers and revolutionary United Irishmen.[31]

Bastille Day Anniversary 1792, Belfast

All of those who founded the Belfast organisation were active in the Volunteers, and on the Bastille Day anniversary 1792, they held a review to celebrate the start of the French Revolution. The *Northern Star* gave a full account of the day's activities. Different corps formed into a brigade of three battalions and marched through High Street carrying a portrait of Dr Franklin emblazoned with Algernon Sidney's motto: "Where liberty is, there is my country."[32] The town's inhabitants cheered the 5,000 marchers, some of whom carried slogans, such as "Can the African Slave Trade, Though Morally Wrong, Be Politically Right?" The flag of America, "the Asylum of Liberty", and the French tricolour hung from many windows.

At a meeting following the parade, a motion demanding immediate and unqualified Catholic emancipation was carried. An amendment which tried to make it gradual was defeated. Among those who supported the original motion were Rev. S. Kelburn, Rev. Thomas Ledlie Birch, Rev. Steel Dickson and Samuel Neilson.[33]

James (Jemmy) Hope of Templepatrick carried one of the banners that day. He held a green flag with the inscription:

> Our Gallic brother was born on the 14th July 1789
> alas we are still in embryo
>   Superstitious galaxy the Irish Bastille let us unite
> to destroy it.[34]

To end a pleasant day, the leading citizens of Belfast to the number of about three hundred in the uniform of the

Volunteers retired to the Donegal Arms for a social evening.

The Chairman proposed a toast to the 14th July 1789. When this has been received with acclamation the toasts came quick and fast. The *Northern Star* reported that amongst the toasts were "The King of Ireland... Lasting freedom and prosperity to the United States of America... The Rights of Man... The Union of Irishmen... The Society for the Abolition of the Slave Trade... Mr Paine: may perverted eloquence ever find so able an opposer... The memory of John Locke... The memory of Dr Franklin... The memory of Dr Price.[35]

The report of the Belfast event seems to suggest that there was much conviviality and drinking involved. This was not a gathering of kill-joy Calvinist Presbyterian conservatives, but of men of the Enlightenment, disciples of Locke, Franklin, Price and Paine. They would fight for an Age of Reason and yet could enjoy themselves at the same time.

The Prosecution of Hamilton Rowan

In the autumn of 1792, Rowan, Oliver Bond and Henry Jackson started a new radical company of Volunteers which they rather provocatively referred to as a National Guard.[36] This identification with the French Revolution alarmed the government, which resolved to suppress the Volunteers.

When the government issued its proclamation of suppression in early 1793, William Drennan wrote an address that began "Citizen soldiers to arms"; this would eventually lead to his arrest and trial on a charge of seditious libel. However, the government's first target was Rowan. He was arrested on a charge of distributing the address at an illegal gathering of Volunteers at Pardon's Fencing Academy. He was admitted to bail, and his trial did not take place until January 1794. Rowan's friends believed the government was delaying the trial in order to pack the jury.[37] It appears the government was hoping to hang him,[38] as Robert Watt had been hanged in Edinburgh that same year for printing, publishing and dispersing "wicked and treasonable" papers. In Rowan's case, their plot for judicial murder failed. Rowan was fortunate to receive a two-year prison sentence and a five hundred pound fine.

Rowan was always interested in labour disputes, and the workers of Dublin, in their turn, supported Rowan in his hour of need. In 1794 when he had been sentenced to Newgate, the Working Manufacturers of Dublin, a proto Dublin Council of Trade Unions, sent Rowan a warm message of support saying: "In our humble station in life we think nothing more dear to a man than liberty, and we are proud to say that to none we will yield it in gratitude."[39]

Even before his arrest, Rowan had been a great hero of the Dublin working class. At his trial he had electrified the courtroom when he told the court that he was proud to be a United Irishman. Now he was the toast of reformers throughout Ireland and Britain as a martyr for liberty.

On Sunday, 2 February 1794, Sarah Hamilton Rowan attended a service at Great Strand Street, accompanied by her son. He was described as "one of the handsomest boys in the city".[40] Mrs Bruce, an elderly female member of the congregation (and mother of Dr William Bruce who had quarrelled with Wolfe Tone), approached Sarah and praised her son's good looks. Most of the congregation "ogled Sarah". Sarah was enjoying celebrity status at the time due to the imprisonment of her husband.

Another elderly female, Mrs Dunn, was the widow of Rev. Dunn, late of the Cook Street congregation. She told Sarah she was sorry for her husband's imprudence.[41] It is not clear whether it was Rowan's ringing endorsement of the United Irish cause at his trial that she felt was imprudent.

Sarah may have been conducting some business on behalf of her husband on that day. The minister's ledger contains four subscriptions attributed to A.H. Rowan – dated February 1794.[42] He donated over £100 to the Great

Strand Street ministers while he was incarcerated in Newgate.

Given the diversity of opinion within Protestant dissent, it is scarcely surprising that not everyone in the congregation approved of Hamilton Rowan's radicalism, although many in the congregation were anti-government and supported the pro-reform party. One such was Travers Hartley, the pro-reform MP for Dublin city. Hartley had been a lifelong incorruptible champion of reform and had always enjoyed the most cordial relationships with his Roman Catholic fellow citizens. When Henry Grattan withdrew from parliament in 1797, the Roman Catholics considered asking Hartley out of retirement to run in Grattan's place.

Alderman Henry Hutton, an elder at Great Strand Street, was the descendant of a Cromwellian officer. He was an anti-government member of Dublin Corporation. He was an uncle to Sarah Swanwick, who married William Drennan in 1800. Hutton was not a United Irishman but had chaired pro-reform meetings which were attended by many United Irishmen. He was once denounced in an anti-radical handbill as: "A religious quack, who used to exalt himself on beer barrels to deal out divinity; but has laterally [sic] become the distributor of Tom Paine's aethistical [sic] pamphlets". [43]

When Hutton tried to swing the Dublin Presbyterians behind the candidacy of Colonel Henry Gore Sankey for the 1797 elections, the in-the-know informer Francis Higgins, the "Sham Squire", who apparently hated Hutton, suggested that the alderman was wasting his time. The Sham believed that no one could succeed to "attach that body [the Dublin Dissenters] to any other than men of republican principles". [44] One result in the election seems to vindicate the Sham's view. The "veteran radical" Alexander Montgomery (brother of Richard, the hero of Quebec) also a Great Strand Street member, was returned for Donegal when the United Irishmen urged the freeholders of the constituency to defy their landlords and support Montgomery.[45]

Hutton was a successful coachbuilder. He was a contemporary of Wolfe Tone's father who had been unsuccessful in the coachbuilding business. Thomas Russell would tease Tone by calling him "Hutton", and eventually Tone used the name Hutton as a *nom de plume* in his diaries. To this day there is a window commemorating the Hutton family in the Unitarian Church in Stephen's Green. Her Majesty Queen Elizabeth II travels to the opening of parliament in a coach that was built in Dublin by that old Cromwellian dynasty, the Huttons.

The William Jackson Affair
In the third month of his sentence, Hamilton Rowan had a visit from William Jackson, an Anglican clergyman who had come from Paris via England. He brought with him an offer of assistance from the French Republic. The French vowed to help "Irish patriots who wished for reform of the abuses under which they suffered". Rowan was immediately interested in this offer, and he asked Wolfe Tone to go to France to explore the matter further. Tone could not go for personal reasons, but he agreed to Rowan's suggestion that he compose a statement on the situation in Ireland for the French.

Jackson's mission was compromised from the beginning. John Cochrane, a spy reporting to Pitt, had accompanied Jackson to Dublin. Rowan made two copies of Tone's statement, gave a copy to Jackson to convey to France and gave the original back to Tone; Cochrane saw to it that one of Rowan's copies fell into the hands of the government. Jackson was arrested, and the government, now in possession of Tone's statement in Rowan's hand, had evidence against both of treason. Although the evidence against Tone was circumstantial, he left the kingdom to avoid prosecution.

The ever-resourceful Rowan convinced his gaoler that

he needed to sign a business document in his own home, and offered the gaoler one hundred pounds if he would bring him to his house in Dominick Street in Dublin to complete this transaction. Once there, he asked to be allowed upstairs to visit his wife and escaped through the bedroom window. Matthew Dowling was waiting with a horse, and they rode to a safe house in Sutton in County Dublin.

Rowan was conscious that he cheated his gaoler but quoted from a novel by William Godwin in justification: "I was not prepared to maintain my sincerity at the expense of a speedy close to my existence."[46] The military mounted a massive search, and a proclamation was issued offering £1,000 for his arrest. Two fishermen from Howth, the Sheridan brothers, evaded the British fleet and brought Rowan to the French coast in a small boat; there he was arrested as a suspected spy and thrown into a dungeon.[47]

Before his Dublin mission, William Jackson had been associating with Thomas Muir and Lord Edward FitzGerald in Paris and Nicholas Madgett, an Irishman based in Paris who was attached to the French Foreign Service. Thomas Muir, who would eventually be transported to the penal colonies, was a lawyer and leader of the Scottish radicals. Lord Edward FitzGerald, a young charismatic former army officer, was a great-grandson of Charles II, a first cousin to the leader of the opposition in the British House of Commons, Charles Fox, and a younger brother of the Duke of Leinster. Within a few years, he would be in overall command of the army of the United Irishmen. By this time, he was already a close friend of Tom Paine and a committed republican.

Madgett was the director of the Jackson operation. He instructed Jackson to make contact with certain English and Irish reformers and democrats to ascertain the likely response of the people of both countries to an invasion by the French. He was also to offer direct French help to Irish reformers. Madgett provided Jackson with a letter of introduction from John Stone, a Unitarian political refugee and friend of Dr Priestley. Jackson's first contact in England was John Stone's brother William Stone, a coal merchant in Middlesex.

Jackson's list of contacts included Dr Priestley, John Horne Tooke, a high profile former clergyman turned political activist, and Richard Brinsley Sheridan, an Irish-born actor and member of parliament in England. The man Jackson was told to consult with in Ireland was Hamilton Rowan.[48] There is an obvious Unitarian connection to this dangerous and treasonable operation. Stone and his brother were seeking to involve their fellow Unitarians, Hamilton Rowan and Dr Priestley.

The arrest of Jackson caused problems for Sheridan, who was a formidable foe of Pitt in the House of Commons. Sheridan had strongly attacked Pitt for his campaign of repression. Pitt would have been willing to let Jackson live if he were prepared to provide evidence to hang Sheridan. Wolfe Tone suspected Jackson of being a double agent, but Tone was wrong. Jackson gave no information to the authorities. Jackson committed suicide in the dock. He swallowed a poison and fell dead in the court room while awaiting his death sentence.[49]

Had Tone been right about Jackson, Pitt would have had the pleasure of silencing Sheridan for good, and the most talented of the British and Irish radicals would have gone to the gallows. Jackson was a secret agent; such people court anonymity, yet thousands of people followed Jackson's coffin to burial at St Michan's churchyard.

Archibald Hamilton Rowan as Fugitive

The Jackson affair brought the open existence of the Dublin United Irishmen to an end, with the government dispersing the society and seizing its funds. There would be no more debates and resolutions or correspondence in favour of reform. The United Irish leadership now adopted a strategy of secret revolutionary activity based on a plan to rise in support of a French invasion. With Tone and

Hamilton Rowan in exile, the initiative had passed to Neilson, Bond and Jackson. Soon two disenchanted members of the Irish House of Commons would link up with these hardened Dissenter revolutionaries. Arthur O'Connor and Lord Edward FitzGerald would direct the United Irish efforts to convince the French to invade Ireland. They also intended to have Irish Roman Catholics, Protestants and Dissenters organised and ready to rise in support of the French and against their oppressors.

The Sheridan brothers landed Rowan safely at Roscoff where he was immediately arrested and incarcerated by the French as a suspected spy. Rowan's democratic credentials were at last recognised and he was released. He met with Jean Bon Saint André, the flamboyant French general and naval commander. Rowan gave Saint André a copy of Tone's statement and was then given an audience with Robespierre. Because Rowan was sick with a fever contracted in prison, this proved an unsatisfactory consultation. The meeting was adjourned with an agreement to reconvene, but by the time Rowan had recovered, Robespierre had been overthrown and would soon be dragged to the guillotine. The leader of the Jacobins suffered the fate he had himself visited on his comrade Danton and which he had tried to visit on Tom Paine.

Paine, who had refused to support the execution of Louis and was imprisoned by the Jacobins, had avoided the guillotine by a matter of hours. The door of his cell had been marked with an "X", the sign for immediate execution. However, the X had been placed on the inside of an open door which, as it had been closed, was unnoticed by the execution party who passed without seeing it. By the next day, Robespierre had fallen from power, and Tom Paine's life was safe.

Rowan did not see Robespierre die, but he saw many of his followers guillotined, and although he was some distance from the scaffold, his shoes were covered in their blood.[50] The coup that saw off Robespierre put an end to

Rowan's plans for a French intervention in Ireland. Such was the state of confusion and uncertainty in France that Rowan concluded that he would do no good for Ireland there and he decided to go to America.

In America Rowan linked up again with Wolfe Tone and Napper Tandy. Despite Tone's determination for security reasons not to be seen in public with Rowan, the informer Leonard McNally described them as having "a kind of seditious convention in America".[51] Tone had great respect for Rowan's "firmness and personal courage" as well as his "great and justly merited popularity".[52] Rowan's reputation with the French was of particular value to Tone when he was attempting to get permission to travel to France to petition the government.

Hamilton Rowan and Mary Wollstonecraft

In France, Rowan befriended Mary Wollstonecraft, who was by this time (1795) a well-known writer. Before coming to France, Mary had spent a few years in Newington Green, which had long been a hotbed of religious and political radicalism. Mary was a close friend of Dr Richard Price, "Newington Green's presiding spirit".[53] Rowan and Wollstonecraft's friendship became close and intense. At the time, Mary was involved in an unhappy love affair with an American, Gilbert Imlay, but she claimed that she had a "corner of her heart where she allowed Rowan a place".[54] Wollstonecraft is said to have taken particular gratification in her friendship with Rowan. Some have interpreted this as meaning they were lovers.[55]

Wollstonecraft was an early pioneer for women's rights. In recent times it has been recognised that she had an essentially religious motive for advocating the emancipation of women.[56] Barbara Taylor, who has given close attention to the role that religion played in Wollstonecraft's work, suggests that Mary believed that virtue was necessary for salvation and that when women are denied liberty to develop virtue, they are denied salvation.

Wollstonecraft's friend and mentor, Dr Price, had men in mind when he said:

> Without moral liberty, man is a wicked and detestable being, subject to the tyranny of base lusts, and the sport of every vile appetite. And without religious and civil liberty, he is a poor and abject animal, without rights, without property, and without a conscience, bending his neck to the yoke, and crouching to the will of every silly creature who has the insolence to pretend to authority over him. Nothing, therefore, can be of as much consequence to us as liberty.

Wollstonecraft went one step further and suggested that what was true for men was also true for women.

Wollstonecraft's personal life was often turbulent and unhappy. She would eventually find happiness when she married William Godwin in 1797, but it was short-lived, for later the same year she died, giving birth to a daughter, Mary. Mary Godwin eloped with Percy Shelley when she was just sixteen years old.[57] She became as well-known as her mother when she wrote *Frankenstein* as Mary Shelley.

When Rowan was pardoned in 1806 and came into his castle and estate in Killyleagh, he sent a substantial sum of money to William Godwin. This may have been to help with the rearing of Mary's children. Perhaps it was to help Godwin to advance his ideas of using children's literature to broaden the minds and improve the education of young people. That Rowan had been long familiar with Godwin's written work is shown by his quoting one of Godwin's novels to justify eluding his gaoler in 1794.

Mary Wollstonecraft and another United Irish Aristocrat

Hamilton Rowan was one of just a small number of aristocrats who joined the United Irishmen. There was yet another aristocratic member of the society who had once enjoyed a close personal relationship with Mary Wollstonecraft. Mary was at one time governess to

Margaret King, later to be Countess of Mount Cashel. In 1786, Caroline, Lady Kingston, was looking for a governess for her daughters, Mary and Margaret. Dr Richard Price was asked for his advice and recommended Wollstonecraft, who was desperate for any position at the time. Mary moved from London to the Kingston estate in Cork, where she enjoyed a very close relationship with Margaret King, who would later say: "I felt an unbounded admiration because her mind appeared more noble and her understanding more cultivated than any others I had known."[58]

Wollstonecraft spent only a year with the Kings, but her influence on Margaret was lifelong. At the age of nineteen, Margaret contracted a loveless marriage to Stephen Moore, Lord Mountcashel. On this occasion, Wollstonecraft's advice against marriage, particularly when it was early and loveless, was disregarded by the young Lady Mountcashel.

In other ways, however, Wollstonecraft's opinions guided Margaret's actions. Although Margaret disliked Roman Catholicism every bit as much as Mary Wollstonecraft had done, like her mentor she was much in favour of universal toleration.[59] Nonetheless, it is surprising that such an aristocratic lady at some point joined the United Irishmen. (In spite of its title, the organisation did not confine its membership to men.)

Margaret Kingston supported the 1798 rebellion, although her brother George, later the Earl of Kingston, was leader of the North Cork Militia. Kingston's torture of defenceless people and his house-burnings did much to provoke the rising in Wexford.

In the days and weeks leading up to the rebellion, when the commander-in-chief of the United Irish army, Lord Edward FitzGerald, was being hunted down by the authorities, it was to Margaret Kingston he would often go, seeking refuge in one of her many properties. On one occasion when Lord Edward was staying with Margaret at Moore Park, Kilworth, Cork, the house was raided by troops searching for him. Margaret diverted them from their task by plying them with food and drink while Edward hid in the cellars.[60]

Wollstonecraft's views on marriage were eventually taken to heart by Lady Mountcashel. When Margaret forsook her title and her aristocratic husband to live adulterously on the Continent, she assumed the name Mrs Mason, Wollstonecraft's alter ego in her book, *Original Stories*. Mrs Mason never forgot her beloved tutor, and many years later when living in Pisa in Italy, she became like a surrogate mother to Mary Godwin Shelley after Mary had eloped with the poet from England in 1814.

Back in 1798, Margaret's sister Mary eloped with her mother's married cousin, leading to a scandal and a sensational murder case. Mary's father, the second Earl of Kingston, was tried and acquitted by his peers in the Irish House of Lords of the murder of his daughter's lover. Lord Edward considered a United Irish attack on the House of Lords on the day of the Kingston trial in order to catch many of the aristocratic enemy at one time in one place. His proposal was defeated by one vote at a meeting of the United Irish Directory.

Mary Kingston and her sister were seen to have gone to the bad, and all respectable society blamed the time they had been under the care of the "notorious Mary Wollstonecraft".[61]

The Trial of William Drennan

Shortly after Rowan had escaped, William Drennan was arrested and charged with being the author of the pamphlet which Hamilton Rowan had been jailed for distributing. His trial for seditious libel began in June 1794. The stakes were high for Drennan, as a conviction might have meant his execution. Drennan was anxious to distance himself from any association with Jacobinism in the address he composed for the jury.

He claimed his father's friend, Francis Hutcheson, and other notable ministers as influences:

I am the son of an honest man, a minister of that
gospel which breathes peace and good will amongst
men, a Protestant Dissenting minister in the town of
Belfast. He [William's father] was a friend and associate of good and may I say great men. Of Abernethy,
of Bruce of Duchal and Hutcheson.[62]

Drennan was invoking the names of the great intellects
of Irish Unitarianism. All of them had been associated to a
greater or lesser extent with the Wood Street congregation.
Abernethy and Duchal had served there as ministers and
Bruce was an elder of the congregation, while Drennan
senior and Hutcheson had run the school.

That William Drennan would seek to defend himself on
a political charge by citing such people indicates how, for
him, his radical politics developed as a consequence of his
religious background. It indicates also that the people
whom he regarded as his influences were not only religious
philosophers, they were republican in politics. In the
address Drennan also identified John Locke, Dr Price and
Dr Priestley as influences on his thinking.[63] This identification with such religious and political radicals would, most
likely, not have helped Drennan to convince the jury of his
innocence of the crime of sedition. Luckily for him, he had
the services of John Philpot Curran as his defence council.
Curran was the most highly regarded lawyer of his day,
and though he had unsuccessfully defended Rev. Jackson
and Hamilton Rowan, he was determined to save Drennan
if he could. Curran urged caution. Had Drennan made that
speech, he would have slipped the noose around his own
neck. The jury never got to hear the address, and Drennan
was acquitted.

Many years afterwards, Drennan published his
defence. Had he not done so, posterity might have
remained in the dark regarding the influence on the
United Irishmen of the Commonwealthmen and the
descendants of the Dublin Cromwellians. A.T.Q. Stewart
describes how, instead of tracing the hidden origins of the

United Irishmen by scraping on a faded mossy headstone, Drennan's words are a slender clue, a key to the door which leads us from the drear churchyard into a well-lit room in the early eighteenth century.[64] This well-lit room where Revs Thomas Drennan, Abernethy, Ducal and Francis Hutcheson discussed the ideas and principles which almost brought the younger Drennan to the gallows, may well have been the vestry room at Wood Street.

Notes to Chapter Eight

1. Barrington 1997, p. 234
2. Herlihy 1996, p. 19
3. *Ibid.* p. 21
4. Orr 1998, p. 226
5. *Ibid.*
6. Lottes in Philip 1991, p. 82
7. Small 2002, p. 34
8. Cullen 2003, p. 133
9. Fitzpatrick 1865, p. 46
10. *Ibid.*
11. *Ibid.*
12. O'Donnell 2003A, p. 25
13. *Ibid.*
14. *Ibid.*
15. Larkin 1991, p. 8
16. Kilroy 1994, p. 46.
17. See Agnew 1998, 1999, vols I, II, and III
18. *Ibid.*
19. Curtin 1998, p. 43
20. Bartlett 1998, p. xvi
21. Curtin 1998, p. 36
22. Drummond 1840, p. 159
23. Armstrong 1829, p. 74
24. Boyd 2006, p. 20
25. Barlett 1998, p. 126
26. J. Hill 1997, p. 176
27. McNeill 1960, p. 34
28. Boylan 1981, p. 21
29. Graham in Barlett 2005, p. 137
30. McDowell 1998, p. 3
31. Curtin 1998, p. 31
32. Clifford 1989, p. 60

33. *Ibid.*
34. Newsinger 2001, p. 53
35. *Ibid.*
36. Clifford 1989, p. 52
37. Drummond 1840, p. 186
38. Curtin 1998, p. 60
39. Drummond 1840, p. 204
40. Agnew 1998, vol I, p. 13
41. *Ibid.*
42. RIA DUC STR 3, final page
43. Dickson 1994, p. 146
44. Bartlett 2003, p. 101
45. Dickson 1993, p. 146
46. Drummond 1840, p. 215
47. Orr in Hill, et al 1998, p. 213
48. O'Toole 1997, p. 288
49. Bartlett 2004, p. 85
50. Drummond 1840, p. 204
51. Bartlett 2004, p. 51
52. *Ibid.*
53. Taylor 2003, p. 103
54. Drummond 1840, p. 248
55. Gordon 2005, p. 383
56. *Ibid.*
57. Todd 2003, p. 228
58. *Ibid.* p. 102
59. *Ibid.* p. 168
60. *Ibid.*
61. *Ibid.*
62. Stewart 1993, p. 71
63. Larkin 1991, p. 128
64. Stewart 1993, p. 71

Chapter Nine

GUNPOWDER JOE

14 July 1791, Birmingham, England
Magistrates Carles, Spencer and Brooke have been plying their Church and King Mob with liquor to prepare them for the duties they are expected to carry out in defence of "the church in danger". The mob arrives at the hotel in Temple Row too late to attack the diners who have finished their celebrations marking the fall of the Bastille. The crowd must content themselves with stoning the now empty hotel and shouting "No Popery". Someone suggests that they should move on to burn the Dissenters' meeting houses, businesses and homes. Dr Joseph Priestley's Unitarian chapel is the first target, but three meeting houses and twenty-seven homes are soon in flames. Dr Priestley listens anxiously to see if his home, his precious library and his laboratory will be spared. At last, as the sun rises on 15 July, the exhausted drunken mob lie down to sleep in the street. As darkness falls next evening, the crowd are again on the march. Priestley knows he will be murdered if he is taken. As he and his wife escape through the back lanes of the city, they look back to see their home in flames. Thus did one of England's greatest scholars and philosophers leave Birmingham for ever.

Dr Joseph Priestley
Joseph Priestley was born in a small village near Leeds in 1733. He was educated at grammar school until he was sixteen, by which time he had mastered several languages, including Greek, Latin and Hebrew. Later he began reading his way into Chaldean-Syriac and Arabic.[1] Besides becoming a Dissenting minister, he had a passion for science; and

although he was not a full-time scientist, he is remembered as one of the foremost scientists of the eighteenth century. He experimented with electricity, and he isolated oxygen, along with seven or eight other gases. Dr Priestley was, therefore, one of the founders of chemistry as a branch of science. As a result of his immense reputation in the sciences, he was elected a fellow of the Royal Society and was awarded their gold medal for his discoveries in chemistry. In a dissertation he wrote as a medical student in Edinburgh in the 1780s, Thomas Addis Emmet identified Priestley as the foremost authority on chemistry in Britain.[2] This is remarkable recognition for a man for whom science was essentially a hobby.

Priestley regarded himself as first and foremost a minister of religion, but he was also a highly regarded educationalist and a philosopher. He became one of England's foremost scholars in spite of the fact that he and his fellow Dissenters were banned from the great universities. While Priestley and his fellows must have deeply resented the discrimination which denied them access to these places of higher learning, neither he nor they had much regard for the system of education promoted in such places.

William Blake was not targeting the mills of the Industrial Revolution but rather the universities of Oxford and Cambridge with the words of his hymn, "And was Jerusalem builded here, Among these dark Satanic Mills?" Adam Smith regarded these institutions as "sanctuaries in which exploded systems and obsolete prejudices found shelter after they had been hunted out of every other corner of the world".[3]

Priestley worked as a tutor at the Warrington Dissenting academy from 1757. As the "dark Satanic Mills" were closed against Protestant Dissenters, they set up their own academies throughout England, of which Warrington was perhaps best known. Similar institutions were established at Daventry, Hoxton and Hackney. Dr Priestley worked at Warrington from its foundation until 1762.

Under Priestley's direction, Warrington provided a broader education than that favoured by the universities. The subjects he taught included history, geography, sciences, modern languages, philosophy and mathematics. This broad curriculum and the scepticism which Priestley impressed on his students about the danger of uncritically accepting received ideas can help to explain how his students were accustomed to free enquiry and had "no bias in favour of established opinions". Warrington and the other academies have been described as "the most effective weapons in the assault on the old order" as they "provided a preparation uniquely appropriate for the new age".[4]

After he left Warrington in 1762, Priestley held a succession of posts, including minister to a congregation at Leeds and private tutor to the family of Lord Shelbourne. He was "called" to a Dissenting congregation in Birmingham in 1780. There Priestley formed a club of intellectuals, scientists and entrepreneurs which, as it met monthly, he dubbed the Lunar Society. Amongst the better-known members of the society were James Watt, the inventor, Josiah Wedgewood, the entrepreneur, and Erasmus Darwin, the polymath intellectual. Wedgewood and Darwin may have passed on their aptitude for science and their intelligence to a future generation, as both were grandfathers of Charles Darwin.

Priestley was also a close friend of Benjamin Franklin, and they worked on electrical experiments together. Another American friend from this era was John Adams, later the second president of the United States of America. Adams said of Priestley that he was "like a comet in the system, this great learned, this indefatigable most excellent and extraordinary man".

Like many other British radicals of his time, Dr Priestley had a strong element of millenarianism in his thinking. He believed that the Book of Revelation contained prophesies that he expected would be fulfilled in his lifetime. This millenarianism informed his interpretation of the American and French revolutions. To Priestley the events were:

> Unparalleled in all human history, [and] make a totally new, a most wonderful, an important era in the history of mankind.... a change from the darkness to light[,] from superstition to a sound knowledge and from a most debasing servitude to a state of most exaulted freedom.
>
> We may expect to see the establishment of universal peace and goodwill amongst all nations... This sir will be the happy state of things distinctly and repeatedly foretold in many prophecies, delivered more than 2,000 years ago.[5]

Such millenarian views were not the preserve of fanatics or cranks in the late eighteenth century. Writing of the American Declaration of Independence, Elie Halevy, the French philosopher and historian, declared that "for the radicals of its day it seemed to foreshadow the fulfillment of the Biblical prophecies, the coming of the age of reason and virtue in which the Gospel of Peace should be better understood and glorified".[6]

Nor were the otherwise modern enlightened thinkers of the United Irishmen immune from these millenarian fantasies. Thomas Russell's biographer, John Quinn, suggests that Russell's career can only be understood in terms of the millenarian elements of his thinking. Quinn also suggests that William Steel Dickson and William Stavely, who formed an important element in the leadership of the United Irishmen in Ulster, and who fused advanced politics and apocalyptic beliefs, preached sermons and published tracts with explicit millennialist themes throughout the 1790s.[7]

Priestley saw these years as "the time of trouble" foretold in the Book of Revelation. There would soon be a thousand years during which there would be no more war or oppression, no more poverty or ignorance, no more superstition or religious animosity, and a millenium of peace, justice and plenty would precede the end of the world. The Fifth Monarchists had believed something very similar in the mid seventeenth century, when they thought they were ushering in the rule of the saints. Even the more secular thinkers of the late eighteenth century such as Paine and Godwin believed "an age of virtue" would be brought about by human benevolence.[8] Twenty-first century Marxists would be amused at such idealism. They should, however, reflect on the genesis of their own utopian notions of the "classless society which was to follow the dictatorship of the proletariat".

When in 1791 Priestley was forced to flee his home in Birmingham, he decamped to London. The Birmingham mob had rioted for three days with the undoubted complicity of several Tory magistrates and clergymen. Although they had burnt Priestley's home, laboratory and two Unitarian meeting houses, their real target had been Priestley himself. They would have gladly murdered him had he not been warned and made his escape. His crime was to infuriate this so-called Church and King Mob by holding a dinner to celebrate the fall of the Bastille. In several English cities mobs burnt effigies of Dr Priestley and Thomas Paine. Such was the climate of repression and violence that both men feared that they would be lynched by the mob if they escaped judicial murder by the state. The fact that the mob, along with shouting "Church and King", also shouted "No Popery" may indicate that Priestley's anti-sectarianism was also regarded as a crime. Perhaps it was, as Daniel Defoe had said of an earlier mob, "they would spend the last drop of their blood against Popery that do not know whether he be a man or a horse".[9]

E.P. Thompson explains the role of the urban poor in the Priestley riots as a kind of latent class hatred against the wealthy Dissenters.[10] If workers were involved for reasons of ideology rather than for free liquor, it is more likely because many in Birmingham worked in the arms and iron industry which prospered as a by-product of the slave trade. Priestley and his fellow Lunar Society members were all well known for their opposition to that trade. The Caribbean slave trade was driven by the need for labour for sugar production. Birmingham produced the guns that were exchanged for African slaves and the shackles that were used to restrain the unfortunate victims of the system. It might be that the workers who produced these items did not appreciate the humanitarianism of Priestley and his associates.

When George III heard of the burning of Priestley's house and chapel, he expressed his pleasure that Dr Priestley had suffered, "for the doctrines he and his party had instilled".[11] Edmund Burke, the Dublin-born British parliamentarian, was openly delighted by Priestley's misfortunes.[12]

Samuel Neilson had this to say in his editorial in the *Northern Star* on 25 April 1792:

> There is not perhaps an instance existing, of a more successful deception, than that practised on the people of Birmingham in exciting their indignation against Doctor Priestley. There is not a doubt that the very people who destroyed his house and its contents, and who would have gladly destroyed him in it, would be among the first to idolize him, if they knew what his sentiments really are and what is the tendency of his meritorious labours. The great endeavour of his life is to soften and ease the condition of mankind: and as the condition of the lower orders of the people stands in most need of amendment... they would consider his protection a debt of justice...[13]

Priestley was now without a position, and thirty years after he first began teaching, he returned to it briefly when Dr Price founded New College Hackney. Priestley only worked there for a short time. This school closed in 1796 in spite of attracting some brilliant scholars, such as the famous essayist William Hazlitt junior. Edmund Burke had called Hackney "an arsenal for manufacturing revolutionary weapons, and a breathing ground for revolutionary ideas". Hackney Academy was also described as "a nursery of riot" and "a slaughterhouse of Christianity".[14]

The Tory press had waged a hate campaign against Dr Priestley, dubbing him "Gunpowder Joe". Priestley first earned the nickname in 1787, when his *Reflections on the Present State of Free Inquiry in this Country* was deliberately misrepresented and some of his remarks were taken out of context. What he wrote was, "We are... laying gunpowder, grain by grain, under the old building of error and superstition." This literary flourish was intended by Priestley to show that scientific enquiry would defeat ignorance, but was used to brand Priestley as a political subversive in the tradition of Guy Fawkes.

The press portrayed him as a violent incendiary. A popular song alleged that, "Priestley would drench the throne in blood" and suggested that his "sires of old had murdered their king".[15]

The king whose murder was laid at the door of Priestley's "sires" was of course Charles I. Charles had been executed many generations before Dr Priestley was born, yet in the 1790s Tories commonly identified Protestant Dissenters such as Dr Priestley as the descendants of the regicides. Tory propagandists never tired of accusing Dissenters of being republicans, Levellers and enemies of the monarchy. One piece of doggerel warned people not to be fooled by the gentle demeanour of Priestley and the other Dissenters and suggested that they were hypocritical subversives.

> Sedition is their creed
> Feign'd sheep, but wolves indeed
> How can we trust
> Gunpowder Joe would
> Deluge the throne with blood

And lay the great and good
Low in the dust[16]

As early as 1780, Priestley had published a pamphlet advocating Catholic emancipation. Eleven years later in 1791, Wolfe Tone recorded in his diary that "Dr Priestley is delighted with the idea of union and has begged six copies of a celebrated pamphlet."[17] The pamphlet was Wolfe Tone's *Argument on Behalf of the Catholics of Ireland*. The reports of an informer to Dublin Castle suggest that Priestley had written to the secretary of the Catholic Committee, Wolfe Tone, and his correspondence had been read out by one, McKenna, to an early meeting of the Dublin United Irishmen.[18] Dr Priestley expressed rejoicing at the union of "the Papists and the Presbyterians".

The Dublin Society of United Irishmen repeatedly discussed Dr Priestley's troubles and also those of his fellow radical Tom Paine. According to an informer at a meeting of the society held on 18 May 1792, "everyone present avowed the principles of these two gentlemen".[19] As Priestley fled Birmingham, the Dublin United Irishmen discussed a proposal that Priestley and Paine be made honorary members of their society. Paine's name was added to the membership list, which was promptly reported to Dublin Castle by a spy.[20] Paine fled England and accepted a seat in the French National Assembly. William Blake had warned Paine that he was about to be arrested on a charge of treason. Conviction would have brought him to the scaffold.

The Dublin United Irishmen were informed by one of their number that Priestley had an invitation from a Dublin Unitarian congregation to take care of them for a salary of £300 per annum.[21] This was a very generous salary in 1792. The invitation is hardly surprising, as the two main Unitarian ministers in Dublin at the time, Rev. Phillip Taylor (Eustace Street) and Rev. John Moody (Great Strand Street) had been students of Priestley at Warrington and Nantwich. Dr William Bruce, who had recently left Dublin for Belfast, had also been a pupil and remained an admirer of Dr Priestley.

We shall never know if Priestley would have been safe from judicial murder in Dublin. However, given the popularity of Oliver Bond and Henry Jackson at Pill Lane, Priestley would have had nothing to fear from the Dublin workers living in the Great Strand Street, Pill Lane district.

Although radicals everywhere expressed sympathy for Dr Priestley, and messages of support came from England, Ireland, France and America, Priestley continued to be hounded and burnt in effigy. Even after his move to London, life was made impossible for him.

William Drennan told his sister that Priestley "could not even get a servant to hire with him he is so terrible an object".[22] Drennan believed that:

> the emigration will be a historical fact that will tell against England the longest day it has to live and I question if he could do so much service to the cause for which he suffers in any way by this action. Indeed if there is an invasion of England he would probably be murdered and it is therefore the highest prudence to go off in time.[23]

As he prepared for exile, the Dublin United Irishmen sent him a testament of support composed by William Drennan. It noted with sadness that Priestley, scientist and man of progress, had been driven from his native land. He would not be buried alongside his reformer friends, Saville, Price, Jebb and Fothergill. They also asked for Priestley's prayers for their own member, the imprisoned Hamilton Rowan, and for the imprisoned Scottish radicals, Palmer and Muir. The address has an air of optimism in that Priestley is seen as going to a better place – the world of Washington and Franklin.[24]

This address is a clear indication that the United Irishmen saw themselves, along with Priestley, Muir and

Franklin, as engaged in a common struggle. The address has many Unitarian associations in that Drennan wrote it for Priestley and mentions other Unitarians Jebb, Price, Rowan, Palmer and Franklin.

Priestley was sixty-one when he arrived in America. He was offered a post in the University of Pennsylvania, but he preferred to settle in a small community in Northumberland, Pennsylvania, about seven days' ride out of Philadelphia. He chose Pennsylvania "because it was free from the curse of slavery".[25] As we have seen, Pennsylvania had abolished slavery through the efforts of Dublin-born George Bryan.

Dr Priestley's Fellow Reformers in England and Scotland
The English and Scottish reformers of the 1790s tried to emulate the Irish Volunteers by holding national conventions to press for reform, but without the back-up of an armed force. However, the British government moved to put an end to conventions. William Pitt insisted that his government would not be subject to internal pressure for reform. His determination hardened when England declared war on revolutionary France in 1793; Pitt outlawed such conventions and brought charges of sedition and treason against anyone who defied these laws.

In England the government rounded up thirty radicals with a view to putting all of them on trial and hanging them for treason. John Thewell, John Horne Tooke and Thomas Hardy were first up. William Godwin made an intervention by writing a letter to the newspapers saying that if opinion was treason, no one was safe. The jury refused to convict, and the prisoners were freed. The collapse of the trials was greeted with great rejoicing by reformers in Britain and Ireland.

Thomas Muir organised a convention in Edinburgh in 1793 which was attended by 150 delegates, including Archibald Hamilton Rowan and William Drennan, who carried an address of solidarity from the United Irishmen.

Shortly afterwards, Muir was arrested and was warned that he would be charged with sedition. He went to France, where he met up with Tom Paine, John Hurtford Stone and Lord Edward FitzGerald.[26]

Returning from France on an American ship, the *Hope*, Muir called to Belfast where he was fêted by the Belfast United Irishmen and made an honorary member of their society. By then he knew a bill had been laid against him, and his father urged him not to return to Scotland. Hamilton Rowan, who was on bail on similar charges, urged him to return to face the charges as a way of getting a political platform for his ideas. Rowan might not have been so cavalier with his advice had he known that his friend would get a savage sentence of fourteen years transportation to the penal colonies.

During Muir's trial the prosecutor, Dundas, claimed that Muir had been in contact with that "notorious democrat and fugitive from justice" Archibald Hamilton Rowan. The term "democrat" was often used in this pejorative fashion by Tories of this era. Rowan certainly was a democrat, but he was not at this time a fugitive, though he soon would be. He immediately travelled to Scotland to support Muir and to challenge Dundas to a duel. Duelling was very much a vice of the aristocracy and was frowned upon by most democrats. Rowan, who was excitable and quick to take offence, particularly on behalf of others who were in difficulty, was always ready to defend his honour and that of his friends by offering challenge. Dundas refused the challenge and, with some justification, accused Rowan of intimidation.

Years later, when Rowan was seventy-four years old, he travelled to London to challenge a Mr G.R. Dawson to a duel for falsely asserting in the British House of Commons that Rowan had been convicted of treason. Rowan had never been charged with treason because he had escaped to France and America.

Muir's trial for treason was a travesty. The judge

whispered to one of the jurors who passed close to the bench, saying, "Come awa', master Horner, and help us hang an o' these damn scoundrels."[27]

The judge was particulary scathing about Muir's propaganda amongst the working class and suggested that the rabble had no right to representation.[28]

On his conviction Muir was quickly taken from Scotland to a prison hulk, the *Surprise*, on the Thames. Before the ship sailed for the penal colony in New South Wales, Muir wrote to the Dublin Society of United Irishmen, expressing his confidence that they would triumph over despotism and achieve the emancipation of Ireland.[29] On board the prison ship, there were four other Scottish radicals, including the English-born Rev. Thomas Fyshe Palmer. Rev. Palmer had been a friend of Archibald Hamilton Rowan from their days in Cambridge.

Rev. Palmer was tried in Perth. His crime had been to encourage the reading of Tom Paine's works amongst a society of "low weavers and mechanics".[30] His real crime may have been that since coming to Scotland he had established a number of Unitarian congregations, which were thriving as long as he was present but quickly declined when he was transported.[31] His sentence was seven years' transportation. Neither Palmer nor Muir were to see their native lands again. Muir escaped from Botany Bay but was badly wounded by a British cannonball during a naval battle while a prisoner on a Spanish vessel. He made it to Paris, where he died in 1798. Rev. Palmer died of dysentery in 1802 on the island of Guam. More than forty years after their deaths, the fate of these Scottish martyrs was invoked by the Chartist press in their campaign for democracy.

E.P. Thompson observed, "an example was made of two gifted professional men who had been unreserved in their willingness to co-operate with plebeian reformers".[32] A half a century later the Chartists were aware of this heritage. They erected a monument to the martyrs Muir and Palmer at Edinburgh.

Notes to Chapter Nine

1. Porter 2001, p. 407
2. Madden 1860, p. 29
3. Cited in Witt Bowden, Industrial Society, p. 61 recorded in Kramnick, 'Middle Class Radicalism" The Online Library of Liberty.
4. Grayling 2001, p. 28
5. Quinn 2002, p. 99
6. Aptheker 1960, p. 110
7. Quinn 2002, p. 98
8. *Ibid.*
9. Thompson 1964, p. 77
10. *Ibid.* p. 80
11. Redmond 2002, p. 1
12. Uglow 2003, p. 446
13. Clifford 1989, p. 53
14. *Ibid.* p. 41
15. Andrews 2003, p. 81
16. Eshet 2001, p. 127
17. Redmond 2002, p. 1
18. McDowell 1998, p. 8
19. *Ibid.*
20. *Ibid.*
21. *Ibid.* p. 121
22. Agnew 1998, vol. II, p. 15
23. *Ibid.* p. 33
24. Small 2002, p. 233
25. Chryssides 1998, p. 20
26. O'Toole 1997, p. 288
27. Thompson 1964, p. 135
28. *Ibid.*
29. *Enlightenment and Dissent*, No 23, 2004–2007, p. 151
30. *Ibid.*
31. Andrews 2003, p. 141
32. Thompson 1964, p. 136

Chapter Ten

ARTHUR O'CONNOR AND CITIZEN EDWARD

January 1793, Irish House of Commons
The shocking news has reached Dublin that Louis XVI has been executed at Paris. Not since the murder of Charles I in 1649 has such a dastardly fate been visited on the sacred person of an anointed king. Every member of the House, with the exception of Arthur O'Connor, is wearing black as a sign of mourning. He alone refuses to honour the royal martyr and condemn the actions of the French. O'Connor tells his fellow MPs, "I am the only one here who has a right to condemn the killing as I have always maintained that Society has no right to take the life of any of its members. Is not this parliament here in Dublin the result of the execution of Charles I?"[1] *O'Connor's refusal to condemn "king-killing" angers his fellow MPs, Whig and Tory alike. It is now clear that French principles have not only seduced the northern Dissenters and the Catholic mob but have insinuated themselves into the parliament of Ireland.*

A Contested Ancestry

Arthur O'Connor was born near Bandon in 1763, and he always maintained that he was descended from Gaelic chieftains, the O'Connors of Kerry, but Arthur's account of his ancestry through the male line is fanciful. He claimed that his ancestor the Gaelic chieftain was murdered by his co-religionists for marrying a Protestant woman, who managed to escape to the walled Protestant town of Bandon with her money and her son. Later historians poured scorn on this story of his ancestry.[2] It was claimed that he was descended from an Englishman, a Connor who had land from the Cromwellian confiscations.[3]

Arthur often cited the legend that the gate of Bandon was inscribed with the motto, "Enter Turk, Atheist, Jew, but do not enter Papist."[4] This has been repeated down the years by many who wished to brand the people of Bandon as intolerant religious fanatics.[5] It is also reputed that a wag responded by writing underneath, "Who ever wrote this wrote it well for the same is written on the gates of Hell." If the story of the bigotry of the Bandon citizens is not apocryphal, it shows they were possessed of a strange form of tolerance. They wanted no Roman Catholics amongst them, yet they pretended to welcome Moslems and Jews, who were not welcome in most of Christian Europe; and atheism was a capital offence nearly everywhere.

O'Connor was resolutely opposed to primogeniture, so though there is doubt about O'Connor's ancestry through the male line, perhaps his mother's ancestry is more relevant. She had the profoundest influence on his religious and philosophical outlook, and influenced and informed his political beliefs and actions. Anne Longfield's ancestors came to Ireland in 1652 and settled in Cork, arriving in Ireland at the time of the Commonwealth when English settlers were regarded as "Cromwellians". There is much evidence in what O'Connor himself said about his mother that she inherited many "Cromwellian" traits.

She held liberal Protestant views. She believed that the individual conscience was answerable to no man but to the "Great Spirit, to God".[6] She advised her son to believe that "no man should abandon reason to the dictates of priesthood".[7] She was familiar with the work of Benjamin Hoadly (1676–1761). Although Hoadly was a bishop of the Established Church, he preached that the scriptures afford no warrant to a visible church authority. The Non-subscribers in Ulster were said to have a mania for Hoadly. O'Connor learned from his mother that "knowledge was acquired honestly through the senses and by rational thought". His mother's influence ensured that "the superstitions of the medieval world were contemptible to him".[8] John Toland had fled Dublin one hundred years earlier after expressing views such as these. These ideas are closer to John Locke than to the teachings of the Established Church, of which O'Connor was nominally a member.

There was an adult male influence on the young O'Connor, his mother's friend Major Acropolis Morris, a descendant of a Cromwellian soldier. Morris had been a soldier in the British army. At the time of his army career, his regiment was "esteemed the best disciplined in the British service".[9] Morris, who became O'Connor's teacher, told him to "concentrate on the laws of nature for those were certainties". Arthur learned from Morris and his mother of the Scottish Enlightenment. The ideas of Hume and Locke were central to his education.[10]

Acropolis Morris was so enthusiastic in the American cause that he slipped out of Ireland and went to America to fight for Washington, enlisting in the American forces under an assumed name. He was arrested on his return to Ireland, but no charges against him could be proven and he was set free.[11]

There is no evidence to suggest that Arthur O'Connor's mother or Morris were members of Rev. William Hazlitt's congregation at Bandon. However, given the similarity of the religious views of Anne Longfield and Hazlitt, and given the strength of Hazlitt's and Morris' enthusiasm for the American cause, it is conceivable that in a small place like Bandon in the mid 1770s, there may have been some connections between them.

Due to the education he received from his mother and Morris, O'Connor had a special affection for the philosophers of the Scottish Enlightenment. An avid reader of economic theory, his hero was Adam Smith, Francis Hutcheson's star pupil. Such was his interest in the work of Smith that he was something of a social bore. Lord

Wycombe complained that, "Arthur O'Connor behaved like an imbecile if not worse. When in company by the aid of a good memory he talks a few pages of Adam Smith in lieu of conversation."[12]

On obtaining his degree from Trinity College Dublin, O'Connor went to London to qualify as a barrister. In London he often attended the public gallery in the House of Commons, where he listened to and was impressed by the speeches of Charles Fox and Richard Sheridan. They were later to be his close friends, and their evidence would save him from the gallows in 1798. He listened to the speeches of William Pitt, but he found that he "could never defend himself from the idea that he sought to deceive."[13] O'Connor admitted that Pitt had studied economics under Dr Richard Price, and it showed. Pitt had only absorbed the commercial aspects – he forgot the lessons about harvesting the resources of the nation through free and liberal policies.[14]

When O'Connor was finished his studies and qualified as a barrister, he returned to Ireland where he worked for his mother's very wealthy brother, Lord Longueville. His uncle gave him a seat in the Irish House of Commons. Many of the seats in the Irish House of Commons were in the gift of individual aristocratic families in this manner, and even Henry Grattan had been given his first break in politics with a gift of a seat from Lord Charlemont. O'Connor's first years in parliament were unremarkable.

O'Connor's uncle was of Cromwellian descent, yet he was typical of the aristocratic place-chasers who dominated the Dublin parliament. He had gone to considerable lengths to secure the position of revenue commissioner from William Pitt for his nephew. O'Connor's refusal of this sinecure was an indication of his emerging radical and democratic politics. In a short time he would move from being a member of parliament and up-and-coming scion of the Protestant Ascendancy to militant collaborator with revolutionary France.

On a visit to London in 1793, O'Connor had a cordial meeting with Edmund Burke. Knowing they would differ on the French Revolution, he avoided the topic. Knowing that O'Connor supported Catholic emancipation, Burke mistakenly assumed that O'Connor was sympathetic to that religion. O'Connor quickly disabused him of this notion. For O'Connor, "Roman Catholicism was the death of mental liberty." He would spend the best years of his life fighting for the political rights of Roman Catholics but would never accept their state of mind.[15] O'Connor believed that political liberty would help Catholics shake off priestly superstition. His discussion with Burke convinced him that, "Burke had a hankering after popery."[16]

The Fitzwilliam Affair

The Fitzwilliam Affair led to the end of Arthur O'Connor's career in parliament. The spirits of the reformers had lifted in December 1794 when the Earl of Fitzwilliam was appointed lord lieutenant. Almost his first act was to dismiss the Castle clique of Fitzgibbon and Beresford. Fitzwilliam, a liberal Whig and a friend to Catholic emancipation, intended to support a bill to introduce Catholic emancipation, but he never got the chance. Fitzwilliam was recalled suddenly in March 1795 after the king had been lobbied by the ousted clique and he had urged Pitt to dump Fitzwilliam.

The Roman Catholics of Ireland were furious. The Protestant students of Trinity College joined the Dublin mob when it vented its anger by rioting and smashing the windows of Beresford's home at Ely Place. There were riots and mob violence amongst the Protestant weavers in the Liberties, orchestrated by the United Irishmen. Fifty mutinous soldiers were induced to desert to the Liberties, where they were stripped of their weapons and accoutrements, provided with allowance money and given employment as weavers.[17]

The Dissenters in Dublin in their various congregations

voted to discontinue their custom of addressing the new lord lieutenant.

The Dissenters had been delighted by the appointment of the Earl of Fitzwilliam. They sent him a glowing address because they believed he would introduce parliamentary reform and Catholic emancipation. In the address of welcome, the Dissenters told the viceroy that from their ancestors they had derived a reverence for the Glorious Revolution and the Hanoverian succession. Fitzwilliam responded by praising their loyalty and pointing out how important such loyalty was when the kingdoms stood threatened by the old adversary, France. [18]

The recall of Fitzwilliam signalled the end to hopes for Catholic emancipation. The hopes that had been raised by the appointment were replaced by furious anger. Many now felt that with no hope of reform, revolution was the only viable option. At a meeting held in the Great Strand Street vestry on 30 March 1795, the "gentlemen" of the congregation voted unanimously not to welcome the Earl of Camden, the new lord lieutenant, to Ireland

The terse vestry minute reads: "The gentlemen of the congregation resolve that it appears to this meeting that the practice hitherto pursued of addressing the lord lieutenant on his arrival be discontinued."

Rev. Dr Moody (the minister) was in the chair. Present at the meeting were: Mr Hone, Mr Crothers, Mr J Hutton, Mr Kennedy, Mr D. Hutton, Mr Vickers, Mr Caldwell, Mr J Hartley (brother of Travers Hartley MP), Mr J Hawksley, Mr Thwaites, Mr Anderson, Mr Bruce, Mr Lyons, Mr Rainey, Mr Holmes, Dr W. Drennan, Mr Lindsay, Mr A. Kirkpatrick, Mr Ewing, Mr Jordan, Mr Ashmore, Mr Armstrong. [19]

Rainey, Drennan, Ewing, Holmes and Jordan are known to have been United Irishmen. Sam Bruce, a brother of Rev. William Bruce, had joined the society but had probably withdrawn from it by this time. Dr Moody's brother, Rev. Boyle Moody, would later fight in the rebellion in County

Down and die in 1799 as a result of the hardship he endured.[20]

Rev. John Moody had delayed opening the meeting to see if the congregation's two most eminent aristocrats would appear. Robert Stewart, Lord Londonderry, and his son, also Robert, later Viscount Castlereagh, were members of the Great Strand Street congregation. The younger Robert Stewart had been baptised at Great Strand Street on 18 June 1769. (The register recording the baptism is still in use today in the Dublin Unitarian Church.) When it became clear that neither Londonderry nor Castlereagh would be joining the meeting, those present resolved unanimously that in common with their Protestant Dissenter brethren of Dublin that they would not welcome Lord Camden.

Both Londonderry and son had been liberal reformers, playing prominent roles in the Volunteers while Robert junior was yet a boy. In 1795, Robert Stewart the younger was not yet a viscount, but he was MP for County Down. Rev. William Steel Dickson of Portaferry had been a great admirer of Robert the younger's grandfather, Alexander Stewart, and had worked for the Stewart family in the elections of 1783 and 1790. Samuel Neilson had been secretary to Stewart's election committee in 1783. For many years, Robert junior had followed his father's practice of subscribing two half-yearly payments of £5. 3s. 9d pew rent to Great Strand Street. This money went towards the upkeep of the ministers.[21]

William Drennan expressed his surprise that Londonderry did not attend the meeting, but Drennan knew that his lordship was married to a sister of the new lord lieutenant, Camden, and had been "very bustling and active preparing the way for the new arrival".[22] Following the fall of Fitzwilliam, father and son "gave in to the lure of ambition and changed their politics and religion".[23] Shamelessly seeking patronage and promotion, they took advantage of the opportunity for personal and family advancement provided by the replacement of Fitzwilliam by their kinsman.

Rev. James Porter of Greyabbey had also helped the Stewarts in the election of 1790. When they changed sides and were being rewarded with honours and titles, Rev. Porter lampooned their rise through the ranks of the aristocracy in a series of brilliant satires in the *Northern Star* entitled "Billy Bluff and the Squire". Even though Londonderry was not good at remembering his supporters and friends, his memory was more fine-tuned when it came to slights. Rev. James Porter would die in 1798 on the gallows outside his meeting house and in front of his congregation for the "crime" of writing "Billy Bluff and the Squire".

Besides being clearly angry that Fitzwilliam, whom they regarded as a Whig and a reformer, had been deposed, the Great Strand Street vestry committee had another cause for concern. They knew that the new viceroy was a descendant of the notorious Judge George Jeffreys, who had presided over the "Bloody Assizes". He had butchered hundreds of Dissenters on behalf of James II in the aftermath of Monmouth's rebellion. He had condemned Algernon Sidney to death.

If the congregation perhaps feared that Camden would have his ancestor's traits, they were soon proven right. The new lord lieutenant was a worthy descendant of the hanging judge. He suspended habeas corpus and introduced the Insurrection Act. He placed the whole of Ulster under martial law.[24] Two years after his appointment, Oliver Bond and Henry Jackson and their United Irish committee at Pill Lane were toasting their hope that Camden would meet the fate of his notorious ancestor.[25]

If the fall of Fitzwilliam caused riots in the streets and disaffection in the meeting houses, the parliament itself was not totally insulated from the sense of outrage. Arthur O'Connor denounced the machinations of the Castle, telling the Irish House of Commons that:

the men who usurp the whole political power of this country, the men who have converted the whole representation of Ireland into family patrimony; to the poverty, to the oppression and to the disgrace of the nation and to the monstrous aggrandizement of themselves, their relatives, and their servile adherents, these are the men who oppose Catholic emancipation and why? Because it would be incompatible with their accursed monopoly.[26]

Wolfe Tone described this speech as "the ablest and honestest [*sic*] speech ever made in that house",[27] but it cost O'Connor dear. Although he had been the chosen heir to his uncle's considerable fortune, Lord Longueville disinherited Arthur and took his parliamentary seat from him. O'Connor then found a new career path for himself; he became a committed revolutionary and a leader of the Society of United Irishmen.

Citizen Lord
At some time in the previous year, Arthur O'Connor made the acquaintance of another member of the Irish House of Commons who had joined the United Irishmen, Lord Edward FitzGerald. He and O'Connor immediately became close friends. O'Connor was thirty-one, the same age as FitzGerald, whom he ever after described as "the twin of my soul".[28] As the Society of United Irishman was by now a secret organisation, it is impossible to say if any other members of parliament became involved. There is, however, a very good case for believing that FitzGerald's much older friend, Alexander Montgomery MP, was also a member of the underground organisation.[29]

By the time O'Connor and FitzGerald met, the latter had long been a committed revolutionary republican. He had experienced the excitement of revolutionary Paris in the company of Tom Paine and had associated with the Priestley/Godwin circle in London in 1791. He had followed Paine to France and lodged with him there at

White's Hotel, the favoured haunt of the English-speaking radicals. In Paris he befriended John Hurtford Stone, a friend of Dr Priestley who had played a part in the failed Jackson mission to the English radicals and the United Irishmen which had caused so much trouble for Hamilton Rowan and Wolfe Tone.

At a dinner in White's Hotel on 18 November 1792, FitzGerald formally renounced his aristocratic title and became "Citizen" Edward.[30]

Before coming to Paris, FitzGerald had been in England where he had a love affair with Richard Sheridan's wife, Elizabeth. She had died of consumption when her and Lord Edward's child, Mary, was just a few weeks old. FitzGerald was still grieving over the death of his lover when one night he accompanied John Hurtford Stone to a theatre in Paris. There he saw a woman who bore a marked physical resemblance to Elizabeth. This was Pamela, daughter of Madame de Genlis, who was mistress to the Duc D'Orleans, Philip Egalité.[31] Madame de Genlis was "the greatest female intellectual and educator of her age".[32] She had always claimed that Pamela had been adopted as a child and claimed the adoption was part of an experiment in the educational theories of Rousseau. These required separating a child from its parents and placing it with a tutor.[33] Everybody else, including Pamela herself, believed that she was the daughter of Duc D'Orleans and Genlis. Horace Walpole, who described Madame de Genlis as "a scribbling trollop", observed that she had "educated Pamela to be very like herself in the face".[34]

After FitzGerald married Pamela, he decided to leave Paris and return to Ireland. Before he left, he met Tom Paine for the last time and discussed the possibility of a French intervention in Ireland. He arrived in Dublin in January 1793 with his new wife, where the couple cut quite a dash. FitzGerald, dressed in the French republican fashion, was accompanied by his young beautiful wife and his giant black American servant Tony Small. The Dublin ladies gossiped that Pamela carried a handkerchief which had been dipped in the blood of a guillotined aristocrat. Pamela was a great favourite of the Dublin men, though it was rumoured also that she hummed revolutionary songs. The Dublin papers asserted that she was the daughter of Philip Egalité and that she was not more than nineteen years old. It has been suggested that Pamela was only sixteen at this time.[35]

FitzGerald's hair was cropped in the democratic style that was to be adopted by many United Irishmen. Indeed, so many of the rebels in 1798 had cropped their hair that they were referred to as "croppies", and one of the mass graves in Dublin where the bodies of so many murdered rebels were dumped is called Croppies' Acre.

FitzGerald and O'Connor would often spend time in FitzGerald's small house in Kildare, which had a portrait of Paine over the fireplace. There they would have political discussions and "O'Connor would try fruitlessly to persuade FitzGerald from his Anglican convictions".[36] O'Connor remained a Protestant to the end of his days, or at least he "was not irreligious, he believed in a benevolent Providence".[37] By the time he was trying to proselytise his friend, he must have regarded himself as a Dissenter in the tradition of his mother and Acropolis Morris.

O'Connor was drawn to Presbyterian republicans of Ulster, possibly due to his upbringing and education, his experiences in the Volunteers and his contacts with enthusiastic pro-American Dissenters in Bandon. He suggested that the Belfast Dissenters were "a population of the best informed people in Europe and of the best public spirit and independence... not a parish that has not a little library and all instruct and regale themselves with reading that excellent journal the *Northern Star*."[38] He believed that the religious ideas of the Presbyterians gave independence to everything they did and said.[39] Such was the cruel tyranny the Catholics had endured that it had, in O'Connor's view, made them timorous.[40]

After losing his seat in parliament, O'Connor went to London, where he considered the possibility of a political career in England. He was very close to the leader of the opposition, Charles Fox, Edward's cousin. O'Connor was also on very good terms with the great opposition orator, the Dublin-born playwright Richard Brinsley Sheridan. However, his dearest friend in England was Francis Burdett, the only radical reformer to hold a seat in the British House of Commons.

FitzGerald soon joined O'Connor in London. He had a mission from the United Irishmen to go to France, and he wanted O'Connor to accompany him. O'Connor and FitzGerald travelled to Hamburg, which was the only open port in northern Europe during the war. An informer reported to Dublin Castle that Colonel Marcus Despard attempted to organise passports for them.[41] They made contact with the French ambassador and then travelled to Basle in Switzerland and had further contact with the French there. FitzGerald was not allowed to enter France due to his connections with the Duc D'Orleans, who had gone to the guillotine some time previously, so O'Connor entered France alone. He met the French general Lazare Hoche, and over a number of days they discussed the best way to approach the invasion of Ireland.

They agreed that Hoche would get the expedition underway as soon as possible. Hoche would be the military leader while O'Connor would exercise the chief command of administration and civil government.[42] O'Connor agreed to lead a Presbyterian army from Belfast to Dublin which would then swing west to meet the French forces which he expected would land at Galway.

O'Connor told Hoche that "The progress of Ireland in establishing her liberty must depend on the influence given to the Presbyterians". He did not conceal from Hoche that "If Ireland contained but the Papist population [he] never would have attempted the separation from England".[43]

O'Connor left France, linked up again with FitzGerald in Hamburg, and they returned to Ireland. O'Connor first went to Belfast to report his success with the French to Samuel Neilson and William Tennant. He struck up an immediate relationship with these Belfast Unitarians whose liberal views on religion would have been similar to those he had imbibed from his mother.[44] O'Connor held Wolfe Tone in the highest regard but denied that Tone had been the "father of the United Irish Society". He declared that "the Society was really begun in Belfast and that the real fathers of the Society were the editors of the *Northern Star*" (Neilson's group). He next went to Dublin and secured enthusiastic commitment from Oliver Bond and Henry Jackson of the Pill Lane group. Henry Jackson told O'Connor that "he was with him to the last drop of his blood".[45]

O'Connor then went to see Thomas Addis Emmet, whom he regarded as being of "extreme timidity of character". He claims that Emmet informed him that he was not of a disposition to take part in the rising that was now inevitable.[46] Thomas Addis Emmet and O'Connor were to become bitter enemies. The enmity and rancour between them, which was to escalate after the rebellion during their long incarceration in Fort George in Scotland, damaged future relationships with the French, who had to deal with rival factions of dis-united Irishmen led by O'Connor and Emmet respectively.

O'Connor, having secured the agreement with the French, was anxious that the northern Presbyterians should be ready to act. There was a parliamentary election due in 1797, and Arthur stood as a candidate for Antrim. When the French fleet was being buffeted at Bantry, O'Connor was in Belfast fighting the election campaign. The French had arrived in Bantry a few weeks before O'Connor was expecting them, and he was not yet ready. The plan had been that the French would muster at Bantry but disembark at Galway. The army would leave Dublin to engage the French, and O'Connor and his Presbyterians would march on Dublin.

The French did not land; after days of heavy storms they returned home, and the army stayed in Dublin. The government closed down the *Northern Star* and arrested O'Connor in Dublin on 3 February. At the same time, Neilson, the Simms brothers and Thomas Russell were arrested and lodged in Kilmainham gaol. They became the first of an ever-expanding group of United Irish leaders who were to become known as the state prisoners.

The United Irishmen and the government were convinced the French would return, and both sides were determined to be ready for that eventuality. The United Irishmen were determined to politically educate and arm the people to take the field with their French allies. The government strategy was to suppress the disaffected with as much brutality as possible, in order to disarm them and to provoke a rising before the French returned.

O'Connor was considered so dangerous that he was kept apart from the other prisoners in the tower of Dublin Castle. The government had no evidence to charge him with treason and were delighted when he asked for permission to go to London.

Arthur O'Connor Cheats the Gallows

In early 1798, O'Connor, John Binns, a Dublin-born radical who was now a leading member of the LCS, and James Coigley, a Roman Catholic priest from Armagh who was a senior United Irishman, were arrested at Margate in Kent while trying to procure a passage to France in order to contact the French government.

John Binns was born in 1772. His mother, Mary Pemberton, was a member of the Established Church. The male Pembertons were successful bricklayers, supporters of the government and holders of a number of civic offices in Dublin Corporation. Mary's cousin Joseph Pemberton was Lord Mayor of Dublin for a time. However Binns's father, who died when John was an infant, was a Moravian and therefore a Dissenter. His father's family was active in the liberal and anti-government politics in Dublin.[47] His paternal uncle, also John Binns, was a member of Dublin Corporation and a political ally of Napper Tandy. A very tall man, he was known to his friends as "Long John Binns" and to his enemies as "the Devil's Darning Needle".[48] Young John adopted the pro-reform and anti-government politics of his father's family.

John Binns emigrated to London, where he worked as a plumber's assistant for his brother, Benjamin,and there he joined the London Corresponding Society. During the "Church and King" riots in London in the early 1790s, he had led a group of one hundred Irishmen armed with shillelaghs to defend the home of Thomas Hardy, founder of the London Corresponding Society. At the age of twenty-two, Binns chaired a public meeting at Copenhagen Fields in London that was attended by 150,000 people who were protesting against the war with France. From the time he left Dublin in 1793 until his departure for America in 1801, he said he was to "see the inside of many a prison including the Bastille and the Tower of London".[49] His reference to the Bastille most likely refers to his incarceration at Coldbath Fields in Clerkenwell, London, which was sometimes known as the English Bastille. His radical colleague Horne Tooke, at a social gathering in the Crown and Anchor, observed that together "they had seen the inside of more prisons than any two horse thieves in England".[50] An informer reported that Binns was giving lectures in the use of the pike against cavalry to workmen in London in the mid 1790s.[51]

Binns had something of a charmed life in Britain, avoiding a plot to have him pressed into the fleet at Portsmouth, escaping conviction for treason on a number of occasions and thus escaping the gallows.[52]

As a member of both the LCS and the United Irishmen, Binns was a significant link between the Irish and the

British democrats. Binns was also a member of the "United Britons" and the joint British and Irish committee that sought to coordinate efforts by the British and Irish revolutionaries. Thomas Russell's brother-in-law, William Henry Hamilton of Enniskillen, and Colonel Despard were also on this committee. Binns organised statements of support from the British groups which his brother Benjamin took to Dublin in early 1798 when he and Coigley (who had just returned from France) came to see the leadership of the United Irishmen. They discussed plans for a republican revolution with Oliver Bond and Henry Jackson and their "committee" of United Irishmen based at Pill Lane.

During Benjamin Binns' visit to Dublin, he also met "the Papists".[53] The Papists may refer to Defenders, but more likely it refers to the Catholic Committee – people who were now an important element in the United Irishmen.

By the time Arthur O'Connor linked up with John Binns, Coigley and Despard, the union between the British and Irish radicals was at an advanced stage. Many of the dealings of the leadership took place in Furnival Inn's cellar in Holborn.[54] O'Connor did not risk attending these meetings. Instead Despard took lodgings in Osterley, Middlesex, where he could receive O'Connor with less risk of being seen by spies.[55]

O'Connor and his friends were being shadowed from London by the Bow Street Runners. On 28 February, the Runners pounced on their lodgings, the King's Head in Margate. Coigley was unfortunate in that an address from United Irishmen and the British radicals was discovered in his pocket. The address had been composed by Dr Crossfield, chairman of the LCS, and was addressed to the French government.

Wolfe Tone read about the arrest in the French newspapers. Tone had met Coigley in Paris and did not like him. When he heard what had happened, he expressed himself "staggered that any man living would leave such a paper of consequence in so careless a place".[56]

After the arrests, the authorities swooped on the British radicals of the LCS and the United Irishmen in London. This may have been as a result of the papers found on Coigley, or perhaps because the authorities knew that John Binns was a leading figure in both organisations. Thirty men were arrested, including Colonel Despard, who with his fellow prisoners was sent to the "Bastille" at Coldbath Fields, Clerkenwell. O'Connor, Binns and Coigley were tried for treason, and Coigley was convicted. He was offered a deal by Pitt to betray O'Connor in return for his life, which he refused. He died bravely on the gallows in July 1798.

Tone was so impressed by Coigley's heroism at the end that he said that if Ireland gained her liberty he would propose a monument in his honour. In his diary, Tone quoted Shakespeare's lines for Coigley: "Nothing in his life became him like the leaving it."[57]

Binns and O'Connor were acquitted. Charles Fox, leader of the Whigs, and Richard Brinsley Sheridan MP gave evidence on O'Connor's behalf, insisting that while he was fully behind reform, he would have no truck with treason. William Drennan had travelled from Dublin to give evidence on O'Connor's behalf, but he was not called. The jury accepted the defence witnesses' version of events, but the Tory newspapers and the satirist Gillray would, a short time later, recall their evidence with glee when the real depth of O'Connor's involvement with the rebellion became known.

No sooner was O'Connor acquitted at Margate than he was rearrested and brought back to Ireland as a prisoner. It must have been a bitter homecoming. As he stepped ashore in Dublin, he knew the rebellion had failed and that his comrade Edward FitzGerald was dead. O'Connor was on his way to join the rest of the United Irish leadership in the long incarceration at Fort George. One small consolation for him was that in passing through Scotland on his way to imprisonment he passed through the native country of

"Hume and Smith and the Presbyterians", where the ideas of the Scottish Enlightenment had been conceived.[58]

Notes to Chapter Ten
1. Hames , J.H., 2001, p. 72
2. *Ibid.* p. 16
3. *Ibid.*
4. *Ibid.*
5. W. O'Brien 1926, p. 121
6. Hames 2001, p. 24
7. *Ibid.* p. 33
8. *Ibid.* p. 33
9. *Ibid.* p. 27
10. *Ibid.* p. 52
11. *Ibid.* p. 30
12. Livesey 1998, p. 9
13. Hames 2001, p. 50
14. *Ibid.*
15. *Ibid.* p. 26
16. *Ibid.* p. 83
17. *Ibid.*
18. RIA DUC EUS
19. RIA DUC STR 2
20. Swords 1997, p. 113
21. RIA DUC STR 3
22. Agnew 1999, vol. II, p. 143
23. Mc Millan, in Swords 1997, p. 88
24. W.A. Maguire 1998, p. 156
25. Bartlett 2004, p. 144
26. Hames 2001, p. 89
27. Bartlett 1998, p. 590
28. Hames 2001, p. 84
29. Mansergh 2005, p. 229
30. Tillyard 1997, p. 139
31. *Ibid.* p. 141
32. Ambrose 2008, p. 9
33. *Ibid.* p. 143
34. *Ibid.* p. 144
35. Byrne 1955, p.131
36. *Ibid.* p. 179
37. Hames 2001, p. 273
38. *Ibid.* p. 50
39. *Ibid.* p. 120

40. *Ibid.*
41. Bartlett 1998, p. 170
42. Hames 2001, p. 120
43. *Ibid.* p. 120
44. *Ibid.* p. 95
45. *Ibid.* p. 122
46. *Ibid.* p. 123
47. Binns 1854, p. 24
48. *Ibid.* p. 25
49. *Ibid.* p. vi
50. *Ibid.* p. 46
51. Wells 1986, p. 71
52. Thompson 1964, p. 187
53. *Ibid.* p. 123
54. Wells 1986, p. 123
55. *Ibid.* p. 124
56. Bartlett 1998, p. 830
57. *Ibid.* p. 860
58. Hames 2001, p. 207

Chapter Eleven

THE SHAM SQUIRE
AND REVOLUTIONARY DUBLIN

12 March 1798, Bridge Street, Dublin

Major William Swan orders his soldiers to surround the elegant house he has kept under surveillance for the past twenty-four hours. Then, accompanied by twelve sergeants in full regalia, he pushes open the front door as he calls out, "Is Ivers from Carlow come?" He confronts a man in the front room and places him under arrest. The arrested man offers no resistance. Then Swan and his men bound up the stair to an annexe, where an informer who gave them the password has told them a treasonable meeting will be in progress. There are a dozen men in the room talking in groups while one man sits at a desk writing. Swan orders all present to put their hands up and he seizes the treasonable paper. Swan then tells Oliver Bond and the Leinster Directory of the United Irishmen that they are now His Majesty's prisoners.

Pill Lane and the Sham Squire

Pill Lane in the 1790s was a bustling commercial street. Calico printers, glovers, pin-makers, silk weavers, skinners and woollen drapers did business there. Many Presbyterian businessmen had shops facing on to the street. Their manufacturing workshops were to the rear, and their families and servants resided in the upper floors of these premises. Oliver Bond set up his woollen business in Pill Lane when he came to Dublin in 1782. Henry Jackson's steel foundry was near by in Old Church Street.

The most elegant and largest building in the area was

the Great Strand Street meeting house, which opened in 1763. With its arched doorway and ornate central window, it was the very essence of Georgian modernity. The more prosperous members of the congregation could alight from their coaches at the broad open space in front of the building when they attended Sunday services.

Thomas Addis Emmet claimed that the United Irishmen organisation in Dublin ceased to exist in 1794 following the Jackson affair and the flight of Rowan. However, whether Emmet was aware of it or not, Samuel Neilson's organisers had been busy everywhere, including Dublin. Pill Lane was the nerve centre of the organisation. Jim Smyth tells us:

> About fifty members of the society met in Henry Jackson's house in Church Street [beside Pill Lane] in October 1795. At this meeting John Sheares proposed reorganising [the society] into fifteen man "sections", which would each delegate a representative to "a council or central committee".[1]

From their nerve centre at Pill Lane, the Dublin United Irishmen were now developing a secret revolutionary conspiracy on a national basis, wedded to the idea that the people of Ireland could establish a democratic republic with the help of republican France.

The Pill Lane group had adopted Neilson's Jacobin approach to organising. Their commitment to building a mass movement which involved businessmen, professionals, workers and peasants was precisely the proposed approach that had frightened the more timid and reformist elements in the Dublin United Irishmen before their organisation had been suppressed.

Oliver Bond "became busy indeed". His extensive business brought him connections in every part of the country, "and he travelled about as much as he could, transacting trade on one hand and administering the oath of allegiance to the brotherhood on the other".[2]

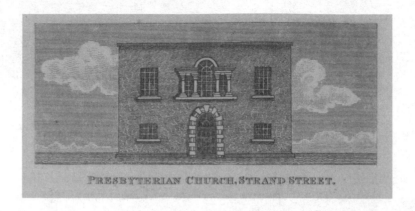

PRESBYTERIAN CHURCH, STRAND STREET.

When Bond and Jackson set up their secret "committee", Neilson had suggested that it should be called the Committee for Public Safety – a clear attempt to emulate the French Jacobins. Samuel Gardiner (a member of the Eustace Street congregation), a tailor from Fisher Lane, off Pill Lane, was described as president of the committee.[3] He was an "opulent citizen" of Dublin who was now being closely watched after having been arrested and released following some over-exuberant celebrating at the Hall of King's Bench following the release of William Drennan.[4]

An informer described Gardiner's "committee" as "the most important republican society". He said it had "about seventy members, men of great property who were extremely cautious whom they admitted to membership". This informer alleged that at their meetings "They imitate the Jacobins of France: they referred to each other as 'Citizen' and even the waiter was referred to in the same manner".[5]

In the spring of 1796 Neilson sent Jemmy Hope, William Putnam McCabe, William Mines of Saintfield and William Metcalfe of Antrim to Dublin to help organise the operatives in the capital.[6] Neilson gave letters of introduction to Hope and Metcalfe recommending them to Edward Dunn, Henry Jackson's foreman.[7] In sending Hope, Neilson was sending his man best qualified to organise the working class. Hope recruited textile workers in Balbriggan, where he lived for a time. He was a weaver by trade and had significant success in organising the weavers of Dublin's Liberties. He possessed the great organising skills of a trade unionist and the class politics of a proto-socialist.

Hope believed that the struggle was between commercial and aristocratic interests to determine which should have the people as its property. Hope held that "the conditions of the labouring class was the fundamental question at issue between the rulers and the people. He said that none of their leaders were acquainted with this fact with the exceptions of Neilson, McCracken, Russell and Robert Emmet."[8]

When the United Irishmen became an oath-bound society, Hope argued that oath-taking was pointless because "an honest man is bound by his word but no oath can bind a knave".[9] However, he helped to develop a mass membership in Dublin under the direction of the Pill Lane group. He particularly targeted the illegal workers' combinations (trades unions), which "would account for the spread of their organisation south of the river into the Liberties and also for its significant Protestant artisan membership".[10] Many of these weavers were Presbyterians, and some of the older men would have been supporters of Charles Lucas. Hope's organisation survived the 1798 rebellion, and he had organised five thousand workers in the Liberties to be ready to rise with Robert Emmet in 1803.[11]

Francis Higgins, the Sham Squire

The Sham Squire was a most effective and sinister government informant, who took particular interest in the activities of the "committee" that met in the White Horse Inn at Pill Lane. Francis Higgins was a disreputable charlatan who had been dubbed "the Sham Squire" by a judge who gaoled him for forgery and deception in 1767. The citizens of eighteenth century Dublin knew a good appellation when they heard one. The "Sham Squire's" name stuck. Thirty years later, the Sham was the editor of the *Freeman's Journal*. He was by this time outwardly respectable, but he remained as venal and corrupt as ever. The Sham reported to Edward Cooke, under-secretary for Ireland, in a series of letters he sent to Dublin Castle. The Sham dubbed the committee "the king-killers of Pill Lane" in a report dated 29 January 1797.

The morale of the Pill Lane committee would have been very high at this point. The government of revolutionary France had promised them support. The "king-killer" jibe may have been the Sham's way to denigrate them as pro-French Jacobins, since the Jacobins certainly brought Louis XVI to the guillotine in 1793. However, Under-Secretary Cooke received other reports which suggest a different explanation for the Sham's allusion to regicide. Another informer, who signed himself "Left Hand", reported that "Oliver 'Cromwell' Bond, Henry Jackson, Pat Ewing (a half pay Officer ... but a violent republican) and Dr William Drennan were meeting almost every night". He added knowingly "For what purpose such meetings are held is easy to guess".[12] A third informer told Cooke that Oliver "Cromwell" Bond was holding a treasonable correspondence with Rev. William Steel Dickson of Portaferry, a well-known radical Unitarian clergyman.[13]

When the Sham called Bond and his committee king-killers he was more likely referring to the killing of Charles I of England, although Charles had been executed a century and a half before the Pill Lane group came into existence. However, the Sham and Left Hand had good grounds for associating the "committee" with the Civil War regicides. All those mentioned in Left Hand's report – Oliver Cromwell Bond, Henry Jackson, Patrick Ewing and William Drennan – were Protestant Dissenters. As far as Tories and Dublin-based Anglicans were concerned, the Dublin Dissenters were never allowed to forget the regicide of their ancestors.

Nor was the Sham the first person to call Drennan a regicide. In December 1792, a few months before the execution of Louis XVI, Isaac Corry, one-time MP for Newry, had greeted William Drennan in the street, asking him, "How many kings did you kill today?" In some ways it was a fair question. Drennan never spilt blood but was a king-killer in the ideological sense. On 30 January 1777, in a letter to his sister, Drennan celebrated the anniversary of the execution of Charles I by welcoming, "the day that makes tyrants tremble".[14] For a number of years, Drennan's Unitarian friends in Belfast celebrated 30 January with a dinner at the Washington. We know this because his sister told him that on 30 January 1793, ten days after the execution of the king of France, the attendance at the Belfast event was a bit thin.[15]

By the time Higgins was becoming obsessed with the Pill Lane group, he was the editor of the *Freeman's Journal*. Earlier he had been a forger, an unscrupulous fraudster, a brothel-keeper, and he was always a semi-literate misanthrope. The known details of Higgins's life are from hostile sources and do not paint a pleasant picture. He was born into a Roman Catholic family from County Down. His father had conformed to the Established Church and worked for an attorney in Dublin. Following the death of his father, Higgins "while yet of tender years worked as an errand boy, a shoe-black and a waiter in a porterhouse".[16] He became a "hackney writing" clerk in the office of Daniel Bourne, attorney-at-law in Saint Patrick's Close. He trained as a calligrapher and found that his skill could be used to best advantage in forgery rather than honest work. He forged a series of documents, warrants and deeds which suggested he was a man of property, the holder of a government position and the heir to a fortune.

Higgins used forged documents to deceive Fr Shortall, a Jesuit priest, into thinking that he was a rich Protestant who wished to convert to Roman Catholicism. The conversion was to be kept secret so as to avoid disinheritance from his fictional Protestant fortune. Higgins pretended to confess his sins to Fr Shortall each Saturday and was presumably given absolution. When he had the priest totally duped, he asked for his help in finding "an amiable wife of the true religion".[17] The priest introduced him to an eminent Roman Catholic merchant, Mr Archer. Archer's daughter Mary Anne was horrified at the repulsiveness and "approach to deformity of Higgins who was reputed to be one of the ugliest men alive". However, Mary Anne's parents forced her into marrying Higgins.[18] The unfortunate girl must have had a shocking experience when he brought her to her marriage bed in Lucan, County Dublin. She fled with "manic wildness" back to her parents.[19] The girl was at her mother's door at Stephen's Green pleading to be admitted when Higgins arrived in hot pursuit. Her mother opened the door and Higgins burst in and broke his mother-in-law's arm.

Higgins stood trial for his crimes, and the bill laid against him alleged that he was "a person of evil name, fame and dishonest conversation and a common deceiver and cheat".[20] He was imprisoned for a short time. The leniency of his sentence may have been a result of the religious prejudice of the judiciary. Robinson, the Protestant judge, may have had little sympathy for the Roman Catholic Archers and their covert efforts to inherit Protestant land and fortune. Mary Anne Archer did not long survive her humiliation, and it is said she died of a broken heart.[21]

Higgins served only a few weeks in prison, but Robinson had unwittingly pronounced a sentence which would follow Higgins to the grave when the judge observed, "'Tis true this Sham Squire is guilty of great duplicity." Higgins would eventually feign respectability, becoming a judge and proprietor of a newspaper. He doctored the legal records to remove all trace of the Archer affair, yet he was always known both to his contemporaries and to posterity as the "Sham Squire".

For a time the Sham made a living by selling smuggled tea to shopkeepers and selling the same shopkeepers to the Revenue. He served two years in prison for assaulting Mr Peck, a shopkeeper of Cornmarket when Higgins was trying to entrap Peck for smuggling. On his release, he became a strong-arm man in a brothel in Smock Alley that was owned by Charles Reilly, who made the mistake of borrowing money from the Sham. After a short time Reilly found himself in the Marshalsea, the debtors' prison, where he went insane. The Sham took control of the brothel and the brothel keeper's wife. She is said to have died shortly afterwards from a sexually-transmitted disease passed to her by the Sham.[22]

The Sham made money in the hosiery industry and became involved in the Hosiers' Guild. He became an attorney and started working for the *Freeman's Journal* in 1770. Using the same tactics that he had used to dispossess the brothel keeper, he gained control of the newspaper. The owner of the paper borrowed money from the Sham, who foreclosed on the loan when he had the owner at his mercy. The proprietor was jailed for the debt, and the Sham gained ownership of the paper at one quarter of its value.[23] The pro-reform newspaper founded by the great Charles Lucas now became a government propaganda sheet. The Sham increased his wealth as the government plied him with money to print its statements and proclamations. In turn he furnished the government with detailed information on the Society of United Irishmen.

When spying on the Pill Lane group, the Sham used many names to describe them, including "the Marats of Pill Lane" and "the Association of Eating and Drinking Democratic Citizens". However, his coining of the title "the king-killers of Pill Lane" is the most telling.

The Sham knew that the Pill Lane republicans were ill-disposed to "George the Last" of Great Britain and all the other monarchs of Europe. Dr Priestley, of whom many of the Pill Lane group were disciples, regarded George III and all the reigning crowned heads of Europe as the ten horns of the great beast in the Book of Revelation, whose days he believed were numbered once the *ancien régime* and the head of Louis had fallen.[24]

Higgins was suggesting these people were enemies to all kings. He reported that their toast called for "all the kings of the earth be in hell" or the scarcely more moderate, "that all the kings of the earth be in heaven".[25] The Pill Lane group were the republican descendants of republicans. He knew their ancestors had made an English republic and their cousins had helped create a republic in America. With the help of the French Republic, and in cooperation with Scotsmen and Englishmen, the Pill Lane Committee were determined to bring republican government once again to these islands.

Dublin, by this time, was a cauldron of revolutionary activity and revolutionary cells, some of which used the cover of reading clubs. Kevin Whelan quotes a contemporary newspaper (most probably the *Hibernian Journal*) thus:

> The younger part of tradesmen and all apprentices of the city have now the mischievous alternative of assembling in clubs instituted for the spurious purpose of improvement under the name of reading clubs but designed for the corruption of their members. Such clubs the emissaries of sedition have fatally succeeded in establishing.[26]

Along with the reading clubs, there were avowedly revolutionary cells such as the Telegraphic Society, Philanthropic Society, the Athenian Society and the Strugglers.[27] Working tradesmen were said to be organising republican clubs under the name of "Houses of Call".[28] Dublin also had a number of Masonic lodges, a myriad of trade union combinations and had recently seen a major growth in Defender lodges. The Ulster United Irishmen had been targeting such groups in the north for proselytising and recruitment since 1791. The Pill Lane group systematically set about subsuming all these diverse elements into the United Irish command structure.[29]

Oliver Bond, Henry Jackson and the Workers
There was nothing timid about Oliver Bond or Henry Jackson, the Pill Lane leaders. They had been members of the Dublin Society of United Irishmen from the beginning. Bond was born at St Johnson, a few miles from Londonderry, in 1757. He was the son of a Presbyterian minister. He had prospered since coming to Dublin in 1782 to set up as a woollen-draper at 54, Pill Lane.

In 1791 on a bright June morning, Bond married Miss Eleanor Jackson, the pretty and accomplished daughter of Henry Jackson. Eleanor was a woman of sparkling courage and proved an ideal wife for this young revolutionary.[30] She became a sworn "Unitedman" and administered the oath to several ladies.[31]

An enemy described Oliver Bond thus:

> Wealthy, popular and of affable manners, made £6,000 a year by his business, had great dominion of all the [black] smiths and other desperate fellows, was called King Bond and would on the downfall of the Government have been at the head of everything.[32]

A friendly observer described him as one of the most opulent merchants in Dublin and as a "fine, comely, well built man with a shapely pair of legs of which he was just a little proud".[33] Lady Lucy FitzGerald regarded Bond as "one of the handsomest and most delightful men to all appearances that ever was".[34]

Eleanor's father Henry Jackson was "a deep man slow in speech but much listened to".[35] He was described by an admirer as "one of our most wealthy and independent citizens, whose wealth and independence were the least enviable of his endowments".[36] Jackson had been an officer in the Volunteers and had served on Dublin Corporation, where he was aligned with the anti-government faction, including Napper Tandy and Long John Binns.[37] A leading industrialist, Henry Jackson owned an iron foundry at 180, Church Street. His company carried out major public contracts but also manufactured pikes. His foundry also produced cannon balls designed to be fired by French cannons. An informer reported that Jackson's workforce were producing "those diabolical instruments called 'Cats' invented for the destruction of cavalry".[38]

Jackson had introduced the first steam engine into Dublin. James Watt, Dr Priestley's friend and fellow Lunar Society member, had invented the rotary steam engine in 1781. Industrial, scientific and political innovation was very much characteristic of the radical Dissenters. One writer has identified the traits, so common amongst the Dissenters, of advanced politics, rational religion and mercantile endeavour, as the Belfast Trinity.[39] Bond and Jackson, though neither was a native of Belfast, were in that mould.

Bond's house was in Bridge Street, south of the Liffey, but his business premises were located north of the river in Pill Lane. It appears that Bond's and Jackson's employees were easily convinced to join their employers in treason. In October 1796, Edward Cooke received intelligence that one of Henry Jackson's young employees, "a violent republican", boasted that there were more United Irishmen in the city than could be imagined.[40] The willingness of employers and workers to form a treasonable alliance is worthy of some consideration.

Capitalism prior to the industrial revolution involved close cooperation between masters and men. They lived in the same streets and neighbourhoods, and they knew each other and each other's families. Apprentices often lived with their masters, and it was not unusual for a journeyman to marry a member of his employer's family. In the case of Presbyterians in the Pill Lane area, they most likely would have attended the same religious services and listened to the same preachers every Sunday.

Perhaps of more significance was the common interest between master and men. For weavers and those in the clothing business, such as Bond, or blacksmiths, and those in the steel business such as Jackson, their economic grievances were about cheap or dumped foreign imports, the restrictions on Irish trade abroad and the corrupt practice of awarding public contracts to friends of government. When workers rioted over these issues, which they sometimes did, it may be that they did so with the blessing, and the active participation, of their employers.

In 1783, Napper Tandy led a campaign for the protection of Irish manufacturing and employment. Several leading United Irishmen, including William Bell, Nathaniel Cartland, Thomas Bacon and John Collins, were publicly associated with the campaign. In 1784, twenty-seven of Collins' employees published an advertisement thanking him for "having employed them during a time of distress and at material injury to his own interests". They said that "all goods sold at 79, Pill Lane are Irish and from the sale of which Irishmen must receive employment". In 1798 Thomas Bacon was executed for his part in the Rebellion.[41]

Many employers had come through the apprentice system and had long-standing loyalty to "the Trade". Trade union business was carried out by a democratic vote of the members. The trade union combinations were illegal and liable to suppression by the magistrates, and in extreme circumstances, the organisers might be sent to the penal colonies or the fleet. It was relatively easy to convince such people that the rights of man applied to them, and that any change in the status quo would be in their interests and to their benefit.

Many of Jackson's foundry workers lived in Church Street and would "often assemble at the George Tavern in Church St and at the gateway of that inn for the purposes of rioting".[42] Leonard McNally, the informer, had reported that Jackson's employees were "very careful and only met in groups of three or four, no minutes are taken and all communications are by word of mouth".[43] The English radical John Thelwell, writing of the reform movement in Britain at this time, said, "every large workshop and manufactory is a sort of political society which no act of parliament can silence and no magistrate can disperse".[44]

There were other Dissenter businessmen in the Pill Lane group who used their considerable business networks to spread the United Irish ideology and organisation both within Dublin and beyond. William and John Orr were muslin manufacturers at 8, Merchant's Quay. They had a major cloth factory in Stratford-on-Slaney in County Wicklow. This operation employed scores of fugitive Ulster republicans and was used by Putnam McCabe and Jemmy Hope as a base when organising south Leinster.[45] Thomas Jordan was a hosier and a manufacturer, and Richard Maxwell was a woollen draper. They both lived in Pill Lane. They had been sworn United Irishmen since 1792 and also had links to the Great Strand Street congregation.[46]

Thomas Houston had been released from prison in Belfast when Thomas Addis Emmett succeeded in having the validity of a writ of habeas corpus upheld in 1797. Houston's relations in Dublin were cambric merchants in 33, Merchant's Quay and were near neighbours to their fellow Pill Lane group members, William and John Orr.[47]

Edmund Burke would have regarded the artisans associated with the Pill Lane group as the "swinish multitude". The Sham Squire was not as much a snob as Burke. Although he described them as "low, working-class artisans, restless drunken and riotous, capable of any mischief", he also observed that, "They are something above the common rabble. They were now reading newspapers and Paine's politics of Liberty and Equality." They were, the Sham Squire bemoaned, "talking of religious emancipation and Union with England quitting their evocations and associating in numbers".[48]

The White Cross tavern in Pill Lane was the main lodging house for Belfast carmen who lodged in Dublin.[49] In this era of coach travel, the Belfast coach departed from White's. Hence communication channels with Neilson's committee in Belfast were excellent.

In the year 1797, Bond (and Jackson) worked tirelessly and cheerfully swearing in recruits and arming them and holding meetings.[50] Perhaps almost inevitably during that year Bond swore in Thomas Reynolds of Kildare, the informer who was to betray him.

Oliver Bond called a meeting of the Leinster directory of the United Irishmen to take place at his home on 12 March 1798. He invited Thomas Reynolds to the meeting and gave him the password. For the sum of £500, Reynolds sold the meeting and the password. Reynolds stayed away himself, pleading the illness of his wife. Sixteen delegates were arrested. They were representing Dublin, Queen's County, Kildare, Carlow, Kilkenny, Wicklow, Meath and Portarlington. This was a bitter but not a fatal blow to the prospects of the coming rebellion. The Wexford leadership was still at large. The commander-in-chief of the United Irish army, Citizen Edward FitzGerald, had also eluded the trap.

The Sham and the Capture of Lord Edward

The Sham Squire's major coup on behalf of Dublin Castle was the information he supplied which led to the capture of Lord Edward FitzGerald in May 1798. This arrest had the effect of preventing a United Irish insurrection in Dublin City. The Sham had good contacts with Catholic members of the United Irishmen, and a number of Catholic priests kept him supplied with information. His best service to the government was to recruit Francis Mangan, a young Roman Catholic barrister, as an informer. Mangan held a senior position in the Dublin United Irishmen organisation. Higgins lured Mangan into betraying his friends with financial blandishments, but Mangan had another motive for his treachery. He feared the consequences of a French invasion, which he felt might damage Ireland and the Catholic Church.[51] A few years earlier, William

Drennan had suspected that such views were common amongst the Catholic United Irishmen. He said that the Presbyterians, "love the French openly and the Catholics almost to a man hate them secretly – and why? Because they have overturned the Catholic religion in that country and threaten to do it throughout the world."[52]

FitzGerald had set 23 May as the date the rising would commence. As the time for action drew near, he was in hiding in Dublin, trying to stay one step ahead of his pursuers. The Castle authorities had a lucky break when Mangan was asked to hide FitzGerald in his own home at Usher's Island. Mangan and the Sham Squire tipped off the Castle. On the evening of 16 May, as FitzGerald's party were moving towards Mangan's house, they were confronted by Major Sirr, the Dublin chief of police. An elite bodyguard consisting of Samuel Neilson, William Putnam McCabe, John Palmer and Pat Gallagher were guarding FitzGerald.[53] As they moved into Watling Street, Major Sirr challenged them. McCabe and Palmer attempted to shoot Sirr, but both of their pistols misfired. Gallagher and McCabe knocked Sirr to the ground, and John Palmer made a stab at the major's neck.[54] Gallagher received a deep sword wound in his leg. Though Palmer's blade was on target, Sirr was unharmed because he was wearing body armour under his shirt and cravat. The FitzGerald party escaped that night.

The evening following the escape, Mangan revealed FitzGerald's new hiding place to the Sham, who again tipped off the Castle. The major took a large body of soldiers to the house of one Murphy of Thomas Street. Sirr managed to arrest FitzGerald on this occasion after a violent struggle. FitzGerald defended himself fiercely and stabbed two of his assailants, Ryan and Swan. Major Sirr shot FitzGerald twice in the shoulder. The badly wounded prisoner was taken to Newgate, where he clung to life for a few days but died in great agony, mental and bodily, on 4 June 1798. The commander of the United Irishmen was betrayed just days before the planned rising in Dublin. This was a fatal blow to the United Irishmen and could be said to have been the point at which their destruction became inevitable.

The planned Dublin rising was now leaderless and thrown into confusion. The fact that an informer had penetrated so close to the leadership convinced the Dublin men that all their plans had been betrayed. The "setters" who earned the blood money were the Sham, who had no motive but greed, and Mangan, who while lining his pockets, believed he was protecting the interests of Ireland and the Roman Catholic Church.

The people of Ireland and the Roman Catholic Church were not aware of his role in the affair, so never expressed their gratitude to Mangan. He was well rewarded by the government, who gave him an annual pension of £200 for life, as well as a sinecure in the Four Courts. Mangan brought his secret to the grave. Many of Edward FitzGerald's loyal companions fell under suspicion of being the traitors in the years that followed. The finger was pointed at Samuel Neilson and Felix Rourke. Rourke, one of Edward's bodyguards, died with Robert Emmet in the aftermath of the 1803 rebellion. It was the great songster Thomas Moore, friend of Emmet and biographer of Lord Edward, who pointed the finger at Neilson. He received a stinging rebuke from a seventy-nine year old Archibald Hamilton Rowan. Moore accepted Rowan's view that Neilson had no case to answer. The Sham Squire's reports clearly reveal that it was he and Mangan who contrived the destruction of Edward FitzGerald, Ireland's most charismatic leader, a man who, even in the view of his enemies, was a person of great "honour, humanity, courage and good nature".[55]

Notes to Chapter Eleven
1. Smyth 1992, p. 148
2. Maher 1950, p. 101
3. Bartlett 2002, p. 100

4. Larkin 1991, p. 31
5. *Ibid.*
6. Newsinger 2001, p. 60
7. Graham in Bartlett 2003, p. 144
8. Newsinger 2001, p. 59
9. *Ibid.* p. 48
10. Graham in Bartlett 2005, p. 140
11. Whelan and Bartlett 1998, p. 173
12. Maher 1950, p. 106
13. *Ibid.*
14. Agnew 1998, vol. 1, p. 35
15. *Ibid.* p. 475
16. Fitzpatrick 1865, p. 5
17. *Ibid.* p. 6
18. *Ibid.* p. 6
19. *Ibid.* p. 12
20. *Ibid.* p. 11
21. *Ibid.* p. 15
22. *Ibid.*
23. *Ibid.*
24. See Garret 1973, p. 51
25. Bartlett 2005, p. 182
26. Redmond 2002, p. 14
27. O'Donnell 2003A, p. 33
28. Bartlett 2005, p. 88
29. *Ibid.* p. 33
30. Maher 1950, p. 98
31. *Ibid.*
32. *Ibid.* p. 98n
33. *Ibid.*
34. *Ibid.* p. 103
35. Bartlett 2005, p. 78
36. Maher 1950, p. 105
37. Binns 1854, p. 23
38. Maher, M., p. 106
39. Blackstock and Wichert 2004, p. 62
40. Smyth 1992, p. 153
41. McDowell 1940, p. 19
42. *Ibid.* p. 78
43. *Ibid.* p. 78
44. Thompson 1964, p. 203
45. O'Donnell 2003A, p. 92
46. Both names appear as the parents of children on the baptismal records of Great Strand Street.

47. *Ibid.*
48. Bartlett 2004, p. 78
49. *Ibid.* p. 100
50. Maher 1950, p. 102
51. Bartlett 2004, p. 48
52. Agnew 1999, vol. II, p. 6
53. Fitzpatrick 1865, p. 111
54. Newsinger 2001, p. 67
55. Fitzpatrick 1865, p. 188n

Chapter Twelve

REBELLION AND RETRIBUTION

23 May 1798, Dublin City
The mail coaches leaving the city have been stopped by armed men. Thousands of men are marching under arms in Kildare, Meath and Wicklow. As darkness approaches in Dublin, "army deployments in College Green and Dame St suggest that something serious is afoot".[1] The city lamplighters have not done their duty, and the streets are in total darkness. When the United Irishmen try to gather at their agreed muster spots, they find the military already in occupation. As dawn breaks, the city streets are deserted of all but the military. In the back alleys and lanes, the only clue to what might have been is the hundreds of pikes and other weapons discarded by the rebels.

The Pikes Come Out
After the arrests at Bond's house, a new leadership cadre of the United Irishmen was formed, consisting of FitzGerald, Neilson and John and Henry Sheares. The Sheares brothers were lawyers from Cork who had done much to spread the United Irish organisation as they toured the country on the legal circuit. FitzGerald was an experienced soldier, and he now believed he had command of 280,000 potential rebels.[2] The Sheares were taken up before the rebellion when they were entrapped by a British officer posing as an English republican.

FitzGerald had decided on 23 May for the rebellion to begin, but his capture on 17 May created utter confusion. As if all this was not bad enough, Samuel Neilson was

233

taken outside Newgate prison where he was apparently planning to rescue FitzGerald.

By 26 May, the Kildare rebels controlled a large swathe of territory in southern Kildare, but the rebels soon suffered defeat in Naas, Carlow and Tara, and they failed to capture Athy. Many of the more determined Dublin men left the city to join their comrades in the surrounding countryside. In north Wicklow and south County Dublin, rebels mustered at Rathcoole, Tallaght, Rathfarnham and Dalkey.

Soon the bodies of rebels were hanging from the bridges over the Liffey in Dublin, and many were hanged from the public lamp-posts.[3] When the Dublin rising collapsed in confusion, the Sham Squire reported that many weavers (mostly those who had been under the influence of Jemmy Hope) "quit the city to join the rebel standard" in the countryside.[4] Castlereagh heard from London that a French fleet had left Brest, and he pleaded for re-enforcements.[5]

The rebels in Wexford took to the field and, after fighting with desperate courage, defeated the North Cork militia at Oulart. When they overcame the Crown forces in this battle, some of the rebels were armed only with stones. When it was over, "a hundred Cork men lay on the plain",[6] and the rebels had one hundred extra muskets, swords, ammunition and bayonets.[7] When word of the rebel success spread, thousands flocked to their ranks. They went on to capture the towns of Enniscorthy and Wexford and held almost the entire county as they waited for a landing of the French. At Ballyellis, pikemen fought a close-quarter battle, defeating a large column of reinforcements and capturing a number of cannon.

Lord Kingston, whose troops had done much to goad the people of Wexford into rising, was captured by the United Irish navy off the coast of Wexford. They treated him well. He was able to return to his murdering and torturing ways after the suppression of the rebellion.

The rebels in Wicklow and Kildare took heart from Wexford, and their resistance stiffened. Michael Quigley

(Archibald Hamilton Rowan's bricklayer on the construction of Rathcoffey) proved to be a great asset to the Kildare men. He was a very talented military leader and fought with distinction, taking a leading part in the battles of Prosperous and Ovidstown.

The Presbyterians in Counties Antrim and Down were in confusion; many of their leaders had been taken up, and many more found they had not the heart to act without French help. Eventually, on 7 June, Henry Joy McCracken and Jemmy Hope brought out the Antrim men, and there was fighting at Larne and Randalstown. As they marched on towards Antrim town, Hope, a fearless soldier, went to the battle of Antrim singing the "Marseillaise" and a merry Irish tune.[8]

McCracken and Hope's pikemen were defeated at Antrim. In County Down, the rebels under Henry Munroe started well with a victory at Saintfield, but were finally overcome at the Battle of Ballinahinch on 13 June. With no French help, with senior leaders incarcerated and with Lord Edward dead from his wounds, the rebellion was over.

In August, a small troop of French soldiers landed in Killala and fought their way inland as far as Ballinamuck, County Longford. Thousands of Irish had joined the French. When the French surrendered, they were treated well and returned to France. The Irish who surrendered were massacred on the field.

The Aftermath

Murder, execution, banishment, and impressments into the fleet was all that were in store for the rebels and civilians as the forces of church and king wreaked a cruel vengeance. Arthur O'Connor reflected that "seventy of the most active of the union had been called in one by one to the Butcher's stake and the people throughout all Ireland had been beaten after a conflict without arms, ammunition, leaders or discipline".[9]

Leading the government terror and reprisal campaign was the apostate from Great Strand Street, Lord Castlereagh. He seemed to bring to his task what an Irishman of a later generation described as "all the added bitterness of an old friend". He was particularly vehement in his pursuit of the Presbyterian clergy.

Seventy-one Presbyterian clergymen had enrolled in the Society of United Irishmen in Ulster in the 1790s.[10] Lord Downshire had informed the government that "the Presbyterian Ministers are unquestionably the great encouragers and promoters of sedition".[11] The democratic element of the "call" to Presbyterian clerical appointment ensured that when they took up their duties as minister they were regarded as leaders of their community. These men believed strongly in the link between public and personal morality, and their sermons were often of a directly political nature as they sought to influence their congregations.

Thirty Presbyterian ministers were involved in the rebellion, most of whom were to pay dearly for their actions. Twenty-seven ministers, licensees and probationers were New Light (Non-subscribers) in their theology.[12] In the wake of the rebellion, "Three ministers were hanged, five ministers fled abroad, seven were sent to prison and four into exile".[13]

Rev. William Steel Dickson held a senior position in the United Irishmen and was reputed to have been the adjutant general of the rebel army in County Down. He was arrested prior to the rebellion, and eventually it was Henry Munroe from Lisburn who led the Down rebels at the battle of Ballinahinch. While being held in custody, Rev. Dickson gave spiritual comfort to Henry Joy McCracken a few hours before McCracken was executed.[14] When a friend of Rev. Dickson approached Lord Londonderry seeking the release of his lordship's former supporter, Londonderry said that everything was being done to procure evidence against Rev. Steel Dickson. This meant that pressure was being exerted on captured rebels and that deals and bribes were being offered for any evidence, no matter how dubious, to hang Dickson. Londonderry had been the beneficiary of Dickson's popularity in the past, but he now pointed out that such popularity made Dickson too dangerous to be released.

However treacherous Londonderry's and Castlereagh's behaviour was in the case of Rev. Steel Dickson, it pales in comparison to their treatment of another Unitarian clergyman who had once been a family friend. James Porter was arrested, tried and sentenced to death. "Billy Bluff and the Squire" must have wounded Londonderry, for although Porter had not taken up arms and had taken no part in the rebellion, Londonderry judicially murdered him out of pure personal spite,[15] Porter was arrested in the aftermath, and on the basis of very dubious evidence was hanged outside his Greyabbey meeting house. Porter's wife, with her youngest child in her arms, had pleaded in vain to Londonderry for the life of a man who had once been his friend. Near the Presbyterian meeting house at Greyabbey, there is stone which reads: "Sacred to the memory of Rev. James Porter, Dissenting Minister of Greyabbey who departed this life on July 2nd 1798."

When Dr Montgomery, a Unitarian minister, visited the place a few years later, he said the stone should have read: "Murdered by martial law for the crime of writing Billy Bluff." After the execution, Mrs Porter and her children were left destitute. When Captain Mercer, a friend of William Drennan and a wealthy member of the Great Strand Street congregation, died in 1800, it was rumoured that he left £300 to Rev. Porter's widow.[16]

Thomas Ledlie Birch, minister at Saintfield, had preached to the victorious rebels at their camp at Creevy Rock after the battle of Saintfield. He was something of an exception amongst the rebel clergy in that he was a Calvinist and not a Non-subscriber. When attending Glasgow, he had not imbibed the liberal religious principles which flourished there, but he did adopt its political radicalism and republicanism. He escaped the gallows through the influence of his well-connected brother and sailed to America.

Rev. Archibald Warwick, who was hanged at Kircubbin, achieved posthumous fame when, long after his death, Florence Wilson mentioned him in her recitation "The Man from God Knows Where". Wilson's ballad tells the story of how the United Irishman, Thomas Russell, was executed for attempting to raise the Ulster Presbyterians to rebellion with Robert Emmet in 1803. The narrator tells how, on a visit to Newtownards, he met a fellow rebel;

> I met McKee in the throng o' the street
> Says he, "The grass has grown under our feet
> Since they hanged young Warwick here."

> And he told me that Boney had promised help
> To a man in Dublin town,
> Says he, "If you still have your pike on the shelf
> Ye'd better run home hot foot by yourself
> And once more take it down.

Not content with the murder of Rev. Porter, Castlereagh continued to hunt down enthusiastically other rebels who had been his former political supporters and in many cases his friends. He was not above using his financial leverage to blackmail congregations into dismissing pro-United Irish ministers.[17]

Castlereagh, who remained a devoted servant of reaction throughout his life, committed suicide by cutting his throat in 1822. His death led to an "extraordinary outburst of public rejoicing" and "was hailed by the entire body of Liberals and Revolutionaries both in England and on the continent as if it had been the death of a tyrant".[18] Thousands of bystanders cheered as his coffin was brought to Westminster Abbey.[19] R.R. Madden called Castlereagh the "Robespierre of Ireland" and said his memory had "the faint sickening smell of hot blood about it".[20]

Percy Bysshe Shelley blamed Castlereagh for the

"Peterloo" massacre of unarmed workers who were attacked by cavalry at a pro-reform meeting in St Peter's Fields, Manchester, in 1819. Shelley was a son-in-law of William Godwin, and when visiting Ireland in 1812 to distribute his radical political tract had contacted Godwin's old friend, Archibald Hamilton Rowan. He therefore knew whereof he spoke when in his poem "The Mask of Anarchy" he wrote:

> I met Murder on the way –
> He had a mask like Castlereagh –
> Very smooth he looked, yet grim;
> Seven blood-hounds followed him:
>
> All were fat; and well they might
> Be in admirable plight,
> For one by one, and two by two,
> He tossed them human hearts to chew
> Which from his wide cloak he drew.

In the light of the terrible retribution visited on the Presbyterian clergy, it seems ironic that the opponents of the rebellion portrayed it as a Catholic sectarian affair from the start. The murder of defenceless Protestant women and children at Scullaboge, by rebels who had been defeated at New Ross, and the murder of Protestant prisoners on the bridge at Wexford by rebels defeated at Vinegar Hill gave credence to this view. Historians to this day battle with each other over this question. At the time, the government supporters had played a strong sectarian card and were anxious to portray the conflict in that light. Five of the leaders of the Wexford rebellion who were executed – Bagenal Harvey, Edward Roach, Esmond Kyan, Anthony Perry and Matthew Keogh – were Protestants, as was Joseph Holt, one of the leaders of the Wicklow rebels who survived the rebellion.

Miles Byrne of Monaseed, a Roman Catholic who fought in Wexford throughout the rebellion and was with Emmet in 1803, was anxious to stress that the rising in

Wexford was not a sectarian affair. He said that the Wexford insurgents had fought for a "perfect toleration for every creed and persuasion".[21]

Rev. Dickson, on his way to a long term of imprisonment at Fort George, was furious when it was suggested to him by visiting Scottish Presbyterian merchants that the rising was a Papist affair. His response was to write down the names of state prisoners and their religious affiliation. His list was as follows:

> **Catholics,** John Sweetman, John Swiney, Dr McNevin and Joseph Cormick
>
> **Presbyterians,** Wm Tennant, Robert Simms, Samuel Neilson, George Cumming, Joseph Cuthbert and Dr Dickson
>
> **Established Church,** T.A. Emmet, R. O'Connor, A. O'Connor, John Chambers, Matt Dowling, Thomas Russell, Edward Hudson, Hugh Wilson, Wm Dowdall and Robert Hunter.

Dickson's list did the trick, and he tells us, "We heard no more of Popish plots."[22]

The Role of the United Irishmen in Wexford

It suited the government at the time to portray the rebellion as a Papists' affair and ignore the fact that it was led and directed by liberal Protestants. It also suited early historians of the rebellion, such as the loyalist Richard Musgrave, to gloss over the participation of the Ulster Presbyterians on the rebel side. Roman Catholic historians were also happy to minimise the role of Protestants in the rebellion. In the nineteenth century, an Irish Roman Catholic priest, Fr P.F. Kavanagh, published a *Popular Account of the Rebellion of 1798* (Dublin 1870), echoing earlier Catholic versions of the story of how a mistreated Roman Catholic peasantry, led by their priests had spontaneously rebelled against that mistreatment. It is suggested that events in Wexford had little to do with the rising that had been attempted in Dublin and that the United Irish organisation was not well developed in Wexford.

However, there is one contemporary account of a witness who had no axe to grind, which suggests that the Wexford outbreak was indeed the work of the Society of United Irishmen and directed from the centre in Dublin. Jonah Barrington was a lawyer who wrote a memoir filled with stories of drinking bouts, duels and hunting squires in Ireland at the close of the eighteenth century. He was also a conservative supporter of government. He had occasion to visit Wexford in April 1798, two months before the rebellion, during which visit he dined at the house of Lady Colclough in Wexford town. In his company that night was Cornelius Grogan, a liberal Protestant and former MP for Wexford, Captain Matthew Keogh, afterwards rebel governor of Wexford, and Bagenal Harvey, who would soon lead the insurgents at the battle of New Ross. Bagenal Harvey invited Barrington to dine at his home, Bargy Castle. In the great banqueting hall, Barrington again met Keogh, John and Henry Sheares, John Colclough and John Hay. When the talk turned to the chances of success of a rebellion, Barrington became convinced he was amongst a group of "absolute though unavowed conspirators".[23]

Barrington made his excuses and hurried away. He immediately wrote to Edward Cooke in Dublin Castle, and while he named no names, he suggested that government troops should be sent to Wexford. His advice was not acted on, and Barrington observed that as a result the government lost Wexford and nearly lost Ireland.

Barrington's fellow diners suffered the chilling consequences of placing themselves at the head of an unsuccessful rebellion. Barrington tells us that besides himself, "every member of that jovial dinner-party was executed within three months". On his next visit to Wexford, he saw the heads of Captain Keogh, Mr Harvey and Mr Colclough on spikes over the courthouse door.[24] Cornelius

241

Grogan's head was on a spike also, but perhaps it was so badly decomposed that Barrington did not recognise him.

The fact that John Sheares discussed the prospects of success for the rebellion in Wexford with Bagenal Harvey before the outbreak not only suggests the Dublin leadership of the United Irishmen were involved in the planning of the Wexford rebellion, but it also connects events in Wexford right back to the nerve centre of the Dublin United Irishmen at Pill Lane.

The Death of Oliver Bond

When the rebellion was suppressed, the government began to execute those leaders against whom they had any evidence. The Sheares brothers were hanged on the evidence of Armstrong, an army officer who had gained their confidence by posing as an English republican.

Oliver Bond stood trial on 23 July 1798 and was defended by Philpot Curran. Armed soldiers in the courtroom constantly interrupted Curran and appeared to offer him violence. He told them, "You may assassinate, but you shall not intimidate me". After nineteen hours, the judge pronounced sentence:

> You, Oliver Bond, are to be taken from this place in which you stand to the gaol from whence you came and thence to the common place of execution, there to be hanged by the neck, but not until you are dead for while you are yet living your bowels are to be taken out and thrown in your face and your head is to be cut off, and your head and limbs to be at the king's disposal, and may the Lord have mercy on your soul.[25]

In order to stop further executions, Arthur O'Connor and the rest of the imprisoned United Irish leadership (the state prisoners) gave detailed statements of their involvement to the government. The deal was done to save the life of Bond. The government promised that in return for a full

242

statement of their involvement in the conspiracy, the prisoners, including Bond, would get a free pardon and be allowed to leave the kingdom.

The state prisoners gave their statements, and executions then ceased, but Bond's lifeless body was found outside his cell on the very day he received his reprieve. The man who "on the downfall of the Government would have been at the head of everything" was dead. Bond was popular with the Dublin artisans, but he had dangerous enemies within the ruling elite. Lords Carleton and Kilwarden had warmly urged the execution of Bond.[26] The authorities claimed that Bond died of natural causes, and his friends did not claim otherwise. However, he was "remarkably robust and not more than thirty-five years of age at the time of his death" [sic].[27] A friend, the Pill Lane silk manufacturer James Davock, had seen Bond in the prison yard the day before his death and found him in good health. William Drennan heard reports that Bond had, around this time, "collared his gaoler and had been clapped in irons in consequence".[28] On the night before his body was "discovered", the prison was reported to be in uproar, and some prisoners had barricaded their doors in fear of violence.[29] It is likely Bond was murdered by Simpson, the under-gaoler, on the orders of the Sham Squire.[30] The Sham had enjoyed an unwholesome relationship with the prison authorities from the time of his own incarceration over the Archer affair.

Because Bond's friends were anxious that his widow Eleanor would inherit his estate worth some £30,000, they did not challenge the official version of events. Eleanor's property was not confiscated, and she remained in business in Dublin until 1809. She then relocated her family to the United States. Following her bereavement, she had the social support of William Drennan and his Unitarian friends. In early July 1800 Drennan invited Mrs Bond to dinner to meet his new wife in the company of some of the more well-to-do families of the Great Strand Street,

Eustace Street circle. Drennan and Sarah entertained Eleanor Bond and her daughter along with the Huttons, the Welds and Rev. Taylor and his family.[31] Although this is the only record connecting Eleanor to the Dublin Unitarians, female names are remarkably few in these record books. However, in October 1785, an Ann Jackson is shown to have made a donation of £100 to the Eustace Street congregation's alms house.[32] Only a very wealthy woman could have made such a donation, which was about half William Drennan's annual income. It is very likely then that the donor was Eleanor Bond's mother, Mrs Henry Jackson.

Eleanor Bond emigrated to America in 1809. Her father had received permission to enter the United States in 1799 and bought land in Pennsylvania, but the urban industrialist could not settle in the country and joined his daughter in Baltimore. Henry Jackson died in Baltimore, Maryland, in 1817.[33] Before Eleanor left for America, she had a stone erected over the grave of her late husband in Saint Michan's churchyard at the western end of Pill Lane. Bond shares this peaceful resting place with Charles Lucas, his executed comrades John and Henry Sheares and the unfortunate Rev. Jackson, the agent of revolutionary France. In a remote, neglected and overgrown corner of Saint Michan's, Bond lies with other members of the Jackson family under a simple horizontal stone.

Eleanor had more than ten years to think about a suitable inscription for her husband. No reference is made to the circumstances of 1798 or the terrible events which led to his murder. To the Sham Squire he was a man of no religion and a Pill Lane king-killer. Bond had been the most formidable amongst the United Irish leaders and the trusted leader of the Dublin artisans, but Eleanor Bond was more concerned with his personal qualities than his political actions or opinions. She chose to inform posterity that "Oliver Bond died in July 1798 in the 39th year of his life" and that he was "the noblest work of God, an honest man". The United Irishmen got a small measure of revenge for Oliver Bond in 1803 when one of the aristocrats who had pressed hard for his execution, Lord Kilwarden, was piked to death in Thomas Street, Dublin, during Robert Emmet's rebellion.

Notes to Chapter Twelve
1. O'Donnell 2003A, p. 81
2. Curtin 1998, p. 259
3. O'Donnell 2003A, p. 83
4. Bartlett 2004, p. 48
5. Hames 2001, p. 183
6. United Irish song. "At the Hill at Oulart he displayed his valour, where a hundred Cork men lay on the plain."
7. Todd 2005, p. 254
8. Newsinger 2001, p. 74
9. Hames 1950, p. 182
10. Curtin 1998, p. 127, table 5.2
11. Campell 1991, p. 74
12. McMillan, in Swords 1997, p. 85
13. Boyd 1969, p. 2
14. *Ibid.*
15. Clifford 1991, p. 9
16. Agnew 1998, vol. II, p. 719
17. McMillan in Swords 1997, p. 94
18. Ingram 2005, p. 205
19. *Ibid.*
20. Fitzpatrick 1865, p. 198
21. Whelan 1998, p. xx
22. Clifford 1991, p. 100
23. Barrington 1997, p. 188
24. *Ibid.*
25. Maher 1950, p. 109
26. Fitzpatrick 1865, p. 147
27. Bond's headstone, in St Michan's, tells us he was in his 39th year when he died.
28. Agnew 1999, vol. II, p. 406
29. Fitzpatrick 1865, p. 147
30. *Ibid.*
31. Agnew 1999, vol. II, p. 609
32. RIA DUC EUS 1
33. Madden 1860, p. 183

Chapter Thirteen

EXILES IN AMERICA AND AFTER

6 February 1804: Northumberland, Pennsylvania
Thomas Jefferson, the president of the United States of America, is concerned to hear that his old friend, seventy-one-years-old Dr Joseph Priestley, has fallen seriously ill and is in danger of death. Jefferson takes a break from his hectic schedule to write to the old man, telling him, "yours is one of the few lives precious to mankind". A short while later, Dr Priestley calls John Binns to his bedside. Dr Priestley open his eyes, smiles at Binns and says, "I have now finished my life's work, I have nothing to be uneasy about, I am ready to depart."[1]

A Heart That Prized His Country's Good

Due to his exile, Archibald Hamilton Rowan did not participate in the rebellion of 1798. His wife Sarah shared his Unitarianism but not his politics, and she worried about his mixing with his radical friends in America. In particular, she had hated Wolfe Tone. She blamed Tone for her husband's exile and the fact that she was forced to remain on in Ireland without him in an effort to retain their property. A less partisan observer might have concluded that Rowan and his fellow Unitarians in the Jackson plot were responsible for Tone's troubles. Mrs Rowan wrote to her husband, pleading with him to stay away from Tone and Tandy. She urged him to shun their company in favour of that of Dr Priestley.

Rowan maintained contact with Dr Priestley and kept his wife Sarah informed by letter regarding Priestley's well-being and such matters as his sadness at the death of his wife, Mary, in September 1796. There is no evidence that Rowan paid any heed to Sarah's advice about his other associates. She felt that her husband was easily led by bad company. He responded that while "association did lead me more into active life than I wished", he also stressed that his sentiments "have always nearly been the same, and from education and principle I was led to assert and attempt to support a reform of parliament and equal liberty to all religious sects".[2]

Despite his biographer Rev. Drummond echoing Sarah and disparaging Tone, Rowan never wrote a critical word about Tone or any of his old comrades. On the contrary, it is clear from his correspondence that he remained loyal to and proud of his revolutionary friends to the end of his days. Even when petitioning for pardon, he stood by his political principles and declared:

> My opinions were not hastily adopted; they were nei-
> ther the result of pride, of ambition nor of vanity;
> they were the result of the most mature reflection of
> which I was capable: they cannot alter, and though I
> must desist from acting on them I never will disown
> them.[3]

Faced with the prospect of having to stay in America, Rowan displayed his humanitarianism. He declared that he would not shoot Indians and he would own no slaves.[4] Rowan eventually moved to Hamburg while Sarah lobbied, eventually with success, for a pardon. While in Hamburg, he offered to give whatever assistance he could to the newly released state prisoners from Fort George, most of whom had come to Hamburg after their release, at the risk of undermining Sarah's efforts on his own behalf. Thomas Addis Emmet acknowledged Rowan's brave, loyal and generous offer but declined to do anything which might damage Rowan.

Unlike many of the United Irishmen, Rowan favoured the proposed Act of Union in 1800. For Rowan, the Union meant the end of the corrupt parliament in College Green. Although a radical and revolutionary democrat, as well as a patriot who loved his country, he was not a nationalist. Rowan's republicanism was for all mankind. He might even have regarded the ethnocentric term "Irish Republican" as an oxymoron in that it subverts the very objective of the United Irishmen, which was to create a union based on universal liberty in the place of ethnic or religious division.

As a result of Sarah's efforts, Rowan was pardoned and allowed home to Ireland in 1806. He came home to his inheritance, Killyleagh Castle, and lived until 1834. He "retained a lively if sometimes clandestine sympathy for reform".[5] He remained loyal all his days to his political and religious principles and to his revolutionary friends, both living and dead. As an old man, Rowan made a typically courageous, but ultimately futile, stand in Killyleagh Presbyterian church against the theological backlash which defeated Protestant liberalism and social radicalism.

In 1828, Rev. William McEwen, a Unitarian minister at Killyleagh, published a poem entitled "Changes", in which he refers to Rowan, who still had another six years to live.

> His virtues knew and loved them well
> A mind with classic lore imbued
> A heart that prized his country's good
> The first to raise the patriot band
> When rose the valiant of the land
> Fair freedom traced his name on history's page
> Her bravest knight in youth, her steadiest friend in age.[6]

Dr Priestley's Last Years in America with John Binns

Following the defeat of the Irish and British reform movements, John Binns went to America in 1801, and there he became, in turn, a publisher, a judge and a successful politician. He moved to Northumberland to be close to Dr Priestley. When he married an Englishwoman, Ann Bagnerin from Shropshire, Dr Priestley officiated at his wedding. Binns and Ann went on to have ten children, all of whom except for a son and a daughter lived to adulthood. The one son who predeceased him rejoiced in a name that would not surprise anyone who understood Binns's politics. The son lost to him was Benjamin Franklin Binns.[7]

During their exile, Binns and Dr Priestley often remembered old times and old friends. Priestley once told Binns how, in the mid 1770s with Benjamin Franklin, he had gone to meet the British Privy Council and defended the revolt of the American colonists. After that meeting, Franklin had locked away his silk waistcoat and said that he would only ever wear it again when he was signing a treaty in which Britain recognised American independence.[8]

In March 1799, Sarah Hamilton Rowan wrote to her husband:

> I hear Priestley has lately published a very absurd book on religion; he has many enemies however, and I think it more than probable that the book is not at all what it is represented. I would thank you to get it for me that I may as I generally do judge for myself.[9]

John Binns published this book, which was entitled *The Doctrines of Heathen Philosophy Compared with Those of Revelation*. In this, his last book, Dr Priestley set himself the task of comparing the ethical systems of Aristotle, Jesus Christ, Plato, Pythagoras, Seneca and Socrates. Priestley had produced this work at the request of Thomas Jefferson. Long before the book appeared, the makers of the American Revolution had split into conservative and radical factions. One important issue between them was their differing attitudes to the French Revolution. Priestley supported the pro-French and anti-monarchist Jefferson. The conservative Federalists, ironically, were also led by another old friend of Dr Priestley's, John Adams, the second president of the republic. Adams was no friend to the

French, and his Federalists were hostile to the exiled United Irishmen who had managed to flee to America.

Though Joseph Priestley's countrymen had burned his house in Birmingham, his American house is still standing. It is said to be the first research laboratory in the United States. It is, to this day, a science museum which is maintained in Priestley's honour. It was a long time before his fellow Englishmen were prepared to honour one of their most learned and extraordinary men. As William Lloyd observed, "No more candid or gentlemanly controversialist ever defended an unpopular cause and no man less deserved the disgraceful treatment he received from his countrymen".[10] Finally, in 1874, Professor Thomas Huxley, the great champion of scientific evidence over religious superstition, sometimes known as "Darwin's Bull Dog", unveiled a statue of Priestley in Birmingham, England. The city of Birmingham finally acknowledged a great injustice and rehabilitated the reputation of its greatest citizen.

Notes to Chapter Thirteen
1. Binns 1854, p. 180.
2. Drummond 1840, p. 290
3. *Ibid*. p. 354
4. *Ibid*.
5. Orr 1998, p. 282
6. Millen 1900, p. 50
7. Binns 1854, p. 179
8. *Ibid*.
9. Drummond 1840, p. 335
10. Lloyd 1899, p. 182

Chapter Fourteen

ROBERT EMMET AND COLONEL DESPARD

23 July 1803, Dublin City
Hundreds of men from Kildare are leaving their places of employment and are drifting in small groups to Dublin city centre. They come on foot by road and along the banks of the Grand Canal. In many parts of the city, there are gatherings of working men who are under the direction of officers they trust. They are waiting for the rocket signal to indicate that the rebel effort to capture Dublin is on. Many of these men are the battle-hardened veterans of 1798, who have been told that this time it would not be pikes against cannon and that they will be issued with firearms. The confusion begins when the promised muskets are not available. Throughout the day the confusion escalates, and by nightfall, in spite of some impressive gallantry by small disciplined groups of pikemen, the signal to abort will be given, and Emmet's rebellion will end in failure. Without the capture of Dublin, without French help and without firearms, the Presbyterians of Ulster will not respond to the urgings of Thomas Russell. There will be no rising in Ulster.

The Endgame
Five years after the defeat of the great rebellion, Robert Emmet, the younger brother of Thomas Addis Emmet, made his attempt to establish a democratic secular republic in Ireland. Robert's brilliant academic career as a student in Trinity College had been interrupted in 1798 when he was expelled on account of his revolutionary politics. Since then he had been active in the revolutionary underground. He had visited Paris and had met and impressed

Talleyrand, Napoleon's minister. Emmet believed he had secured yet another pledge of French help for the United Irishmen.

Emmet had arrived back in Ireland from France and reorganised the revolutionary movement, concentrating his efforts on those who had proven their worth in '98. One of the many '98 veterans who flocked to Emmet was the redoubtable Jemmy Hope, the veteran of the Battle of Antrim. However, Emmet made a tactical error by asking Jemmy Hope to leave his power base amongst the Dublin weavers to help raise the Ulster Presbyterians. Wolfe Tone's old friend Thomas Russell risked execution by defying the Banishment Act when he returned to Ireland to help Emmet, as did Michael Quigley, the Kildare bricklayer. Under the favourable surrender terms won by the Kildare rebels, Quigley had emigrated to France in 1798.

Emmet had established secret weapons depots in various parts of Dublin city. An accidental explosion in one of his depots had forced Emmet to bring his planned rebellion forward. On 23 July 1803, pike-carrying working men from Dublin and Kildare briefly held their own against the 21st North British Fusiliers. However, Emmet's rebellion disintegrated from an organised uprising to a street riot in a matter of a few hours.

Three thousand men were incarcerated in the aftermath of the rebellion. Emmet's "Citizen Soldiers" were carpenters, weavers, tanners, chemical workers and bricklayers. More than six hundred of them were lodged in Kilmainham and Newgate. Twenty men were executed, including '98 veterans Felix Rourke, Henry Howley, and Owen Kirwan. The corpses of the executed were dumped in a mass grave at Bully's Acre, a paupers' burial ground at Kilmainham in Dublin.

Emmet stood trial in front of John Toler, the notorious "Hanging Judge" known to posterity as Lord Norbury. Although harassed and interrupted by Norbury and insulted by the prosecutor William Plunket, Emmet delivered a speech from the dock which is justly regarded as one of the greatest trial speeches in the English language. He was quickly dispatched to the executioner's block on 20 September 1803. His corpse and head were dumped into a pit in Bully's Acre. It is believed that his family had the body removed from there the following day. Irish nationalists would later make Emmet an icon. He wanted no epitaph, and the fact that his burial place is unknown has added to his mystique. No epitaph or marker of any kind marks the spot where his working-class followers are buried.

Emmet's rebellion was to have been supported by an uprising of British and Irish radicals in London under the leadership of the enigmatic Colonel Edward Marcus Despard. Despard was born in County Laois, Ireland in 1751, the youngest of six brothers, all of whom had careers in the British military. The Despard family has been described as a Cromwellian dynasty.[1] Despard had had an impressive career in the British military service in the Caribbean. In 1782, along with his young comrade Horatio Nelson, Despard had fought with distinction against the Spanish in territory known then as the Bay of Honduras, now Belize.

Although Nelson and Despard both emerged from this conflict as heroes, Despard gained the bigger reputation as Nelson had been wounded and so did not see the conflict through to the final British victory.[2] While still in his early thirties, Despard was made governor of the territory. In many conflicts between the propertied white interests and the interests of the dark-skinned natives, he was consistently determined that the native population should be treated fairly.[3] His enemies amongst the propertied interests lobbied against him and were scandalised when he married a native of the place, his dark-skinned wife Catherine.

In 1790, Despard and Catherine arrived in London so that Despard could answer to the authorities for a dispute he had with his opponents in the territories. He was also seeking payment of money owed to him by the government. Things did not go well for him. The government strung him along and refused either to deal with his financial claims or to confirm him in his post. As a result, in 1792 he went to a debtors' prison for two years. When he emerged from prison, he joined the United Irishmen and the London Corresponding Society. By 1797, the Sham Squire in Dublin was reporting that Despard was a spy for the French, and had applied to get a passport for Lord Edward FitzGerald and Arthur O'Connor to travel to Paris.[4] It was claimed that Despard had an officer's commission from the French and enjoyed the confidence of the Paris-based United Irishmen.

Despard was arrested in the round-up of radicals which followed the arrest of Binns, O'Connor and Coigley at Margate, and he was sent to prison at Coldbath Fields in Clerkenwell. This so-called "English Bastille" was a terrible place, where he was held in dreadful conditions for nearly three years without trial. Thirty inmates had been incarcerated for more than two years before Despard's arrival for their part in the naval mutiny on the Nore.

The Catholic aristocrat and United Irishman, Lord Cloncurry (Valentine Lawless) was most likely dissembling when he claimed in his memoirs not to have known Despard until he visited him in Coldbath Fields, but he was clearly telling the truth when he described the conditions:

> We found the Colonel, who had served many years in tropical climates, imprisoned in a stone cell six feet by eight furnished with a truckle bed and a small table. There was no chair, no fireplace, and no window. Scanty light was admitted into this abode through a barred but unglazed aperture over the door, which opened directly onto a paved yard at the time covered in snow.[5]

The floor of the cell was below ground level and was subject to flooding in wet weather. Catherine, who "was becoming distraught at his condition" as his near starvation diet "wizened him",[6] campaigned hard to have his conditions of confinement improved. Arthur O'Connor's close friend, Francis Burdett MP, who had known Despard in the LCS, supported her in her efforts. They were the only two gentlemen members of that organisation, most of the rest being artisans and tradesmen. Burdett's campaign on behalf of the prisoners made him very popular with the people of London.[7] The popular slogan was "Burdett and no Bastille".[8] When another MP, John Courtnay, visited the prison, he hailed a cab and said "take me to the Bastille".[9] The cabby knew exactly where to take him. This suggests that the democratic cause still had support in London during the worst times of oppression.

The poets Samuel Taylor Coleridge and Robert Southey, who were flirting with both Unitarianism and political radicalism at this point, may have been supporting Despard when they published "The Devil's Thoughts" in September 1799, which contained this verse.

> As he went through Cold-Bath Fields he saw
> A solitary cell;
> And the devil was pleased, for it gave him a hint
> To improve his prison in hell

Despard's conditions improved a little, for which Lord Cloncurry claimed some credit, but when Despard was finally released in 1801 it was due to the efforts of Catherine Despard and Burdett. After his release, Despard dropped out of sight and he may have paid a short visit to Ireland. One informer suggested that Roger O'Connor (a younger brother of Arthur O'Connor) had intended to move back to Bandon, and that his friend Colonel Despard would stay with him there.[10]

In November 1802, Despard was arrested with thirty of the "lowest order of people" in the Oakley Arms in Lambeth, London. His arrest was probably the result of the loose talk of William Dowdall, the former state prisoner who had come to Dublin as an agent for Despard. Dowdall's mission was to liaise with the United Irishmen, who were by now deeply involved in planning Emmet's rebellion. Jemmy Hope was horrified when he heard Dowdall speak openly of Despard's plans in the company of suspected informers. He warned Dowdall that he had placed himself in extreme danger.[11] The government was on to Despard, whether because of Dowdall's imprudence or otherwise, and it was clear at Despard's trial that he had been closely watched and his organisation infiltrated by spies and *agents provocateurs*.

At the trial Despard had three major problems, the first one being the question of what could a gentleman be doing in the company of bricklayers, carpenters and soldiers, if not planning treason? This example of circumstantial evidence also neatly captures what the Tories most hated about the democrats. That a man of high standing, in this case a British officer and war hero, was prepared to associate with the working class could not have an innocent purpose in Tory eyes.

Despard's second problem was that copies of an oath pledging support for the independence of Ireland and Britain and promises of support for those who fell in the conflict, were in the possession of the prosecution. The oath also contained a commitment to the equalisation of civil political and religious rights. This oath was similar to the United Irish oath, but it is clear that the objective was the independence of Britain as well as Ireland. Finally, there was a succession of witnesses to swear that Despard had discussed with them the logistics of attacking the king and killing him on his way to open parliament. Despard's old comrade, Horatio Nelson, appeared as a character witness at the trial, but to no avail. Despard and six others were sentenced to be publicly hanged, drawn and quartered.

Much of the evidence against Despard was fabricated. Rather than organising an attack on the king, Despard had been trying to forestall any action from the London militants until an expected French landing had taken place in Ireland.[12] Despard then intended to stage a diversion in England to support an uprising in Ireland, which was to occur the moment the French landed on Irish soil. The executive of the United Irishmen had given Despard these instructions, probably transmitted through John and Benjamin Binns.[13]

Despard maintained his innocence of the particular charges to the end, though he did admit that he had endeavoured with all his power to achieve freedom. It may be that Pitt knew what Despard's plans were, and his spies fabricated or part-instigated this particular plot as a pre-emptive strike.

It appears that in the months before his arrest he had travelled widely in England. If the trial witnesses were telling the truth, and if Despard had told them the truth, he had travelled on foot through Leeds, Birmingham, Sheffield and other cities, and was satisfied that the people were ripe for revolt. However, he may also have been to Ireland and may have met with Emmet's group.

Lord Cloncurry and William Dowdall had been the key intermediaries of the United Irishmen on the British mainland since 1797.[14] Cloncurry met Despard again after his release from Coldbath Fields in 1802 and claimed that Despard was deranged, driven mad by the injustices and the harsh imprisonment he had endured.[15]

However, nothing said either by Despard himself or by anyone else at this trial, or indeed in his dignified speech and demeanour at his trial and execution, suggests mental instability. To the end he was regarded by his fellow United Irishmen as being completely trustworthy. Why would Cloncurry put this claim of Despard's insanity on the record, if it were not true? Cloncurry was very likely involved with Emmet and Despard, but he had escaped detection. Better for him that the record should show that the British government had murdered an unfortunate man they had first driven mad than acknowledge one's own involvement with a conspiracy to organise a rebellion in Britain and Ireland.

Cloncurry did his comrade Despard one service that, perhaps, made up for the damage he did to his reputation. After Despard's death, Catherine Despard and her young child were alone in the world, far from her native land. A black woman and her child, the family of a disgraced traitor, they faced utter destitution. Cloncurry gave Catherine and her child a home at his Lyons estate in Newcastle, County Dublin.[16] Lord Cloncurry's reference to Lyons confused both of Despard's biographers, who assumed he was talking about the city in France rather than his estate in Dublin.

One remarkable difference between the Irish end of the plot run by Emmet and Despard's English operation was that Emmet took the authorities completely by surprise while Despard was compromised almost from the beginning. James Connolly, in *Labour in Irish History*, suggests that the reason the government was so much in the dark about Emmet's plans was because Emmet had relied on the workers, whom Connolly clearly regards as more trustworthy than the propertied, business and professional men who were the leaders in 1798. Yet Despard had also relied on the workers, and the government knew everything it needed to know about his plans. The reason for Emmet's success in keeping his plans secret may have a class basis. Certainly many of his co-conspirators had been members of the well-organised Dublin trade combinations that were well-used to keeping their activities secret and guarding against infiltration. Emmet brought into his confidence only those who had proven themselves in 1798, and this was an important aid to his security.

Despard had clearly proven himself in 1798, and before, and had worked with the Lord Edward, John Binns, O'Connor and Coigley. In his soldiering days, Despard had been a heroic officer who had always commanded the loyalty of his men in battle.[17] Most of the working-class democrats he had recruited remained steadfastly loyal to him. Only a few betrayed him, and some of them did so to save their own lives, and some were paid government agents from the outset.

Despard, who was aged fifty, was followed to the gallows by John Francis, a private soldier, aged twenty-three; John Wood, a private soldier, aged thirty-six; Thomas Broughton, a carpenter, aged twenty-six; James Sedgwick Wrageten, a shoemaker, aged thirty-five; John Macnamara, a carpenter, aged fifty; and Arthur Graham, a slater, aged fifty-three. The religion and nationality of this group was as follows: Despard was an Irishman of Cromwellian stock who was at the end "not particularly attached to any form of religion".[18] Macnamara was an Irishman and a Roman Catholic. The other five were Englishmen – Broughton and Francis were members of the Established Church and Graham, Wood and Wrageten were Dissenters.

When refusing an offer of religious consolation, Despard told the Rev. William Winkworth that "he believed in a Deity and that outward forms of worship are useful for political purposes", but that "the opinions of Churchmen, Dissenters, Quakers, Methodists, Catholics, savages and even atheists were equally indifferent".[19] Macnamara was comforted in his last hours by the same priest who had accompanied Coigley to the gallows. However, this priest attended Macnamara and Coigley for the same reason: he hoped to get information from the condemned men's confessions which would be useful for the government. Rev. Winkworth was up to the same dirty business in relation to Despard, but neither effort succeeded.

Upwards of twenty thousand workers stood in silent protest as Despard and his comrades were executed. The silence was only broken when the crowd cheered his references to liberty and justice. Despard told them:

> Fellow Citizens, I come here as you see after having served my country faithfully honourably and usefully served it for thirty years and upwards, to suffer

death upon a scaffold for a crime of which I must protest I am not guilty. I solemnly declare that I am no more guilty of it than any of you who may now be hearing me. But though his Majesty's ministers know as well as I do that I am not guilty, yet they avail themselves of a legal pretext to destroy a man because he has been a friend to truth, liberty and justice [there was a loud cheering from the populace] because he was a friend to the poor and the oppressed.

But Citizens, I hope and trust notwithstanding my fate and the fate of those who will no doubt soon follow me that the principles of freedom, of humanity and of justice will finally triumph over falsehood tyranny and delusion and every principle hostile to the interests of the human race. I have little more to add, except to wish you health, happiness and freedom, which I have endeavoured as far as was in my power to procure for you and mankind in general.[20]

Despard and his follow prisoners were executed on 21 February 1803. They were the last men to be hanged, drawn and quartered in England. In Ireland seven months later, Robert Emmet and twenty men of the lower orders were hanged and had their heads severed from their bodies in front of a throng of onlookers. Thomas Rusell was hanged at Downpatrick and then beheaded at the gate of the gaol on 21 October 1803, one month short of his thirty-seventh birthday. Jemmy Hope's extraordinary good luck held. He was never captured, he never surrendered, and he lived until 1847. In the last paragraph of his autobiography, which he narrated to R.R. Madden when he was eighty-one years old, he paid a tribute to two of his former leaders who were also his friends – Henry Joy McCracken and Robert Emmet.[21]

John Newsinger summed up the life of Hope after the defeat of the United Irishmen as follows: "He lived out the rest of his life as a working man remaining both a

Protestant and a republican, committed to social equality and social justice and the interests of working people both Catholic and Protestant."[22]

Robert Emmet's rebellion was the last stand of the United Irishmen. It has been portrayed as a hopeless, poorly organised farce that may have been encouraged by *agents provocateurs*. Recent study has suggested that it was a serious effort involving sophisticated planning, tight security and hardened revolutionaries. There had been a real chance of success. It was a lost opportunity undone by bad luck.

Some of Emmet's working-class citizen soldiers escaped to England and brought their democratic politics into the Luddite and Chartist movements. Within twenty years, Daniel O'Connell had led Roman Catholic Ireland to a nationalism that equated the cause of Ireland with the cause of Roman Catholicism, where there was no space for Dissenters or their universal republicanism. After Emmet, Irish politics fractured along sectarian fault lines, and the divisions persist today. Non-sectarian republicanism in Ireland died with Emmet and twenty working men in Dublin in 1803.

Notes to Chapter Fourteen
1. Butler 2007, p. 108
2. Jay 2004, p. 119
3. *Ibid.*
4. Bartlett 2004, p. 170
5. Cloncurry 1850, p. 36
6. Jay 2004, p. 289
7. Thompson 1964, p. 191
8. *Ibid.*
9. Jay 2004, p. 289
10. Conner 2000, p. 205
11. Madden 1860, p. 293
12. Connor 2000
13. Connor 2000, p. 207
14. Weber 1997, p. 147
15. Cloncurry 1850, p. 38
16. *Ibid.*

17. Jay 2004, p. 119
18. Despard Trial notes, p. 70
19. Linebaugh, p. 654
20. Madden 1860, p. 299
21. Newsinger 2001, p. 109
22. *Ibid*. p. 37

Chapter Fifteen

THE EMMET FAMILY
AND GREAT STRAND STREET

21 September 1799, Great Strand Street Meeting House
*Rev. Dr John Moody greets Mary Anne Emmet as she
arrives to marry Robert Holmes. Mary Anne is accompanied by her father and mother, Robert and Elizabeth, and
Robert Emmet junior, her younger brother. Mary Anne's
older brother Thomas Addis cannot attend the nuptials as
he is a prisoner at Fort George in Scotland.*

*Lord Castlereagh continues his reign of terror against
the defeated rebels and has displayed particular hatred for
those ministers who sided with the people. Rev. Moody has
recently learned that his brother, Rev. Boyle Moody, has
fallen victim to the fatal vengeance of Castlereagh. Thirty
years earlier, John Moody had baptised Castlereagh in this
very meeting house.*

*No public announcement of this wedding has been
made. A warrant has been issued for Robert Emmet, and
he risks arrest in order to be present. Robert Holmes has
been ostracised by his colleagues in the legal profession
because of his suspected sympathy for the rebellion. His
isolation will increase if it becomes public knowledge that
he is marrying into this notorious rebel family.*

The Emmets and the Dublin Dissenters
The Emmets were perhaps the pre-eminent republican fam-
ily in Ireland in the era of the United Irishmen. Robert
Emmet has no equal except for Lord Edward FitzGerald in
the pantheon of eighteenth century republican heroes. The
Emmets were members of the Established Church but seem

263

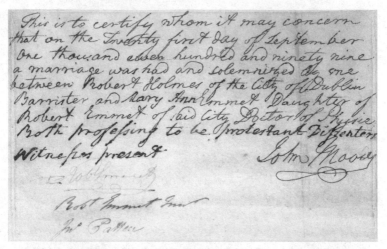

The signature of Robert Emmet as witness to the wedding of his sister

to have had many connections to the Great Strand Street Dissenters.

Thomas Addis Emmet was married to Jane Patten. Thomas and Jane were married in Great Strand Street and had their children baptised there. Jean was the daughter of a Dissenting minister, Rev. John Patten from Clonmel. Jane's mother, Margaret Colville, was herself a minister's daughter.

Jane's brother, John Patten, was a close friend of Robert Emmet.[1] He lived in the Emmet's home at St Stephens' Green and participated in secret political meetings with Robert prior to 1798.[2] He also accompanied Robert on a number of missions for the United Irishmen, including a visit to the state prisoners at Fort George in Scotland in 1801. Patten carried a brace of duelling pistols to Fort George so that Thomas Addis Emmet could settle his differences with Arthur O'Connor. It took all of Robert Emmet's considerable diplomatic skills to prevent this duel from taking place.

The Colville family had a long association with Great Strand Street and New Light Presbyterianism. Margaret Colville Patten's uncle, Rev. Alexander Colville, had been ousted from his post by the Dromore Presbyterian congregation of County Down in 1725. This was during the Non-subscription crisis when the Non-subscribers were ejected from the Synod of Ulster. Rev. Colville was supported at the time by the Dublin Dissenters.[3]

By the 1790s, Rev. Colville's nephew, William (Margaret's brother), was a wealthy merchant living in Dublin. William Colville had been guardian to Jane Patten Emmet following the death of her father.[4] William Colville contributed a large sum of money each year for the up-keep of the minsters, which entitled him to a family pew.

Colville may have sat in his pew on 21 September 1799, when Mary Anne Emmet married Robert Holmes. If Colville was present at the nuptials, he would have met Robert Emmet senior, Robert junior and John Patten, all three of whom stood as witness.[5] Just one day short of four years later, on 20 September 1803, Robert Emmet was executed in Thomas Street, Dublin.

In the aftermath of the Emmet rebellion in 1803, John Patten and Robert Holmes were arrested on suspicion of involvement and lodged in Kilmainham gaol. Patten described himself on the arrest sheet as "a merchant in partnership with Mr Colville".[6] Colville had several business interests, and he and Travers Hartley MP, another Great Strand Street committee man, were directors of the Bank of Ireland. Robert Emmet senior was an investor in the bank.

Colville employed a young man, Joe Palmer, in his business in Merchant's Quay. Major Sirr captured Robert Emmet in Joe Palmer's home in Harold's Cross on 25 August 1803. John Palmer, Joe's brother, was one of the men who had attempted to kill Major Sirr a few years previously, when he tried to apprehend Lord Edward FitzGerald in Watling Street.[7] Might William Colville have been involved with his employee in procuring Robert Emmet's hiding place? William Colville continued to be held in high regard by the surviving members of the Emmet family. Thomas Addis and Jane named the last of their eleven children, a boy born in 1807, William Colville Emmet.

The imprisonment of Robert Holmes in 1803 was hard on Mary Anne Emmet. Her parents had died and one of her brothers had been executed within a short space of time. Her surviving brother, Thomas Addis, had been banished from Ireland on pain of execution. Mary Anne had two children in her charge, her own daughter and her orphan niece, Katherine or Kitty. Mary Anne was pregnant at this time, and though she appears to have been unaware of it, she was also dying of consumption. On 2 February 1804, her son Hugh was baptised in Great Strand Street. Robert Holmes had been liberated from Kilmainham gaol just two days before the birth of his only son and is recorded as the child's parent.[8]

William Drennan informed his sister in September 1804 that baby Hugh Emmet Holmes had died. Less than six months later, on the evening of Sunday, 10 March 1805, Mary Anne herself succumbed to her illness.[9]

The Great Strand Street register also holds a clue to the resentment which many felt at the behaviour of William Plunket, the prosecutor at Robert Emmet's trial. Plunket's father was a Unitarian minister, and Plunket himself had defended the Sheares brothers when they were sentenced to death in 1798. By the time Emmet came to trial, Plunket had changed sides and was anxious to please his new masters in Dublin Castle.

When Plunket rose to sum up for the prosecution, Emmet had, in effect, conceded defeat and was already doomed. Plunket gratuitously berated and insulted the prisoner before the inevitable verdict and death sentence. He sneered at Emmet's provisional government of "the bricklayer, the baker and the old clothes man". His diatribe annoyed Emmet, and for the only time during the trial, Emmet's resolute demeanour was shaken. Martha

McTier thought Plunket's behaviour "a servile disgusting imitation".[10] Whether Plunket was betraying an old family friend or his own politics to impress his masters remains a matter of dispute.[11] Plunket ever after claimed he was never a family friend of the Emmets, but the Great Strand Street register reveals that he was a member of the same congregation as Thomas Addis, Jane Patten, and Mary Anne Emmet.

Christopher Temple, the son of Thomas Addis and Jane, was baptised in the Great Strand Street meeting house on 16 October 1790.[12] Plunket's children were baptised there also, and their names appear in the same register as young Hugh Emmet Holmes and Christopher Temple Emmet. Rev. John Moody officiated at the baptisms, the wedding and also the funeral service of Mary Anne.

William Drennan denounced Plunket in verse.

> When Emmet self convicted stood
> In fate already hung
> Plunket still longed to taste the blood
> And piked him with his tongue
> Now which of these Barbarians, say,
> Waged the most cruel war
> The savage of the bloody fray
> Or the savage of the bar?

In 1805, with most of the Emmet family dead and Thomas Addis banished, a refuge had to be found for Robert's orphaned niece Kitty. She was subject to nervous attacks, and according to William Drennan, "her terrors increased much at night since her Uncle Robert's lamentable end".[13] Drennan's wife Sarah had wanted to offer Kitty a refuge in her own home, but he was warned by his sister Martha not to take Kitty in "as her name in your house would rivet calumny".[14] Drennan always felt that his reputation for political radicalism had prevented him from making a decent living as a physician in Dublin, so he followed Martha's advice. Drennan advised that for medical reasons

Kitty should reside outside of Ireland, and she was taken to Sarah Drennan's home town, Wem, in Shropshire. These were the circumstances which resulted in Kitty Emmet going to live in Bath with the redoubtable Unitarian minister, Rev. William Hazlitt.[15]

If the Emmet family were the pre-eminent upper-class republican family in Dublin, Joe Palmer's family, who sheltered Emmet after the rebellion, have a similar claim in terms of the common folk who made up the ranks of the Dublin United Irishmen. Other than that Joe Palmer worked for William Colville, there is nothing to directly link the Palmer family to the Dublin Unitarians, but they were almost certainly Protestant Dissenters, and they had many New Light Presbyterian friends.

There is no mystery regarding their politics. The lord lieutenant described John senior as "the father of a notorious rebel" and suggested old John himself had been engaged in seditious activity in 1798.[16] Old John had helped Samuel Neilson to escape to America on a ship that left Ringsend in 1802.[17] He had a grocery business in the Coombe, and he it was who supplied the food for Emmet and his fellow conspirators as they planned their rising in the hideout at Butterfield Lane, Rathfarnham, County Dublin. He seems to have resented the expense of providing for sometimes as many as thirty people, and he called the house "the palace".[18]

John Palmer junior had accompanied Putnam McCabe, another Belfast Presbyterian, on many foreign ventures on behalf of the United Irishmen. Their travels took them to Hamburg, to France and to Fort George. Miles Byrne, who was a participant in many of the battles in Wexford in 1798 and an important staff officer in Emmet's rebellion, described Biddy Palmer, sister of John and Joe, "as like a heroine of olden times".[19] She had carried out dangerous missions in 1803 on behalf of Robert Emmet and Thomas Russell.[20] The Palmers were close friends to yet another Presbyterian radical, Jemmy Hope, whom they sheltered when he was a fugitive following his escape to Dublin after the Battle of Antrim in 1798.[21] The Palmer family were also associated with Patrick Gallagher, a United Irish colonel who had been wounded by Major Sirr when he, Putnam McCabe and John Palmer were protecting Lord Edward FitzGerald in the Watling Street incident.

Notes to Chapter Fifteen

1. O'Donnell 2003A, p. 41
2. *Ibid.*
3. "A short history of the First Presbyterian Church of Dromore"
4. RIA DUC STR 3
5. Marriage Certificate DUC
6. O'Donnell 2003B, p. 220
7. Newsinger 2001, p. 67
8. Dublin Unitarian Church Baptismal register
9. Agnew 1999, vol. II, p. 332
10. Agnew 1999, vol. III, p. 153
11. Ryan 2007
12. Great Strand Street Baptismal records from 1750
13. O'Donnell 2003B, p. 162
14. *Ibid.* p. 181
15. Elliot 2003, p. 126
16. O'Donnell 2003A, p. 228
17. *Ibid.* p. 190
18. Byrne 1955, p. 177
19. *Ibid.* p. 168
20. *Ibid.* p. 28
21. *Ibid.* p. 130

Epilogue

In August of 1827, Archibald Hamilton Rowan, by now seventy-six years old, stood up in his pew in the Presbyterian church at Killyleagh in County Down. Reacting to a fundamentalist onslaught from Rev. Henry Cooke, he tried to defend his Unitarian Protestant principles. Cooke was leading a crusade to purge New Light Presbyterian ministers and to lead their congregations into the Presbyterian mainstream. Cooke ordered the congregation to abandon Rowan and to leave the church. These people had once been fiercely proud and independent and at one time would not have been dictated to by a priest or prelate. Some of the older members of the congregation would have been veterans of the battles of Saintfield and Ballinahinch, but they were demoralised by the crushing defeat they had suffered in 1798.

They obeyed Cooke's instruction and walked away, leaving their former Volunteer leader, their United Irish hero who had also been their neighbour and benefactor, "standing erect in the pew alone his testament unread".[1] Thus was liberal Dissenting Protestantism defeated by what it most abhorred, "an intolerant high priest" and a submissive congregation. That day in Killyleagh meeting house, freedom of conscience bowed before the dictates of a priest. The millenarian hopes of Dr Joseph Priestley and Thomas Russell were well and truly shattered. The Book of Revelation did not contain prophecies after all but fantastical illusions. There would be no "age of virtue" and no time of plenty for humankind. There would be no non-sectarian democratic politics for modern Ireland.

Archibald Hamilton Rowan's liberal religion and

revolutionary politics were the product of a long tradition. His fellow United Irishmen Robert Emmet and Colonel Despard had been killed and their bodies mutilated on the executioner's block. One hundred and forty-three years previously, Hugh Peter was treated with comparable barbarity in revenge for Charles I. Hugh Peter, John Cooke, Algernon Sidney, William Lord Russell, Marcus Despard and Robert Emmet were republican martyrs, links in a chain through two hundred years of struggle for religious toleration, an end to arbitrary power and liberty for humankind.

The Protestant Dissenters in the era of Oliver Cromwell had established and then lost their republic. Throughout the seventeenth and eighteenth centuries in the reign of the Stuarts and the Hanoverians, the Dissenters continued to demand religious toleration and political reform, which they referred to as civil and religious liberty. The Commonwealthmen John Toland, Rev. John Abernethy, William Bruce, Rev. James Duchal and Francis Hutcheson were the champions of reason and enemies of "priestcraft" and tyranny. Their ideas were transmitted to several generations who made up the congregations at Wood Street/Great Strand Street and New Row/Eustace Street.

Archibald Hamilton Rowan, William Drennan, Oliver Bond, Henry Jackson, Arthur O'Connor and Samuel Neilson were brought up to believe that freedom of conscience, and civil and religious liberty, were the birthright of every citizen who would not be a slave.

The Dublin Dissenters had come to the city in 1649 with Oliver Cromwell. One hundred and forty years later, their descendants were still republicans. They were men of enlightened democratic politics and liberal religion. They created a non-sectarian organisation which reached out to Irishmen of every creed. They were dedicated to achieving the Rights of Man. They called their organisation "The Society of United Irishmen". Less noble spirits called them "the king-killers of Pill Lane".

The United Irishmen were utterly defeated in their own time. For two hundred years, both their ideological foes and their would-be admirers have overlooked the importance of their Cromwellian heritage. However, the values they held dear, such as the right to individual conscience and opinion, the right of people to choose or change their government, the rights of man and civil and religious liberty are the foundation stones of modern secular democracy.

Notes to Epilogue
1.   Orr 1998, p. 225

Appendix 1

In a letter dated 12 July 1802, some months before his death, Samuel Neilson wrote the following to Archibald Hamilton Rowan:

> Neither in the eight years' hardships I have endured, the total destruction of my property, nor the forlorn state of my wife and children, the momentary failure of our national exertions nor the still more distressing usurpation in France, has abated my ardour in the cause of my country and general liberty. You and I my dear friend will pass away but truth remains. Christ was executed upon a cross, but his morality has been gaining ground this eighteen hundred years in spite of superstition and priest-craft... I lodge at Jacob Heuserman's little Fisher Street no. 248 and will remain ever your sincere friend
>
> Samuel Neilson.[1]

Notes to Appendix 1
1. Drummond 1840, p. 436

Primary Sources

Royal Irish Academy
The Dublin Unitarian Church Collection
STR 2
STR EUS 1
EUS 2
EUS 3
EUS 4
EUS 5
Marriage and Baptismal register, 1750–1810, Unitarian Church, St Stephen's Green

Note: EUS = Eustace Street; STR = Strand Street

Bibliography

Ackroyd, Phillip. *Blake*. London: Sinclair Stephens, 1995.

Agnew, Jean, ed. *The Drennan McTier Letters 1776–1819* (3 vols). Dublin: Irish Manuscript Commission, 1998,1999.

Ambrose, Tom. *Godfather of the Revolution:The Life of Phillip Egalite Duc D'Orleans*. London: Peter Owen, 2008.

Andrews, S. *Unitarian Radicalism: Political Rhetoric 1770–1814*. New York: Palgrave Macmillan, 2003.

Aptheker, Herbert. *The American Revolution*. New York: International Publishers, 1960.

Armstrong, Rev. James, M.A. "Presbyterian Congregations in Dublin, in the Ordination Service of James Martineau", Dublin, 1829.

Ashley, Maurice. *England in the Seventeenth Century 1603–1714*. London: Penguin, 1960.

Barnard, Toby. "The Government and Irish Dissent", in Herlihy, K. (ed), *The Politics of Irish Dissent, 1650–1800*. Dublin: Four Courts, 1997.

Barnard, Toby. *Cromwellian Ireland: English Government and Reform in Ireland*. Oxford: Clarendon Press, 2000.

Barnard, Toby. *Irish Protestant Ascents and Descents 1641–1770*. Dublin: Four Courts, 2004A.

Barnard, Toby. *The Kingdom of Ireland 1641–1760*. New York: Palgrave, 2004B.

Barrington, Jonah. *Personal Sketches and Recollections of His Own Time*. Dublin: Ashfield, 1997.

Bartlett, Thomas. *Theobald Wolfe Tone*. Dublin: Lilliput, 1998.

Bartlett, Thomas. *Revolutionary Dublin 1795–1801: The Letters of Francis Higgins to Dublin Castle*. Dublin: Four Courts, 2004.

Bartlett, Thomas. *1798: A Bicentenary Perspective*. Dublin: Four Courts, 2005.

Binns, John. *Recollection of a Life, Twenty-Nine Years in Europe and Fifty-Three Years in America*. Philadelphia: Parry and M'Millen, 1854.

Blackstock, Alan. "The Rector and the Rebel" in Wishert, Sabine, ed. *A Festschrift for A.T.Q. Stewart*. Dublin: Four Courts, 2004.

Bonwick, Colin. "Joseph Priestley, Emigrant and Jeffersonian", *Enlightenment and Dissent*, no. 2, 1983.

Bibliography

Bonwick, Colin. *The American Revolution*. New York: Palgrave, 1991.

Boyd, Andrew. *Holy War in Belfast*. Tralee: Anvil, 1969.

Boyd, Andrew. *Montgomery and the Black Man*. Dublin: Columba, 2006.

Boylan, Henry. *Wolfe Tone*. Dublin: Gill and Macmillan, 1981.

Brown, Michael. *Francis Hutcheson in Dublin*. Dublin: Four Courts, 2002.

Burke, Edmund. *Reflections on the Revolution in France*. London: Penguin, 2004.

Butler, David J. *South Tipperary 1570–1841: Religion, Land and Rivalry*. Dublin: Four Courts, 2007.

Byrne, Patrick. *Lord Edward FitzGerald*. Dublin: Talbot Press, 1955.

Campbell, Flann. *The Dissenting Voice, Protestant Democracy in Ulster from Plantation to Partition*. Belfast: Blackstaff, 1991.

Campion, Justin, ed. *Nazarenus/John Toland*. Oxford: Voltaire Foundation, 1999.

Campion, Justin. *Republican Learning: John Toland and the Crisis of Christian Culture 1696–172*. Manchester: Manchester University Press, 2003.

Childs, John. *The Williamite Wars in Ireland, 1688–1691*.

Chryssides, G. *The Elements of Unitarianism*. New York: Element, 1998.

Clifford, Brendan. *Belfast in the French Revolution*. Belfast: Historical and Educational Society, 1989.

Clifford, Brendan. *Scripture Politics the Works of William Steel Dickson*. Belfast: Athol, 1991.

Cloncurry, Lord. *Personal Recollections of Life and Times*. Dublin: McGlashan, 1850.

Conner, Clifford D. *Colonel Despard: The Life and Times of an Anglo Irish Rebel*. Conshohocken, PA: Combined Pub., 2000.

Connolly, James. *Collected Works vol. I*. Dublin: New Books, 1987.

Connolly, S. J. *Religion Law and Power: The Making of Protestant Ireland 1660–1760*. Oxford: Clarendon, 2002.

Connolly, S.J. *Divided Kingdom: Ireland 1630–1800*. Oxford: Oxford University Press, 2008.

Connolly, James. "Labour in Irish History", *Collected Works*, vol l. Dublin: New Books, 1987.

Cullen, Sheamus. *The Emmett Rebellion in Kildare*. Naas: Leinster Leader, 2003.

Curtin, Nancy. *The United Irishmen: Popular Politics in Ulster and Dublin, 1791–1798*. Oxford: Clarendon Press, 1998.

Dickson, David, et al, eds. *The United Irishmen: Republicanism, Radicalism and Rebellion*. Dublin: Lilliput, 1994.

Dillon, Patrick. *The Last Revolution: 1688 and the Creation of the Modern World*. London: Jonathan Cape, 2006.

Bibliography

Donlan, Sean Patrick, ed. *Edmund Burke's Irish Identities*. Dublin: Irish Academic Press, 2007.

Doyle, David Noel. *Ireland, Irishmen and Revolutionary America, 1760–1820*. Dublin: Mercier, 1981.

Dutton, John. *The Dublin Scuffle*. Dublin: Four Courts Press, 2000.

Drummond, William, ed. *Autobiography of Archibald Hamilton Rowan*. Dublin: Thomas Tegg, 1840.

Elliott, Marianne. *Robert Emmet: The Making of a Legend*. London: Profile Books, 2003.

Emlyn, Thomas. *Emlyn Tracts* Volume 11 Darby Browne. London: 1731.

Eshet, Dan. "Rereading Priestley: Science at the Intersection of Theology and Politics", *History of Science*, vol. 39, 2001.

Esson, D.M.R. *The Curse of Cromwell: a History of the Ironsides Conquest of Ireland 1649–53*. Chesham: Combined Academic, 2009.

Fauske, Christopher J. *Jonathan Swift and the Church of Ireland, 1710–1724*. Dublin: Irish Academic Press, 2002.

Ferguson, Frank, ed. *Ulster-Scots Writing: an Anthology*. Dublin: Four Courts Press, 2008.

Fitzpatrick, W.J. *The Sham Squire and the Informers of 1798*. Dublin: M.H. Gill and Son, 1865.

Fraser, Antonia. *Cromwell Our Chief of Men*. London: Weidenfeld & Nicolson, 1977.

Gabriel, Micheal P. *Major General Richard Montgomery: The Making of an American Hero*. London: Associated University, 2002.

Garret, Clarke. "Joseph Priestley, the Millennium and the French Revolution", *Journal of the History of Ideas* 34.1, 1973.

Gilchrist, Alexander. *The Life of William Blake*, 1863.

Gordon, Lyndall. *Mary Wollstonecraft: A New Genus*. London: Little, Brown, 2005.

Greaves, R.L. "Radicals, Rights and Revolution: British Nonconformity and the Roots of the American Experience", *Church History*, vol. 61, no. 2, June 1992.

Grayling, A.C. *The Quarrel of the Age: The Life and Times of William Hazlitt*. London: Phoenix, 2001.

Gregg, Pauline. *Free-born John: The Biography of John Lilburne*. London: Phoenix, 2000.

Gribben, Crawford. *God's Irishmen: Theological Debates in Cromwellian Ireland*. New York: Oxford University Press, 2007.

Hames, Jane Hayter. *Arthur O'Connor: United Irishman*. Cork: Collins Press 2001.

Hanna, W.A. *Intertwined Roots: An Ulster-Scots Perspective*. Blackrock: Columba Press, 2000.

Bibliography

Harris, Tim. *Revolution: The Great Crises of the British Monarchy 1685–1720*. London: Penguin, 2006.

Harrison, Alan. *John Toland (1670–1722)*. Baile Átha Cliath: Coiscéim, 1994.

Herlihy, Kevin, ed. *The Politics of Irish Dissent, 1650–1800*. Dublin: Four Courts Press, 1997.

Herlihy, Kevin, ed. *Propagating the Word of Irish Dissent, 1650–1800*. Dublin: Four Courts Press, 1998.

Herman, Arthur. *How the Scots Invented the Modern World*. New York: Three Rivers Press, 2001.

Hibbert, Christopher. *Charles I: A Life of Religion, War and Treason*. New York: Palgrave, 2007.

Hill, Christopher. *The World Turned Upside Down*. London: Penguin, 1991.

Hill, Christopher. *Society and Puritanism in Pre-Revolutionary England*. London: Pimlico, 2003.

Hill, Jacqueline. *From Patriots to Unionists: Dublin Civic Politics and Irish Protestant Patriotism, 1660–1840*. Oxford: Clarendon Press, 1997.

Hill, Jacqueline. "Dublin Corporation, Dissent and Politics, 1660–1800", in Herlihy Kevin, ed., *The Politics of Irish Dissent 1650–1800*. Dublin: Four Courts Press, 1999.

Holmes, Clive. *Why Was Charles I Executed?* New York: Hambledon Continuum, 2006.

Houston, Alan Craig. *Algernon Sidney and the Republican Heritage in England and America*. Princeton: Princeton University Press, 1991.

Hume, David. *"To Right Some Things That We Thought Wrong...": The Spirit of 1798 and Presbyterian Radicalism in Ulster*. Belfast: The Ulster Society, 1998.

Hunt, Tristram. *The English Civil War*. London: Phoenix, 2002.

Ingrams, Richard. *The Life and Adventures of William Cobbett*. London: Harper Perennial, 2005.

Jay, Mike. *The Unfortunate Colonel Despard*. New York: Bantam, 2004.

Kennedy, Brian. *The Scots-Irish in the Mountains of Tennessee*. Londonderry: Causeway, 1995.

Kilroy, Phil. *Protestant Dissent and Controversy in Ireland, 1660–1714*. Cork: Cork University Press, 1994.

Larkin, John, *The Trial of William Drennan*. Dublin: Irish Academic Press, 1991.

Livesey, J., ed. *Arthur O'Connor: The State of Ireland*. Dublin: Lilliput, 1998.

Lloyd, Walter. *The Story of Protestant Dissent and English Unitarianism*. London: Phillip Green, 1899.

Bibliography

Macaulay, T.B. "The Monmouth Rebellion", in *History of England*. London: 1851.

McBride, Ian. "William Drennan and the Dissenting Tradition", in Dickson et al, *The United Irishmen: Republicanism, Radicalism and Rebellion*. Dublin: Lilliput, 1993.

McBride, Ian. *Eighteenth Century Ireland*. Dublin: Gill & Macmillan, 2009.

McDowell, R.B. *The Personnel of the Dublin Society of United Irishmen, 1791–4*. Dublin: Irish Historical Studies, 1940.

McDowell, R.B. *The Proceedings of the Dublin Society of United Irishmen*. Dublin: Irish Manuscripts Commission, 1998.

McFarland, E.W. *Ireland and Scotland in the Age of Revolution*. Edinburgh: Edinburgh University Press, 1994.

Mac Giolla Easpaig, T. *Tomás Ruiséil*. Baile Átha Cliath: Cló Moran, 1957.

McKeiver, Philip. *A New History of Cromwell's Irish Campaign*. Manchester: Advance Press, 2007.

McNeill, Mary. *The Life And Times of Mary Ann McCracken, 1770–1866: A Belfast Panorama*. Belfast: Blackstaff, 1960.

Madden, R.R. *The United Irishmen: Their Life and Times*. Dublin: The Catholic Publishing and Bookselling Co., 1860.

Manning, Brian. *Revolution and Counter-Revolution in England, Scotland and Ireland*. London: Bookmarks, 2003.

Maguire, William J. *Irish Literary Figures*. Dublin: Metropolitan, 1945.

Maher, Maura. "Oliver Bond", *Dublin Historical Record*, September–November, 1950.

Mansergh, Danny. *Grattan's Failure; Parliamentary Opposition and the People in Ireland, 1779–1800*. Dublin: Irish Academic Press, 2005.

Maguire, W.A., ed. *Up in Arms: The 1798 Rebellion in Ireland*. Belfast: Ulster Museum, 1998.

Miller, Kerby A., et al. *Irish Immigrants in the Land of Canann: Letters and Memoirs from Colonial and Revolutionary America, 1675–1815*. Oxford: Oxford University Press, 2003.

Moody, T.W. and Vaughan, W.E. *Eighteenth Century Ireland, 1691–1800*. Oxford: Oxford University Press, 1986.

Moore, Susan Hardman. *Pilgrims: New World Settlers & the Call Home*. New Haven and London: Yale University Press, 2007.

Morgan, W. "Memoirs of the Life of Rev. Richard Price, London 1815, in *Enlightenment and Dissent*, vol. 22, 2003.

Moyne, E. J. "The Reverend William Hazlitt: A Friend of Liberty in Ireland during the American Revolution", *William and Mary Quarterly*, third series, vol 21, no 2, April 1964.

Murphy, Sean. *Forgotten Patriot: Charles Lucas, 1713–1771*. Bray: Irish Centre for Genealogical Studies, 2009.

Bibliography

Nash, Gary B. *The Unknown American Revolution*. London: Viking, 2005.

Nelson, Craig. *Thomas Paine: Enlightenment, Revolution, and the Birth of Modern Nations*. New York: Viking, 2006.

Newsinger, John, ed. *United Irishman: The Autobiography of Jemmy Hope*. London: Merlin, 1992.

Ní Mhurchú, Maire agus Breathnach, Diarmuid. *1560–1781 Breathaisnéis*. Baile Átha Cliath: an Clóchmar, 2001.

O'Brien, Conor Cruise. *The Great Melody: A Thematic Biography of Edmund Burke*. London: Sinclair Stevenson, 1993.

O'Brien, William. *Edmund Burke as an Irishman*. Dublin: M.H. McGill and Sons, 1926.

O'Donnell, Ruán. *Robert Emmett and the Rebellion of 1798*. Dublin: Irish Academic Press, 2003A.

O'Donnell, Ruán. *Robert Emmett and the Rising of 1803*. Dublin: Irish Academic Press, 2003B.

Orr, Phillip. "Doing History", in Hill, Myrtle; Turner, Brian; Dawson Kenneth, eds, *1798 Rebellion in County Down*. Newtownards: Colourpoint, 1998.

Orr, Philip. "The Ingenious Mr Hutcheson", Down County Museum, 2000.

O'Toole, Fintan. *A Traitor's Kiss: The Life of Richard Brinsley Sheridan*. London: Granta, 1997.

Paine, Thomas. *Rights of Man*, in Foot, Kramnick, eds. *The Thomas Paine Reader*. London: Penguin, 1987.

Paulin, Tom. *The Day Star of Liberty: William Hazlitt's Radical Style*. London: Faber and Faber, 1998.

Philip, Mark, ed. *The French Revolution and British Popular Politics*. Cambridge: Cambridge University Press, 1991.

Pincus, Steve. *1688: The First Modern Revolution*. New Haven and London: Yale University Press, 2009.

Porter, Roy. *Enlightenment: Britain and the Creation of the Modern World*. London: Penguin, 2001.

Priestley, Joseph. *A free address to those who have petitioned for the repeal of the late Act of parliament in favour of Roman Catholics*, 1780.

Quinn, John. *Soul on Fire, a Life of Thomas Russell*. Dublin: Irish Academic Press, 2002.

Redmond, Sean. "Partners in Revolt", published by author, 33 Lindsay Rd., Dublin, 2002.

Reilly Tom. *Cromwell: An Honourable Enemy*. Dingle: Brandon, 1999.

Robbins, Caroline. *The Eighteenth-Century Commonwealthman*. Indianapolis: Liberty Fund, 1987.

Bibliography

Robertson, Geoffrey. *The Tyrannicide Brief: The Man Who Sent Charles I to the Scaffold*. London: Chatto & Windus, 2005.

Rodgers, Nini. *Equiano and the Anti-Slavery Movement in Eighteenth-Century Belfast*. Belfast: Belfast Society and Ulster Historical Foundation, 2000.

Ryan, Maeve. "The reptile that had stung me: William Plunket and the Trial of Robert Emmet", in Dolan et al, *Reinterpreting Emmet*. Dublin, University College Dublin Press, 2007.

Small, Stephen. *Political Thought in Ireland, 1776–1798: Republicanism, Patriotism and Radicalism*. Oxford: Oxford University Press, 2002.

Smyth, Jim. *Men of No Property: Irish Radical and Popular Politics in the late Eighteenth Century*. New York: St Martin's Press, 1992.

Shannon, Millen. *History of the Second Congregation of Protestant Dissenters in Belfast*. Belfast: Baird, 1900.

Smyrl, Steven C. *A Dictionary of Dublin Dissent: Dublin's Protestant Meeting Houses, 1660–1920*. Dublin: A&A Farmar, 2009.

Stewart, A.T.Q. *A Deeper Silence: The Hiddens Origins of the United Irishmen*. Belfast: Blackstaff, 1993.

Swords, Liam, ed. *Catholic, Protestant and Dissenter: The Clergy and 1798*. Dublin: Columba, 1997.

Taylor, Barbara. *Mary Wollstonecraft and the Feminist Imagination*. Cambridge: Cambridge University Press, 2003.

Thompson, E.P. *The Making of the English Working Class*. London: Penguin, 1964

Tillyard, Stella. *Citizen Lord: Edward FitzGerald 1663–1798*. London: Chatto & Windus, 1997.

Todd, Janet. "Ascendancy: Lady Mount Cashel, Lady Moira, Mary Wollstonecroft and the Union Pamphlets in Eighteenth Century Ireland", vol. 18, Dublin, 2003.

Todd, Janet. *Daughters of Ireland: The Rebellious Kingsborough Sisters and the Making of a Modern Nation*. New York: Ballantine Books, 2005.

Twomey, Brendan. *Dublin in 1707: A Year in the Life of the City*. Dublin: Four Courts, 2009.

Uglow, Jenny. *The Lunar Men: The Friends Who Made the Future*. London: Faber & Faber, 2003.

Weber, Paul. *The United Irishmen in Hamburg, 1796–1803*. Dublin: Four Courts, 1997.

Wells, Roger. *Insurrection: the British Experience, 1795–1803*. London: Alan Sutton, 1986.

Whelan, Kevin. *The Tree of Liberty: Radicalism, Catholicism, and the Construction of Irish Identity*. Cork: Cork University Press, 1996.

Whelan, Kevin and Bartlett Thomas. eds. *The Memoirs of Miles Byrne*. Wexford: Duffy Press, 1998.

Bibliography

Williams, G.A. *Artisans and Sans-cullottes.* London: Edward Arnold, 1968.

Withers, Henry. *Oliver Cromwell the Champion of Liberty.* London: Religious Tract Society, 1930.

Worden, Blair. *Roundhead Reputations: The English Civil War and the Passions of Posterity.* London: Penguin, 2002.

STEPHEN MACDONOGH

*Barack Obama – The Road From Moneygall**

"The first full account of the US president's links with Ireland... is also a thought-provoking study of what it means to be Irish, and how the Irish story goes beyond any simplistic identification with a single religion." *The Irish Times*

"What makes the book so fascinating is not just the way it brings Obama's Irish ancestors to life. This is not just the story of one family, it's the story of how America was made, starting before the American Revolution and following the creation of the country by the pioneers who moved out from the east into the frontier to settle the land. It's a story of hardship, courage and great adventure." *Irish Independent*

"This superb book [is a] riveting reconstruction of Barack Obama's Offaly ancestors... a brilliant book". *Sunday Independent*

"A thoughtful and scholarly work that traces the exodus of several generations of Irish Protestants to the US... and their role as pioneering settlers in the western territories... Obama should be grateful to ... Steve MacDonogh for researching his family history so thoroughly." *Books Ireland*

ISBN 9780863224133

* published in the USA as
Pioneers: The Frontier Family of Barack Obama
(ISBN 9780863224331)

TOM REILLY
Cromwell: An Honourable Enemy

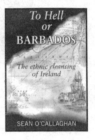

"This is an important book. He is scrupulous in his examination of evidence, he has the necessary scepticism, he is assiduous in research and he quotes primary sources extensively." *Sunday Times*

"Make no mistake, this is a very important reappraisal of Cromwell's nine-month tour of Leinster and Munster." *Sunday Tribune*

ISBN 9780863223907

SEAN O'CALLAGHAN
To Hell or Barbados
The ethnic cleansing of Ireland

"An illuminating insight into a neglected episode in Irish history... its main achievement is to situate the story of colonialism in Ireland in the much larger context of world-wide European imperialism." *Irish World*

ISBN 9780863222870

GERARD RONAN
'The Irish Zorro' The extraordinary adventures of William Lamport (1615–1659)

"Comprehensive and enthralling... Burned at the stake by the Mexican Inquisition at the age of 44, after a 17-year imprisonment, Lamport's story is truly extraordinary... Sometimes historical biography can be a dry read. Ronan's is anything but. He provides interesting insights into the lives of large Irish enclaves in France and Spain in the first half of the 17th century along with harrowing ones of those accused of heresy and subjected to the auto-da-fé of the Inquisition. Ronan's passion and sympathy for his subject shine through so it reads like a novel. A 'must read'." *Irish Independent*

ISBN 9780863223297

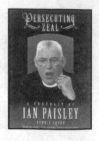

DENNIS COOKE
Persecuting Zeal: A Portrait of Ian Paisley

"A rounded and authentic picture... an insight into the life and times of Ian Paisley that cannot but be of help to anyone trying to understand or ameliorate the lethal depths of sectarianism that have nurtured and still sustain Ian Paisley... A very valuable book."
Eric Gallagher, *Methodist Recorder*

ISBN 9780863222221

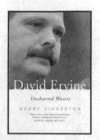

HENRY SINNERTON
David Ervine: Uncharted Waters

"Sinnerton is strong on explaining recent history from a loyalist political perspective... David Ervine played a key role in deliveriung the loyalist ceasefire... He humanised unionism... He stopped Mo Mowlam undermining the consent principle. He did all this under fire from mainstream unionism and under a very real IRA death threat." *Fortnight*

ISBN 9780863223129

JOE GOOD
Enchanted by Dreams
The Journal of a Revolutionary

A fascinating first-hand account of the 1916 Rising and its aftermath by a Londoner who was a member of the Irish Volunteers who joined the garrison in the GPO.

ISBN 9780863222252

ALAN SIMPSON

Duplicity and Deception: Policing the Twilight Zone of the Troubles

"Admirably even-handed and considered."
Sunday Tribune

"This is the story of an honest cop trying to do a decent job and maintain professional standards and ethics in the middle of a very dirty war… told with a remarkable lack of rancour or bitterness." *Irish Independent*

ISBN 9780863224287

ADRIAN HOAR

In Green and Red: The Lives of Frank Ryan

"The work is of a high standard, well documented, with index, a list of sources and copious notes… there is hardly a dull moment in the account from beginning to end."
Irish Independent

"Splendid… Instead of a cardboard cutout of an Irish hero, we get a hugely complex and beautifully written portrait of a man who struggled against his own marginality."
Scotland on Sunday

ISBN 9780863223327

GERRY ADAMS

An Irish Eye

A unique book reflecting the Sinn Féin president's involvement in events between 2004 and 2007.

"Overall, Adams comes across as an intelligent man with a inexorable passion for writing, history and politics." *Sunday Business Post*

"Intelligent writing… Mr Adams is a fine writer and an equally fine orator." *Irish World*

ISBN 9780863223709

GERRY ADAMS

Before the Dawn: An Autobiography

"One thing about him is certain: Gerry Adams is a gifted writer who, if he were not at the center of the war-and-peace business, could easily make a living as an author, of fiction or fact." *New York Times*

ISBN 9780863222894

Hope and History: Making Peace in Ireland

"A fascinating account of his journey through the peace process, from the first tentative discussions with a priest called Father Reid, to his present position charing the pages of *Hello!* with The Corrs, the international stage with Nelson Mandela." *Daily Mirror*

ISBN 9780863223303

An Irish Journal

"Gives an almost personal feel for the peace process as it develops, from Sinn Féin's first meeting with Britain's new prime minister Tony Blair to the build-up to the Good Friday agreement." *Sunday Tribune*

ISBN 9780863222825X